COMPARATIVE DELINQUENCY

CURRENT ISSUES IN CRIMINAL JUSTICE
VOLUME 18
GARLAND REFERENCE LIBRARY OF SOCIAL SCIENCE
VOLUME 1071

CURRENT ISSUES IN CRIMINAL JUSTICE

FRANK P. WILLIAMS III AND MARILYN D. MCSHANE

Series Editors

COMPARATIVE DELINQUENCY
INDIA AND THE UNITED STATES

CLAYTON A. HARTJEN
SESHA KETHINENI

GARLAND PUBLISHING, INC.
NEW YORK AND LONDON
1996

Library of Congress Cataloging-in-Publication Data

Hartjen, Clayton A., 1943–
    Comparative delinquency : India and the United States / by
Clayton A. Hartjen and Sesha Kethineni.
        p.   cm. — (Garland reference library of social science ;
vol. 1071. Current issues in criminal justice ; vol. 18)
    Includes bibliographical references and index.
    ISBN 0-8153-2137-6 (alk. paper)
    1. Juvenile delinquency—India.   2. Juvenile delinquency—United
States.   I. Kethineni, Sesha.   II. Title.   III. Series: Garland reference
library of social science ; v. 1071.   IV. Series: Garland reference library
of social science. Current issues in criminal justice ; v. 18.
HV9198.H37   1996
364.3'6'0954—dc20   96-17196
                                                                    CIP

Printed on acid-free, 250-year-life paper
Manufactured in the United States of America

Contents

Tables and Figures

Preface

The research reported in this volume was initially intended to expand the self-reported delinquency survey carried out as a part of the research conducted by Hartjen and Priyadarsini (1984) in India more than a decade ago. Persons familiar with that earlier inquiry might note some similarities between it and the present work. That is both intentional and unavoidable. This inquiry, however, is considerably more focused as a direct comparison of the similarities and differences in the delinquent behavior of Indian and American youths. In addition, we explore the possibility of explaining the etiological origins and epidemiological patterns of behavior across socially/economically/culturally diverse environments. In so doing we sought to place the India/United States comparisons in broader context by referring to available data from and criminological research on delinquency in countries around the world.

The 1987 survey of Madras and New Delhi respondents was supported by the American Institute of Indian Studies. The 1990 Madras survey was financed by the authors. We are grateful to Dr. K. Chockalingam, Mr. K. P. Senthilathiban and the criminology students of Madras University, and Dr. K. S. Shukla of the Delhi Institute of Public Administration for the assistance they provided in helping us complete our various inquiries. Dr. S. Priyadarsini acted as a consultant, critic, and source of encouragement from the start. James Hackler and Donald Shoemaker made valuable comments on an earlier draft of the manuscript and Phyllis Schultze of the Criminal Justice Collection at Rutgers University was an invaluable reservoir of information and source materials. We thank them and the numerous others who helped make this work possible.

COMPARATIVE
DELINQUENCY

CHAPTER ONE

Introduction

This book is an exploration in comparative criminology. The comparison is largely between India and the United States, although data and commentary regarding other countries are included throughout. In addition, this book is an inquiry into criminological theory. This inquiry takes place at two levels. On the one hand, we address the generalizability of causal theory by testing the cross-national explanatory ability of a causal model that incorporates dimensions relating to major etiological theory. On another level, our inquiry is primarily concerned with the international distribution of delinquent behavior and the kinds of sociocultural arrangements that lead to high or low rates of offense behavior.

Much of the discussion in the pages to follow, however, centers on Indian youths. India commands criminological attention for at least two reasons. For one, very little is known about the delinquent behavior of young people outside North American and western European societies. India, the second largest country in the world, with a juvenile population larger than the entire population of most countries, should be of interest to international criminologists for its own sake. But also, the unique social-economic-cultural characteristics of India make it an ideal social laboratory for cross-national or comparative criminological inquiry. As such, a comparative study of Indian and American delinquency provides insight into the etiological and epidemiological dimensions of delinquent activity among almost one-fourth of the world's young people. In addition, it may also help criminologists primarily concerned with the delinquent behavior of "western" youths to more fully understand and adequately explain their behavior than single-society research has yet enabled us to achieve.

Criminology's ability to understand delinquent behavior has historically been hampered by three problems: (1) the concept of the delinquent, (2) sources of data, and (3) the scope of criminological inquiry (see Gibbons, 1994; Pepinsky & Jesilow, 1984; Shoemaker, 1990; Vold & Bernard, 1986; Wilson & McShane, 1988).

From the days of Lombroso, criminals and young offenders have typically been viewed as somehow different (usually defective) from "normal," supposedly non-delinquent, others. These differences (or defects) in turn were thought to be responsible for the offender's aberrant behavior. Ideas like Sutherland's differential association theory did much to undermine this common perspective (Sutherland & Cressey, 1978: 80–83). However, the vast bulk of delinquency research has still sought to locate the differences in delinquents that are believed to account for their misconduct. A large number of claims purporting to identify the assumed causally-related peculiarities of offenders have been published and still occasionally appear in the literature. Not surprisingly little empirical support for these ideas has been produced (see Gibbons and Krohn, 1991; Gibbons, 1994: 128–150; Shoemaker, 1990: 14–74). Nevertheless, criminological theory and especially programs designed to rehabilitate offenders still often reflect this way of thinking.

Such thinking was perhaps plausible since almost all research on young offenders until the late 1960s focused on known (official) offenders and/or involved analyses of official arrest statistics and similar criminal data. Thus, it was reasonable to assume that the characteristics of incarcerated and otherwise processed youths were distinctive and representative of offenders generally. However, with the advent of "self-report" techniques, the idea that a distinction could be made between delinquents and non-delinquents has become difficult to sustain. Study after study shows that few respondents to these surveys report no involvement in misconduct whatsoever and that most report at least some involvement in often serious forms of illegality (Empey & Stafford, 1991: 93–121). Rather than think of them as delinquent or non-delinquent, most criminologists today would concur that youth are basically more or less delinquent. As a consequence, the focus of research and theory has shifted in recent decades away from explaining the causes of delinquency to accounting for variations in its frequency and forms throughout the juvenile population. Considerable progress in criminological understanding of delinquency, if not in its control, has been the result.

However, the third problem—the scope of inquiry—has received comparatively little attention. Investigations of crime and delinquency by criminologists in societies throughout the world have been conducted, and information on crime and criminal justice in diverse societies is increasingly being made available to western criminologists (e.g., Adler, 1983; Archer & Gartner, 1984; Barak-Glantz & Johnson, 1983; Chang & Blazicek, 1986; Clinard, 1978; LaFree & Birkbeck, 1991; Newman, 1976, 1980; Shelley, 1981). But a coherent body of cross-national research does not yet exist and very little of this inquiry has anything whatsoever to do with delinquency and youth crime or systems of juvenile justice. The vast bulk of the available research upon which our image and understanding of youthful offenders is to be based still centers on North American and western European juveniles. As a result, while we may now know a lot about delinquent behavior and the persons engaged in it, we have almost no idea of the extent to which this understanding extends beyond the borders of "western" societies.

Criminologists have exhibited a growing recognition of the importance of comparative (or cross-national, international) inquiry and a number of individuals in the field are directing their efforts to that end (Friday, 1995). In addition, international criminological organizations have been formed and journals and publications devoted to international and comparative crime and justice have begun to appear. Articles dealing with criminological topics in diverse countries are occasionally published in general criminological journals. And American textbooks on crime and delinquency have increasingly included discussions of, or at least reference to, other countries. But international/ comparative criminological research still lacks depth and theoretical integration.

INTERNATIONAL INQUIRY

Essentially two kinds of investigations on crime, justice, and delinquency throughout the world can be found in the English-language criminological literature. On the one hand, a small amount of "international" research (and/or commentary) exists. These publications offer a kind of global discussion of crime and related matters typically employing official data (usually police or court statistics) to describe world-wide distributions or trends in crime or various forms of criminal conduct. In some cases this information is used in efforts to construct or test "global" theories of criminality (e.g., Adler, 1983; Archer & Gartner, 1984).

Certainly ambitious and often suggestive, the data sources used in this kind of inquiry (if not necessarily inadequate) are of unknown quality, reliability, and validity. Moreover, the categories used to organize this data in theoretically meaningful ways (e.g., developed vs. developing nations, etc.) leave much to be desired. Nevertheless, to the extent that data for this kind of inquiry are at least reasonably reflective of reality, international criminological research holds considerable promise for providing a broader and more comprehensive picture of the epidemiological dimensions of crime and delinquency throughout the world, and it could do much to advance theoretical understanding of the forces that shape crime rates as such. Unfortunately, little of this research focuses on delinquent behavior and youth crime or offers much by the way of information to advance our knowledge of why youths engage in delinquency at all or do so with varying frequencies.

The second kind of inquiry might be referred to as "comparative" research, although relatively little of it actually offers much by the way of comparisons (but see e.g., Evans et al., 1993; Walter & Wolfgang, 1989). Essentially this kind of inquiry consists of more or less sophisticated and in-depth case-study investigations of single countries. Occasional comparisons of findings derived from these inquiries are made with findings from other countries (sometimes in the form of data comparisons, more often mere observational commentary). But few attempts at systematic "comparative" research involving two or more countries can be found in the literature. However, the growing number of such investigations offer much richer and more in-depth data on the delinquent behavior of youth in various countries than "international" inquiry could (at present) hope to achieve. In addition, theoretically relevant characteristics of societies can be compared to more directly test epidemiological theory. In this regard also, comparative research holds promise for testing etiological theory in a way that single-society research renders impossible.

Yet, as with international research, the bulk of the comparative research relies on official statistics, interviews with police and judicial officials, and less than systematic observations regarding societal reactions to delinquency or variables relevant to causal theory. A growing body of this research reports the findings of criminologists native to the countries studied and (more often in non-western countries) by American criminologists engaging in pseudo-anthropological research on crime and related phenomena. Collaborative efforts by criminologists both native and foreign to the country under investigation are almost non-existent.

The volume of information derived from international and comparative research has become fairly sizable. But very little of this research exclusively focuses on delinquency and youth crime or the machinery of juvenile justice/corrections in the world's diverse nations. In one exception, a special edition of the *International Journal of Comparative and Applied Criminal Justice* in 1992 contained articles exclusively focusing on aspects of delinquency in twelve countries throughout the world. This volume provides considerable information on delinquency in these diverse societies. However, the various articles also clearly reveal the extensive lack of our present knowledge about delinquent conduct and juvenile justice in even western, economically developed, countries, much less in Third World nations. In addition, these few articles illustrate the extreme difficulties criminologists face in attempting to develop a truly international picture, much less understanding, of the criminal and delinquent behavior committed by the world's youth or how various societies react to it.

Given the available research, at least in terms of broad dimensions relating to variables such as gender, age, economic development, offense types, etc., considerable similarities probably exist in the offense behavior of young people throughout the world. Extreme differences exist in the laws defining legal status by age, the nature of the offense behaviors for which juveniles can come to legal attention, and the manner in which and degree of effort countries expend in reacting to youth crime and delinquency (Hackler, 1991; Shoemaker, in press). And real differences in the kind and frequency of this behavior undoubtedly also exist. Yet, there appears to be a universality to delinquency such that young people throughout the world exhibit this behavior in roughly similar patterns and frequencies. In this respect, youth crime and delinquency require no special explanation at all. It is something that young people universally seem to do. What is also clear is that even though universal, the epidemiological dimensions of delinquency are by no means universally identical. Considerably more research and considerably more intensive research are still required before we can even begin assessing the true similarities and differences in delinquency phenomena internationally. This book is one effort to advance that kind of inquiry.

INDIAN DELINQUENCY: A REVIEW OF RESEARCH
Research on delinquency and related phenomena in India has received scant attention by criminologists both within and outside India. In contrast to the voluminous literature found for other countries, a coherent body of research and thought relating to delinquency in India is simply not available. Since much of this discussion focuses on Indian juveniles, a review of the research so far available on Indian delinquency may be instructive. For example, in one inquiry a leading Indian criminologist (Shukla, 1982) reviewed all the available publications on delinquency produced in India between 1937 and 1982. During this period a scant 91 publications (including Ph.D. dissertations and government reports) on delinquent behavior and related topics appeared in India. Most of these were produced during the 1960s-1970s. But, on the average, only about two publications of any kind were published during this period per year—hardly an overwhelming outpouring of scholarly or policy-relevant inquiry.

In scrutinizing the 91 publications reviewed, Professor Shukla observed that they constituted a hodgepodge of inquiries and commentaries on the spectrum of delinquency phenomena. Many concentrated on delinquency causation, typically using official statistics (such as arrest or disposition records) as primary data sources. Other studies involved samples of juveniles. Often these consisted of samples of incarcerated juveniles or "comparative" samples of high school and incarcerated youths. In most instances, where official statistics were used, simple correlations of demographic variables with arrest or other rates were presented. Where juveniles were investigated directly, normally one or a few dimensions (reflecting the academic interests of the investigator) were measured and simple comparisons of the "delinquent" and "non-delinquent" (usually called "normal") samples were made to demonstrate the causal impact of the dimension on delinquent behavior. Most of these inquiries used small samples with few if any control variables.

A handful of publications regarding various treatment or corrections programs were also produced during this period along with speculations and commentaries regarding the problem of delinquency or juvenile justice. However, overall, Shukla suggests that the following characterizes the body of knowledge made available in these publications:

> The major findings of the studies have been that the delinquents are generally drawn from the families with low socio-economic status, parents having low prestige occupations, from the families having lower scholastic achievements, broken families, where the modes of discipline were erratic and inconsistent as well as the behavior modes of parents were disdainful, some form of over-crowding was present at home. There was lack of physical space at home, family discord, etc. All these factors alone or in combination affected the socialization process and created maladjustment in children. However, further insight into the factors as well as processes does not seem to have been provided in these studies (Shukla, 1982, p. 108).

Since this review, research on delinquency and juvenile justice in India has, of course, continued and, apparently, at a somewhat accelerated rate. A survey of published studies and commentaries appearing between 1982 and 1988 (termination of the 1987 research) conducted by the authors reveals that more than two dozen delinquency-related articles appeared in the criminological literature produced within India, and a handful of studies were published on Indian delinquency by criminologists from other countries.

Of the post-1981 publications, the bulk of the inquiry has centered on one psychological dimension or another following the research strategy used in the earlier period (i.e., comparing samples of "delinquents" with samples of "normals" to test the causal effect to the variable being investigated). A number of factors appear to distinguish delinquent from supposedly non-delinquent youths. Among the findings from this research Krishna and Kumar (1981) report that school truants exhibit more "adjustment problems" than non-truants. Higher levels of "anxiety" were found to be exhibited by school "cheaters" compared to "non-cheaters" by Sinha & Krishna (1982). In a comparison of 30 incarcerated and 30 high-school youths, Kundu and Bhaumik (1982) found that incarcerated youths had significantly higher neuroticism scores than did high-school youths (also see Sen, 1982). Similarly, Maitra (1981) found that delinquents differed significantly from non-delinquents in "body image" and "self concept" while Misra (1981) reports incarcerated youths were "ego-defensive." Using an inventory to measure 14 different personality traits, Lahri (1983) observed significant differences between delinquents and non-delinquents on nine. Similarly, Kaliappan and Senthilathiban (1984) argue that delinquent and destitute children are more "anxious" than are "normal" children. And more recently, Thilagaraj (1987) tested dimensions relating to strain theory by measuring goal aspirations and expectations and found a number of discrepancies between delinquents and non-delinquents in this regard. A few studies (e.g., Sekar et al., 1983; Shariff & Sekar, 1982; and Kannappan & Kaliappan, 1987; Ravinder Nath & David, 1982) have sought to test the applicability of various measurement instruments developed in western societies to samples of Indian youths. All have found that the instruments are useful to discriminate between delinquent and non-delinquent samples.

In short, like much of the early research in western criminology, inquiries of various psychological correlates of delinquency in recent Indian criminological research have routinely found that "delinquent" youths (typically incarcerated offenders) differ in one way or another from "normal" (non-incarcerated) youths and, presumably, these differences are what explain the delinquent behavior of the incarcerated samples. However, this research has usually focused on relatively small samples, involved rather crude statistical techniques, and generally failed to control for or incorporate other dimensions that could confound the findings.

Similar to research findings from a variety of other countries, investigations of incarcerated Indian juveniles also indicate that these youths often come from home environments marked by abuse, disruption, and other ills (Ram, 1977). However, the extent to which non-incarcerated youths may also suffer from such circumstances is not discernable from this research.

Along the same lines, a number of inquiries have sought to correlate various "social characteristics" with the delinquency of incarcerated youths. For example, Channabasavanna et al. (1981) document the age, religion, social class, and other characteristics of incarcerated boys in Bangalore. This study found that most of the boys were under fifteen years of age, lived in urban areas, resided in nuclear families whose household head was typically poorly educated, unskilled, and earned a small income. Jejurikar & Shonvi (1985) surveyed 371 incarcerated boys and girls in Bombay to find that "adverse home environments"—poverty, illiteracy, and large family size—were common in the backgrounds of these youths. Similar findings are reported by Kulshrecktha and Bhushan (1981), Lakshmanna (1982), and Nagla (1981) from studies conducted throughout India.

Relatively little research has focused on delinquency rates in India, although commentary referring to arrest and other official statistics is fairly common in the media and professional literature (e.g., Nagla, 1981; Nagpaul, 1984). One inquiry by Sandhu (1987) concludes that low arrest rates in India suggest that these figures are a function of the strong family social controls in Indian society. Similarly Hartjen (1986) argues that differences in arrest rates between American and Indian juveniles and women are at least partly a function of differences in the use of informal social controls in these two societies. Yet while arrest and other criminal justice data have been available in

India for several decades, remarkably little use of this information has been made by criminologists in assessing the dimensions and possible correlates of delinquency and youth crime in that society (see Panakal & Gokhale, 1989).

Taken together the published research and available data on delinquent behavior in India paints a sketchy but suggestive picture of the epidemiological dimensions and causal forces behind such conduct among Indian youth. Quite clearly, as measured by arrest and court data, criminality on the part of Indian juveniles is either extremely infrequent (compared either to Indian adults or juveniles in other countries) or a matter of little reactive concern on the part of Indian society or law enforcement officials. The Hartjen and Priyadarsini (1984) research suggests that probably both factors are operative (i.e., relatively infrequent involvement on the part of Indian juveniles in, at least, serious delinquency as well as a general reluctance on the part of Indians to invoke the law in dealing with wayward youths). But much more research along the lines of that inquiry is still needed before any firm assessments in this regard can be made.

The rather more extensive body of literature focusing on incarcerated juveniles (and comparisons with non-incarcerated youths) also implies that those youths officially recognized as offenders in India are largely drawn from the margins of Indian society. Few youths (both absolutely and relatively) wind up being processed by Indian courts, and even fewer are placed in some kind of correctional facility. But those who are so handled are almost invariably drawn from impoverished families, are the victims of neglect or abuse, often suffer from malnourishment, disease, and various handicaps, and generally are among the cast-off children of an impoverished society. Undoubtedly they contribute more than their fair share to the number of illegal acts Indian youths commit, although the seriousness of their offense behavior is difficult to discern from available data or research. But how representative they are of law-breaking juveniles is simply not determinable from existing inquiries. Impressionistic information leads the authors to speculate that poverty and lack of supportive family structures are as much responsible for their incarceration as delinquency. Thus, attempting to draw any kind of conclusions about the etiology of delinquent behavior in India based on previous research would be premature.

PURPOSE OF THIS RESEARCH

One of the problems with our present knowledge about misconduct on the part of youths outside the United States and western European countries is the fact that almost all of what we know is based on either official records or small studies of "official" delinquents. What is absent from this inquiry are alternative measures that more directly allow us to (1) assess the epidemiological dimensions of delinquent behavior that are not biased by the contingencies of citizen reporting and police reaction and (2) that enable us to directly tap various theoretical dimensions concerning the etiological causes of delinquent behavior. Ideally these measures would enable criminologists to conduct cross-national investigations essential to a full understanding of the causes and frequencies of delinquent behavior. At present, only one such research technique—self-reported delinquency surveys—offers these qualities. While also limited in various ways, combined with official data and information gained from various other forms of research, findings from self-reported delinquency surveys broaden our perspective and allow us to obtain the kinds of information necessary to more fully address both epidemiological as well as etiological questions regarding delinquent behavior both within and across societies.

This book is one contribution to the literature on comparative (international) criminology. In the pages that follow we attempt to cast light on both the dimensions of and causal forces behind delinquency and youth crime among juveniles in a Third World society. In so doing, we also describe delinquency law and the juvenile justice/corrections system in India. In addition, we assess the dimensions of official delinquency by analysis of arrest statistics and describe in depth the findings of two self-reported delinquency surveys we conducted among urban high-school aged respondents in India. The results of those inquiries allow us to make some assessments of both the epidemiological and etiological aspects of delinquency in a Third World society.

By itself a discussion of delinquent behavior and juvenile justice in India would do much to advance general criminological understanding of the epidemiology and etiology of delinquency. Our interest here, however, is broader than a study of one country. As such, the official statistics and the findings from the Indian surveys are cast into comparative perspective by analyzing the Indian data in conjunction with the findings from similar research conducted in other countries; particularly Uniform Crime Report statistics and samples abstracted from the 1978 sampling wave of the National Youth Survey (NYS) carried out in the United States.

Thus, besides informing readers about the new system of juvenile justice now operating in India and placing the topic of Indian delinquency into a larger comparative framework, our concern in this volume primarily centers on two key issues. One of these is the extent and distribution of delinquent behavior and youth crime among Indian juveniles in the last quarter of the twentieth century compared to that of youths in the United States and various other countries. The other is the ability of major criminological theories largely constructed to explain criminality among western (primarily male) offenders to explain the epidemiological patterns and etiological causes of offense behavior among young people in a social-economic-cultural environment distinctively different from the western context.

The data available to us in assessing these issues lack the depth and rigor we might want in drawing firm conclusions regarding cross-national patterns of delinquency, much less the universal explanatory relevance of causal theory. However, other than being informative, we hope this report has implications for cross-national research generally and suggests some avenues that more extensive and sophisticated research of this kind might follow in the future.

It is the purpose of this volume then to not only report the findings we obtained from the two self-report surveys discussed in following chapters but to integrate these findings with official statistics, criminological research, and personal observations on India to attempt a more thorough assessment of delinquency and its causes among Indian youths. In addition, we hope to cast these observations into a broader comparative perspective by incorporating (to the extent possible) official statistics and self-report findings concerning American youths as well as research on delinquency in countries throughout the world.

CHAPTER TWO

Methodology

The following chapters report data drawn from a variety of sources regarding the delinquent behavior of Indian youths as well as juveniles in the United States and other countries. In so doing, this inquiry draws upon multiple sources of information including original research conducted by the authors, official statistics reported by various governments, and published reports of research carried out by criminologists throughout the world. The published reports are readily available and the various official statistics reported throughout these pages can be obtained from libraries and the reporting agencies directly. However, the self-report studies completed by the authors and the official crime statistics on India used in this report require more description. This chapter discusses the Indian research sites and the methodologies used in the self-report surveys in some detail. In addition, critical discussion is provided concerning the data sources upon which much of the discussion is based and the comparability of the findings we draw from these data.

RESEARCH SITES

Official statistics used in this report largely cover the particular country in question. The two Indian self-report surveys were carried out in the cities of New Delhi and Madras. For persons unfamiliar with India or the localities in which the surveys were conducted, this section offers a brief discussion of the country and the cities of Madras and New Delhi.

India

The population of India now exceeds 800 million, making it the second largest nation in the world (population data used in all statistical analyses is based on *Census of India,* 1981). Approximately 35 percent of the nation's inhabitants are below eighteen years of age, bringing them under the jurisdiction of the national juvenile justice act passed in 1986. Almost 60 percent of the population is classified as illiterate, although among juveniles the rate of illiteracy is considerably lower (males = 21 percent, females = 34 percent), suggesting that national education efforts have been making some progress. Close to 50 percent of juvenile males and 19 percent of juvenile females are officially employed, although the actual number of "working" (illegally) juveniles is undoubtedly much higher than this estimate.

The country is primarily a rural society with an agrarian economy; almost 70 percent of the working population of India is directly employed in agriculture, and nearly 80 percent of the population live in villages. Nevertheless, the urban centers are growing rapidly and an estimated 27 million persons reside in the country's four major cities of Bombay (8,227,332), Calcutta (9,165,650), Madras (4,276,635) and New Delhi (4,884,234). And while classified as "rural," populations in many towns throughout India's countryside number in the hundreds of thousands.

Fifteen officially recognized distinct languages and hundreds of dialects are spoken by the country's people. About 80 percent of the population is Hindu. Approximately 11 percent are Muslims and the remainder Christians or individuals of different faiths. Given its caste system, the country is further divided into a large number of subcastes (jatis) locally recognized as distinct "communities." Jatis are largely responsible for channeling interpersonal relations and economic activities and provide Indians with their most meaningful social identity. Indeed, few Indians probably use "Indian" as a self-identity label of first choice, instead using their major "community" (religious affiliation, or place of origin—such as a village—identity) as a way of indicating group membership.

Although it is not difficult for Indians to readily determine who belongs to another "community" and their relative social rank thereby, it is illegal to discriminate against someone on the basis of caste and impolite to inquire about one's caste membership. Nevertheless, the government has promoted a highly controversial "affirmative action" program for so-called "scheduled castes and tribes" so that many people seek special advantages (e.g., admission to college or government jobs, etc.) by virtue of their membership in what have traditionally been stigmatized population groups.

But, in addition to jatis, the country's population is increasingly being divided into class groups based on occupation and income and is beginning to experience the disruptive effects of modernization and industrialization that plague most Third World societies today (Groves & Newman, 1986).

The world's largest parliamentary democracy, India is made up of 22 states and 9 union territories (areas directly governed by the central government). These jurisdictions are largely organized along linguistic lines and were created by combining various districts and independent principalities after British rule.

New Delhi

India's capital city, New Delhi, is situated in the Union Territory of Delhi, which, like Washington, D.C., is an autonomous territory carved out of segments of various states. The territory houses almost 6.5 million people with a population density of over 4000 people per square kilometer. Being a desert city located at about 25 degrees north latitude, New Delhi experiences extremes of weather, from dry, stifling summers, often reaching temperatures over 110 degrees at midday, to below-freezing nights during the winter. Irrigated by the Ganges river, the city and its surrounding areas are still dependent on the annual monsoons, the failure of which can spell disaster for entire populations.

The city experienced a decennial growth rate of over 53 percent. With an unbalanced sex ratio of 808 females per 1,000 males, the city has a literacy rate of over 62 percent. About 32 percent of the population is listed as employed, many in clerical occupations in government service. The per-capita income is more than double the national average and the highest of any region in India. In this respect, the city is both actually and visually prosperous and modern compared to many other areas in India. Because it is at the same time modern and traditional, housing a highly heterogeneous Indian population, New Delhi provides an excellent locality for cross-cultural comparative analysis, both with other locations in India as well as with cities in other societies.

Madras

The northern region of India in which New Delhi is situated is predominantly Hindi speaking and populated by descendants of the Aryan, Muslim, and other invaders that swept through the region over the millennia (Kosambi, 1969). In contrast, the southern city of Madras is the capital city of Tamil Nadu (land of the Tamils), housing a population of largely Dravidian descendents speaking a distinct language called Tamil (the oldest continuously spoken language in existence). The state is one of the few jurisdictions in India that independently enacted and actually implemented special laws and a system of juvenile justice/corrections for delinquent and needy children as early as 1920. More than 50 million people live in Tamil Nadu's 130,058 square kilometers. Between 1971 and 1981 the state experienced a population growth rate of about 18 percent. Although housing one of the country's major urban centers, almost 67 percent of the state's inhabitants are classified as "rural." About 2 million residents (4 percent) are categorized as "marginal" workers and over 56 percent (28 million persons) are "non-workers." Often electing political candidates outside the national political mainstream, the state has exhibited a well-known alienation from the central government for many years, and Tamilians pride themselves in being distinctly different from their northern compatriots.

Almost 5 million of the state's inhabitants reside in the 128 square kilometers of the city of Madras. The city was founded by the British East India

Company in the early 1600s. Its literacy rate of over 65 percent is among the highest in the country although, as elsewhere in India, the city has a high unemployment rate and its inhabitants are burdened with a substantial dependent population.

A major urban center in South India, Madras also exhibits a much more rural flavor than New Delhi and is generally considered to be more socially conservative and less westernized than New Delhi. A coastal city on the Bay of Bengal, Madras is located about eight degrees off the equator and has a climate typically referred to by residents as "hot, hotter, and hottest." Although the climate is tropical and there are practically no tall buildings and considerable vegetation, the city's population growth has steadily outpaced its ability to maintain its infrastructure so that water shortages, electrical failures, and deteriorating roads and sewage systems are a constant plague throughout the metropolis.

Being racially, linguistically, and culturally distinct from New Delhi, Madras provides a contrasting location to assess differences and similarities in both the epidemiology and etiology of delinquency in a large, highly diverse society as well as an additional dimension for cross-cultural comparative inquiry.

SELF-REPORTED DELINQUENCY SURVEYS

In 1978 Hartjen and Priyadarsini (1984) carried out a limited self-reported delinquency survey among high school and institutionalized boys in Tamil Nadu in order to augment official statistics and other data sources used in their inquiry and to test the feasibility of such research in a Third World setting. The results of that survey suggested that self-reported delinquency research could indeed be conducted on samples of respondents internationally and provide a sound basis for comparative inquiry (also see Hartjen, 1983). Two similar surveys comprising major data sources for this book were carried out by the authors in 1987 and 1990. The 1987 survey was an attempt to expand the original 1978 inquiry both in regard to questionnaire items and populations sampled. Subsequently, the 1990 survey employed a still more extensive questionnaire and directly sought to solicit data for cross-national theory testing. For comparative purposes, sub-samples corresponding in demographic characteristics to the Indian samples were abstracted from the 1978 version of the National Youth Survey. This section reports the methodologies used in conducting the Indian surveys as well as the procedures employed to select respondents from the National Youth Survey and address some of the strengths and limitations of the data.

The 1987 India Survey

The 1987 survey was designed as a follow-up and extension of the 1978 study conducted by Hartjen and Priyadarsini (1984). The design of the 1987 survey, therefore, was to some extent dictated by the original investigation. The central focus of the 1987 survey was to assess the epidemiological dimensions of delinquent behavior among a large sample of high-school and institutionalized respondents drawn from urban areas in geographically (and in many other ways) distinct regions of India.

A self-administered questionnaire (see Appendix A) was administered to samples of male and female high-school and institutionalized respondents in the cities of Madras and New Delhi during the fall and winter of 1987–88. Juveniles in twenty-one schools and institutions participated in the survey yielding a total sample of 2600 respondents (2077 high school and 523 institutionalized). Table 2.1 presents data on the demographic characteristics of the respondents for the 1987 and 1990 India surveys as well as the comparative samples extracted from the National Youth Survey 1978.

Table 2.1
Demographic Characteristics of Indian and United States Samples

| | 1987 Comparisons | | | | 1990 Comparisons | | | |
| | India | | U.S. | | India | | U.S. | |
	#	%	#	%	#	%	#	%
Gender								
Boys	1446	56	663	53	221	52	371	53
Girls	1124	44	584	47	207	48	330	47
Age								
<14	825	32	490	39	95	22	155	22
15	609	24	249	20	85	20	234	33
16	618	24	221	18	139	31	218	31
17	526	20	287	23	114	27	94	14
N	2570		1247		428		701	

In both Madras and New Delhi, high schools were purposively selected to correspond as closely as possible to those studied in the 1978 research and include respondents from diverse social and economic backgrounds. The schools were chosen from districts throughout the geographical boundaries of the city and were selected as representative of the three categories of high schools found in India (private, private-aided, government).

Generally, these school categories reflect broad social class distinctions (upper, middle, working) in India so that sampling students from each type of school insured that respondents of diverse social-class backgrounds were included in the sample. The respondents in correctional institutions were drawn from the facilities in and around the two cities in which delinquents from each city are normally incarcerated and constituted a census of the governmental institutions in the area.

In Madras respondents were sampled in eight high schools (four male, three female, one coeducational) and four institutions (three male and one female). In most instances the male facilities chosen were the original schools and institutions surveyed in the 1978 research. To include girls in the survey, schools for females were chosen to match the male schools as closely as possible.

High schools in New Delhi were selected to match the Madras sample to the extent possible. One school for females and males from each of the three social-class categories was selected from the various districts in the city. To insure geographic representation, a random procedure was employed to determine the district and the type of school (e.g., male-private vs. female-government) to be surveyed in each district of the city. Following that determination, an appropriate school was then chosen for the specific district. In most instances this constituted the only such school within the particular district. In contrast to Madras, private schools in New Delhi are largely coeducational. Thus, to insure an appropriate mix of male and female respondents, two such schools were chosen according to the random determination of geographical area. Similar to Madras, one male and one female private-aided and government school were chosen for sampling. The institutions studied constituted a census of the correctional facilities for juveniles then existing in New Delhi. Thus, the New Delhi respondents were drawn from two male, two female, and two coeducational high schools and three (two male and one female) correctional institutions.

In all the high schools, respondents were solicited from one section of each grade (9 through 12), providing samples of respondents from approximately fourteen through seventeen years of age. In some schools only one section of each grade existed; in others the section was chosen at random. All students present in the classroom at the time of the survey were requested to participate. In the institutions, respondents of comparable ages (fourteen through seventeen) were chosen regardless of the actual school grade to which they may have been assigned. This meant that practically every ward then confined in the institution completed the survey instrument. Clear instructions as to the nature and purpose of the survey were given by the researcher and assistants and all students were offered the option of not participating. Almost all participants treated the study as a novel and compelling undertaking. Any questions asked by respondents or difficulties encountered in completing the questionnaire were handled by graduate assistants fluent in the local language and familiar with survey techniques.

Offense items used in the questionnaire were modeled after those used in the National Youth Survey (NYS) of 1978 (Elliott et al., 1983). As in the 1978 India survey, questions regarding sexual delinquency were excluded because of opposition on the part of school officials and general taboos about discussion of such matters in India. Since an extensive vocabulary of terminology for various drugs simply does not exist in either Tamil or Hindi, it was impossible to include the long list of substance abuse offenses used in the NYS. Instead, two categories of substance abuse—"soft" (ganja or hashish) and "hard" ("brown sugar" or heroin)—were employed. In addition, in those instances where the NYS used several questions to tap one offense type (e.g., vandalism), the Indian questionnaire collapsed these into single-item offenses to limit the instrument's length and complexity so that it could be self-administered by groups of respondents.

The questionnaire was first constructed in English and then translated into colloquial Tamil (for Madras). Several persons fluent in both languages reviewed the questionnaire, and a small number of high-school age individuals pre-tested the instrument for readability and cultural relevance. It might be noted that both Kethineni and Dr. S. Priyadarsini who acted as a consultant for the research are both fluent in Tamil and English.

For New Delhi, a Hindi questionnaire was constructed based on both the Tamil and English models. Several persons fluent in all or at least two of the languages verified the translation, and informal interviews with high-school youths were conducted to pre-test the instrument. Tamil- and Hindi-speaking graduate student assistants from local universities assisted in administering and coding the questionnaires. Data were subsequently computer analyzed in the United States by the authors.

The 1990 India Survey

The results and limitations of the 1987 survey led us to design a second investigation employing a smaller sample but a more extensive questionnaire to allow us to study various etiological aspects of delinquency not tapped in the 1987 study (see Appendix B). Given funding and other constraints, this study sampled high-school boys and girls from the same schools surveyed in the 1987 Madras inquiry. With a smaller target sample of 400–500 respondents, it was impossible to resample all the schools included in the 1987 survey. Thus, the 1990 survey drew a stratified sample of male and female high schools from those surveyed in the 1987 study. Two schools of each category were randomly selected. Within each school two classes of 9th- through 11th-grade students were randomly selected for interviewing. As with the 1987 survey, all students attending each selected section on the survey date were asked to participate, instructed in the nature and purpose of the survey, and assured of the anonymity of their responses. Questionnaires from a total sample of 428 respondents were returned (see Table 2.1).

The questionnaire was again constructed in English and translated into Tamil and pre-tested on a small sample of students. More elaborate than that used in 1987, the questionnaire was closely modeled after the NYS instrument, although with a number of modifications. Again questions regarding sexual delinquency were excluded, and multiple offense items were combined into single items. Whereas the 1987 instrument employed ordinal measures of incidence (frequency of commission) rates, this questionnaire solicited the actual number of times each offense was committed in the prior year. However, since there was reason to believe that few respondents could indicate precise involvement rates of weekly and daily conduct, the questionnaire provided pre-coded response frequency intervals of "1" through "10 or more times." Similarly other questionnaire items departed from the NYS model as appropriate (e.g., religious affiliation and income).

Some items of no relevance to the survey's purposes were excluded for the sake of brevity. The number of items in the final version of the questionnaire totaled 172 as compared to the 390 contained in the NYS instrument. Although modified, considerable effort was expended to make the instrument as analytically comparable to the NYS study as possible and to include questions concerning the relevant theoretical variables of interest to our inquiry.

The National Youth Survey

Of particular interest to our inquiry was the extent to which major theories of delinquency typically investigated by research on American delinquents applied as well to youths in other countries. To explore this interest we endeavored to compare the results of our findings from India with those of one of the most analyzed self-report surveys carried out in the United States to date, the National Youth Survey (NYS). The design of the NYS survey has been extensively detailed by Elliott et al. (1983, 1985), and it would be redundant to review that literature here. Given differences in both sampling design and instrument administration, we do not presume here that the Indian and American data sets are directly comparable in the same sense that a simultaneous replication investigation would be. Nevertheless, until such research becomes funded, findings from the two surveys provide the only comparable information on self-reported delinquency in a large developing and a large developed country that also allows us to generalize beyond the often dubious meshing of official statistics that is characteristic of comparative criminological research.

To draw samples from the NYS that corresponded as closely as possible to the populations investigated in the separate Indian surveys, slight variations in how samples were abstracted from the NYS respondents were necessary. In both instances, the 1978 NYS sampling wave was selected for study since it contained respondents more closely corresponding to the Indian age group (e.g., ages thirteen to nineteen years) than did any of the other NYS sampling waves. Respondents attending high schools within the age range desired were drawn for the 1987 sample comparison. This provided a total sample of 1247 respondents, of which about equal proportions were males and females. Mean ages for the two samples were almost identical (fifteen years) and this was consistent by gender. For the 1990 comparison, NYS respondents aged thirteen to nineteen in high school grades 9, 10, and 11 were drawn. A sample of 701 respondents was selected, about equally proportionate by grade and gender. Table 2.1 presents the sample characteristics of the NYS respondents used in the comparative analysis.

OFFICIAL STATISTICS

Responses to the self-report surveys described above comprise the primary data analyzed in this report. Although it is now generally agreed by criminologists that self-reported delinquency is a valid and reliable measure of delinquency involvement, these surveys tend to emphasize the less serious forms of misconduct and do not necessarily reflect the kinds of activity of interest to authorities (Akers et al., 1983; Hardt & Peterson-Hardt, 1977; Hindelang et al., 1979; Krohn et al., 1975; Paternoster & Triplett, 1988; Smith & Davidson, 1986). Therefore, findings from these inquiries tend to "overemphasize" the incidence and prevalence of "delinquent" behavior by reporting a goodly amount of trivial activity; even though in a broad legal sense that behavior is technically delinquent in some jurisdictions (e.g., smoking cigarettes). At the same time, they "underemphasize" the more serious forms of criminality (of interest to legal authorities, such as armed robbery) since such acts typically represent a relatively small proportion of the acts queried in self-report surveys (Elliott & Ageton, 1978). Samples of respondents likely to be heavily engaged in this conduct are also less likely to be included in survey samples, and/or respondents may be less likely to report involvement in this conduct as such. Nevertheless, self-report surveys are the only way criminologists have of directly estimating relative rates of delinquent forms of behavior and comparing such findings cross-nationally. Other data sources, however, may be used to augment self-report findings and to tap other dimensions (i.e., societal reactions) relating to delinquency. Among those used in this study are official arrest and disposition data.

Arrest Statistics as Measures of Behavior

Arrest statistics are not only direct measures of criminalization activities but possible measures of crime/delinquency rates as well (see Hartjen, 1978). Thus, provided they are even available at all, such data, while not directly measuring the involvement of persons in specific acts, offer another means to assess differences and similarities in rates of illegal conduct cross-nationally. However, since arrest statistics tap an arena of delinquency somewhat different from that of self-report research as well as actually measuring a different order of phenomena (arrests rather than acts), direct comparisons of findings from the two sources of data are impossible. Obviously, differences in recording techniques, offense categorization, and legal systems make any cross-national comparison of official delinquency statistics tenuous at best. Even then, reliable and comparable data of this kind rarely exist so that such data are of only auxiliary value for general cross-national criminological research. These rejoinders notwithstanding, some sense of the dimensions of the delinquency problem within any country as well as differences and similarities in criminality among various countries, can be gained from arrest statistics.

The government of India publishes an annual report titled *Crime in India* that is roughly comparable to the publication *Crime in the United States* (Uniform Crime Reports) compiled by the Federal Bureau of Investigation in the United States. A considerable literature exists detailing the strengths and weaknesses of *Crime in the United States*. Thus, this discussion is limited to a description of the Indian document. The tables in Chapter Four reporting data abstracted from *Crime in India* show the offense categories used, both for arrests as well as cases recorded (charges filed) by the police (Verma, 1993b). Arrest statistics are largely used in this report.

These statistics provide annual counts of the number of arrests made each year for persons of all ages as well as for "juveniles" (up to twenty-one) grouped under arrests for Indian Penal Code (IPC) crimes and Special and Local Laws (SLL). The latter category consists of nationally applicable offenses not included in the IPC as well as criminal violations peculiar to specific states (e.g., prohibition). Tables regarding the gender and age characteristics of persons arrested for each crime category are detailed as well as distributions by states and major cities. Some information on the socio-economic backgrounds and the disposition of arrestees is also presented.

Unfortunately rate information is not systematically presented and had to be computed from census statistics. Similarly, in the section titled "juvenile delinquency" age categories using broad groupings of unequal size are presented. These categories are not used for all arrests however so that age by age comparisons are difficult to make with arrest data from other jurisdictions. Annual trends are presented over ten-year intervals. But with the legal changes enacted in 1986, no comparisons in trend data after the 1987 report can be made with any earlier period both because of the addition of new offense categories as well as the changes in the age designations used for boys and girls. In short, *Crime in India* offers an available source of crime data for India that has many of the advantages as well as limitations that criminologists recognize in similar documents published by other governments (e.g., the UCR). Yet, in spite of these limitations, not only can we gain some idea about the relative extent and distribution of criminal behavior on the part of juveniles throughout India, it also (with reservations) allows us to make rough comparisons between India and delinquency rates in other societies.

As discussed below, differences in laws, offense categories, and reporting methods make direct comparisons of these data with data from other arrest reports difficult. In the present inquiry, some direct offense comparisons can be made (e.g. murder, theft) when comparing Indian and American arrest statistics. Generally, however, it is more meaningful to collapse offenses into broad types, such as personnel, property, public disorder, and substance abuse offenses, even though some loss of precision occurs as a result. It is this strategy that is followed when making cross-national comparisons in this analysis (see Appendix C). In so doing, official statistics collected for the time period in which the 1987 self-report survey was conducted were selected for analysis from both countries.

Disposition Statistics as Measures of Behavior

In addition to the arrest statistics presented in Chapter Four, Chapter Three reports data on juveniles processed by the criminal justice system or incarcerated as offenders to cast further light on the extent and distribution of delinquent behavior throughout India and, where possible, make comparisons with similar data from the United States and other countries. Since considerable changes were being implemented following the passage of *The Juvenile Justice Act 1986*, only statistics compiled up to 1987 were employed in this analysis.

Indian court and corrections data are available in a variety of sources. A brief description of these data sources is offered here. *Crime in India*, for example, records the dispositions received by "juveniles" sent to court by state, union territory, and city. Also The National Institute of Social Defense under the Ministry of Social Welfare records information on the number of juvenile courts, welfare boards, correctional, and probationary facilities in the various states and union territories. Information on the disposition of cases sent to juvenile courts is also compiled. However, the disposition and processing categories used in these various publications are not necessarily compatible. Also the age ranges and offender status of the juveniles processed is not the same in various reports. Similarly, some reports only cover youths processed by "juvenile courts" even though persons of similar ages could also be dealt with in adult courts or courts with a different title. Moreover, some states had courts that exclusively dealt with juveniles, but since the courts may have had a title different from that used to compile data for the report, statistics for an entire state may be absent. One of the authors, for example, had actually observed cases processed in juvenile courts in the state of Tamil Nadu. But, no such courts are included in the list of juvenile courts existing under the *Juvenile Justice Act 1986* for that state in recent Social Defense statistics. Apparently this is because in Tamil Nadu the court processing juveniles under one of the oldest Children's Acts in the country is not categorized separately as a "juvenile" court and, therefore, is not included in the disposition data. Thus, the extent to which the data are inclusive of juveniles processed or disposed in any state, much less throughout India, is not always clear. Finally, due to the considerable time-lag that often follows between the reporting and publication dates, data pertaining to years as nearly close to the survey period and arrest statistics are reported here, although often this means a difference of several years. To help deal with this problem, the authors were able to collect preliminary (not yet published) data from Indian authorities in some cases. But these are by no means complete.

Clearly, criminologists generally agree that as measures of rates of delinquent behavior, disposition data are the least desirable of all available statistics given the slippage, shrinkage, and redefinition of offense behaviors that occur between the acts of interest and the processing received by those who come to the attention of authorities. But, besides offering a picture of how societies handle youths deemed worthy of official intervention, if employed with considerable reservation, court and corrections data can also offer further clues to the relative "delinquency problem" posed by youths in various societies. Indeed, one country's heavy use of dismissals and probation in contrast to another's reliance on incarceration, for example, could mean that the first is for some reason much more lenient towards wayward youth than the second. Or, it could also mean that the juveniles processed in the first society are less serious offenders than are found in the other. Court and corrections data alone can not tell us this. Combined with self-report, arrest, and other information, however, they can help to round out the epidemiological picture we might draw of a country's youth and their delinquency. Besides offering us a picture of the systems of juvenile justice/corrections found in India and elsewhere, it is in this respect that court and corrections data are used in this report.

Other Data

Where possible, the primary data sources discussed above are augmented by research by criminologists throughout the world published in English-language books and journals. Also, in India observations of correctional institutions and numerous informal discussions with criminologists, criminal justice personnel, high-school officials, young people, and others were conducted by the authors. In addition, newspaper accounts, magazines, and other popular media were all tapped in the course of the research. Generally information from these various data sources is used to contextualize and substantiate the impressions we gain from the primary data sources.

GENERALIZABILITY OF FINDINGS

This book is primarily a comparison of the delinquent behavior of youths in India and the United States along with commentary on other countries. In describing and attempting to explain that behavior we draw upon national arrest data, court and corrections data of unknown national generality, empirical research of unequal quality and quantity on youths conducted by criminologists throughout the world, informal observations and inquiries by the authors over the past ten or more years in India and the United States, and two self-report surveys of youths in the Indian cities of Madras and New Delhi carried out over a time interval of three years. In discussing our findings from the India data we refer to Indian youth in general. But, the extent to which we might generalize from these data to the entire country could be questioned. In the analysis to follow we are by no means insensitive to this problem. But some discussion of the extent to which any conclusions we might draw from these data can be applied to youth in India generally is in order here.

Notwithstanding the limitations of self-report data as such, samples of urban Indian high-school and incarcerated youths can hardly be called representative of Indian juveniles, most of whom live in rural areas and/or may neither be attending school or found in correctional populations. We have no statistical way of assessing the national representativeness of our self-report samples. However, we have no reason to assume that our findings are not generally descriptive of young people throughout the country. For one, our self-report findings are not inconsistent with information gotten from different sources concerning offenders and offense behavior throughout India. Either all these data sources are in error, or the self-report data provide a more refined way of measuring a phenomenon similarly detected by official statistics and less rigorous observations. Surely, a national survey similar to the NYS that samples randomly selected respondents whose representativeness of Indian youth of all types in all parts of India could be estimated would be the desired self-report research technique. Available funding sources and the methodological contingencies of conducting such a survey in a multilingual nation with some regions involved in violent conflict make such an undertaking impossible at this time. Thus, until more extensive and more exhaustive research demonstrates otherwise, the self-report data described in the present inquiry provide the only data of this kind from which any generalizations about "delinquency in India" can be made at all.

Official arrest reports do provide a national data source that offers clues to the relative extent of delinquency among India's youth by state, as well as by urban compared to rural areas. Research in the United States based on the UCR has revealed that crime and delinquency are by no means equally distributed throughout that country. Similar studies in India produce similar results. But, as with self-report research in the United States, our self-report findings also suggest that delinquency in India is not only probably more widespread but also more equally distributed than official statistics indicate.

In any case, the two cities surveyed for the self-report research (and the districts in which they are located) fall in the median range of arrest-rate rankings in India. Nationally India's annual rate for IPC crimes is about 200 per 100,000 population with a range of about 75 to 350 for different states. The state of Tamil Nadu (in which Madras is located) has an annual rate of around 220 each year. Similarly, both New Delhi and Madras fall slightly below the average IPC rate for the 12 major cities of India, with rates in the low to mid-300's while the city average is around 400 per 100,000 population (largely because of extreme rates for two medium-sized cities). Since local laws vary from state to state, relative rankings on the bases of special and local laws are meaningless.

How accurately arrest statistics reflect the actual criminality of the populations included in the state and union territory reports is anybody's guess. If, indeed, this were known, a national self-report survey would be superfluous. In fact, state and city comparisons of arrest rates in India may be of questionable significance anyway. In the authors' opinion, arrest and offense rates reported for some cities and even states are simply unbelievable as measures of actual relative rates of offense behavior. For example, it somehow stretches one's imagination to believe that the 34 "juveniles" arrested in Calcutta for all forms of crime during 1987 represent a truly minuscule delinquency problem in that city of almost eight million people. Similarly, Punjab state reports arrests of a mere 596 juveniles in 1987, less than 2 percent of the number arrested in Tamil Nadu. It is possible that juveniles in Punjab are less delinquent than their Tamilian cousins, but the disparity appears a bit extreme. In short, our ability to generalize from national arrest data is as debatable as our ability to do so from less than national self-report surveys. Taken together, some reasonably supportable judgments about the epidemiological dimensions of delinquent behavior in India can be made.

From the point of view of methodological purity, of course, we could make no general statements about delinquency in India at all from the self-report and official data we obtained (even more so, draw any cross-national comparisons). But, at least with regard to India's delinquency, a third source of information seems to help confirm the picture of India's delinquency problem presented in this volume. Although few in number, the research reported by criminologists and ethnographic descriptions of specific cases of offenders or offense situations in diverse parts of India present remarkably similar findings. This suggests that while the involvement of young people in delinquent forms of conduct is by no means likely to be identical throughout India (as is probably also true of youth in countries throughout the world), it is not so varied that reasonable general discussions cannot be based on what are admittedly less than ideal sources of data. It is in this light that we employ these resources to talk about "delinquency in India" throughout this book.

CROSS-NATIONAL COMPARISONS

It does not take an international conference to realize that cross-cultural criminological research is fraught with difficulties beyond those researchers face while conducting inquiries within their own societies (Klein, 1989). Even given the additional problems encountered, comparative criminological research is not methodologically impossible. But, no methodologically perfect study has ever been completed in criminology, although many grand conclusions have been drawn from the rather sketchy data criminologists have often collected. Yet, as with the issue of generalizability, the comparability of the data sources we use for the cross-national comparisons made in this volume warrants discussion. Since the direct comparisons most frequently made in this report involve official arrest statistics for India and the United States and the findings from the two self-report surveys compared to the 1978 version of the National Youth Survey, the present discussion is limited to addressing these resources.

Comparing Arrest Statistics

Most of the comparative analysis using official data in this report is based on arrest statistics. Since any comments we could make about arrest statistics pertain as well to disposition and corrections data, our discussion focuses on arrests. As persons familiar with *Crime in the United States* would quickly realize, substantial differences exist between *Crime in the United States* and *Crime in India* both in how the reports organize the data presented as well as the offense types included in the reports. Organizational differences present a hair-pulling problem of "putting it together" in some comparable way. But of particular concern are the differences in the offense categories in the two reports.

First, given the variability of laws across the many jurisdictions within the United States, the UCR uses generic offense categories that do not necessarily correspond to specific criminal laws. Indian offense categories, on the other hand, reflect offenses defined by specific laws. Most of these are uniformly defined for the country as a whole, but others (SLL) apply in only some states and these states are not so identified in the report.

Second, both the number of offenses as well as the specific acts included in the two reports are not the same, or, at least, similarly designated. The Indian report, for instance, lists 13 offenses as IPC crimes and 12 under the special and local law title (including the category "other" for SLL crimes only). The offense categories are included in tables reporting both offenses recorded by police as well as arrests. The American report, on the other hand, lists eight crimes in the "known to police" section and 29 separate offenses in the arrests portion of the report (also including an "other" category). In both reports, "other" makes up a sizable portion of the offenses or arrests reported. Of the 20–odd offenses listed in each publication, data for 11 could be directly compared without much contention on the part of criminologists. Two or three other offense categories in each report could, with some hedging, be combined to form one or two other comparable offenses. Thus about one half of the offenses for which data is recognizably recorded in each report could be compared. However, each report also contains a number of acts having no direct counterpart in the other. These include such crimes as assault, arson, vagrancy, and runaways in the American document and riots, dacoity (group armed robbery), violations of the "arms act," and the "Indian railways act" in the Indian report. While these offenses are included under broad offense types for comparative purposes in Chapter Four, we do so only with considerable reservations.

Third, breakdowns by age and other relevant variables differ for the two reports. The Indian report records the ages of arrested juveniles in broad groups of unequal size ("7–12," "12–16," "16–18," "18–21") while annual ages are recorded in the UCR. Also, although both provide gender breakdowns, the ethnicity categories used by the UCR are not found in the Indian volume. Conversely, this publication provides limited information on the family background, economic set-up, religion, "community" (caste) membership, and educational attainment of arrestees not found in the American publication.

Finally, the degree to which the validity of the data presented in each report is subject to extraneous forces cannot be estimated. Political considerations, simple differences or changes in reporting procedures, or variations in routine policing activities can have considerable effect on reported crime rates. To assume that officials in all Indian states and union territories uniformly and accurately report offenses and arrests would be naive given the highly localized and volatile social and political situation in India.

In this respect, direct comparisons between Indian and American official crime-rate data are, if not impossible, highly limited. This does not mean that such data are useless for comparative inquiry. Indeed, almost all comparative/international research has so far been based on such information. Our purpose in reviewing the disparate nature of these official crime statistics is to emphasize the caution we must follow in attempting to draw any conclusions about crime/delinquency rates on the basis of statistics from one report as compared to those of another.

Yet, if not direct or necessarily directly comparable, official statistics can, in fact, be used as direct measures of official criminalization activities across societies. If, for example, we find that one society has extremely low arrest rates for juveniles compared to another, we could conclude that real differences exist in the relative criminal/delinquent involvement of young people in the two societies or that considerable differences exist in the use of official mechanisms of social control between the two countries, or that both are true. The official statistics alone would not allow us to determine which of these possibilities is the case. Nevertheless, such differences do imply that real differences exist in the "delinquency" problem experienced in the two societies. Thus, although it would be erroneous to draw conclusions about precise differences and similarities in the behavior of juveniles from official statistics, gross generalizations about (apparent) relative rates, patterns, and distributions can legitimately be based on the information they provide particularly when augmented by various other sources of data. In short, if one finds that the arrest rate for similar age groups in two countries is very similar (or even very different), one could conclude that the statistics are meaningless and simply argue that juveniles in the two societies are (or are not) alike as far as their delinquency is concerned, depending upon one's beliefs or particular agenda. Lacking other data on which to base such an assertion, however, the official rates (even if not directly comparable) can be employed with reasonable caution as a basis for judging the epidemiological dimensions of delinquency in the two societies. Indeed, it would be unreasonable to assume otherwise. Until criminology has better data collection techniques and far greater knowledge of the operation of criminal justice agencies throughout the world, we, in effect, have no other choice but to use available data albeit with appropriate caution. The official crime-rate data presented in Chapters Three and Four of this volume and the conclusions we draw from it should be read in this light.

Interpreting Self-Report Data

The second major source of data employed in this inquiry was the 1987 self-report survey of Madras and New Delhi high-school and institutionalized boys and girls and the 1990 survey of Madras high-school students. To cast the findings from these surveys in comparative perspective, subsamples of the National Youth Survey completed in the United States in 1987 were abstracted to match the Indian samples as closely as possible. The respective survey procedures were described above. Here we seek to comment on the extent to which findings from these surveys can reasonably be compared.

Sampling and Data Collection

Table 2.1 presents the demographic characteristics of respondents sampled in the various surveys. As far as the crucial variables of age and gender are concerned, the samples are very similar. As we discussed in an earlier article (see Hartjen and Kethineni, 1993) ideally, of course, a cross-cultural comparative analysis would involve a simultaneous replication of matched samples. However, such was not possible here for various reasons. Thus, as with official statistics, the National Youth and Indian surveys are not strictly comparable since they were conducted in different ways, at different times, and draw upon sampling universes that are not matched. However, while this requires us to interpret the findings with caution, we do not feel sampling and data collection differences seriously compromise the analysis.

For one, research shows that interview and questionnaire procedures produce essentially the same results in self-report surveys (Hindelang et al., 1981: 117–133; Krohn et al., 1975; Junger-Tas, 1994). Secondly, although the Indian survey involves an urban sample and the NYS a national sample, the urban residence of the Indian sample need not bias the findings. Indeed, Elliott et al. (1983: 83–93) found no major or consistent differences in the self-reported delinquency of urban, suburban, and rural respondents. And Hartjen and Priyadarsini's (1984: 57–82) earlier survey in India suggests that urban and village juveniles are probably not significantly different from one another either in overall delinquency or patterns of behavior. Also, since "urban" residence does not hold the same meaning in India and the United States (Vatuk, 1972; Wiebe, 1975), the differences in sampling universes are unlikely to profoundly affect the comparability of the survey findings. Finally, the nine-year difference in survey dates also seems to make little difference as far as the veracity of the results are concerned. The general finding from self-report surveys in the United States since the 1960's is that no substantial increase or decrease has taken place in American delinquency over the past three decades (see e.g., Empey & Stafford, 1991: 101–104). Similarly, a comparison of the 1978 and 1988 Indian surveys also indicates no major changes in Indian delinquency occurred over that decade. Moreover, although Elliott et al. (1983: 52–59) found that both prevalence and incidence rates among NYS respondents had decreased between 1976 and 1980, major reductions were not recorded. And arrest rates and proportions for juveniles show no consistent difference from 1978 to 1987. Thus, because the ages of NYS respondents sampled in later years did not match those included in the Indian survey, the 1978 survey date was selected for comparison purposes.

In short, while far from methodologically ideal, we have no reason to believe that major problems in data interpretation arise from comparative analysis of the Indian and National Youth Survey data investigated here. Thus, keeping the limitations of interpretation imposed by the data sets firmly in mind, it is possible to use the data analyzed here to assess differences and similarities in delinquent behavior in quite socially, culturally, and economically distinct societies (see Klein, 1994: 381–385).

Survey Instrument Compatibility

Some individuals may be skeptical about using a survey instrument developed in one society with samples of respondents in another (but see Junger-Tas et al., 1994). The grounds for such a concern are not clear. However, independent of the comparability of samples drawn for separately conducted surveys, the extent to which self-report questionnaires can be used cross-culturally warrants discussion.

Elaborate tests carried out in numerous countries of a common self-report instrument would be an ideal way to develop a universally applicable questionnaire or interview schedule, and the thirteen-nation study of western youths is a major advance in that regard. Lacking such a standard instrument at the time of our inquiry, the Indian survey instrument was designed after a model generally recognized as valid, reliable, and useful in the United States— the one used for the National Youth Survey. An instrument specifically designed for the Indian population could supposedly have been developed. But it is highly doubtful if a substantially different questionnaire would have been produced. Virtually no Indian consulted about the matter (students, criminologists, officials, general public) thought the ones used were culturally foreign. Nevertheless, it was not possible in carrying out the self-report surveys to assess response validity or reliability by comparing survey responses with police records, polygraph inquiry, elaborate test-retest strategies, and the like. Thus a statistical assessment of how truthfully Indian respondents answered the questionnaire similar to those carried out in tests of American surveys, for example, cannot be provided. However, considerable care went into the construction of the Indian instruments to insure that respondents not only understood but could respond to the questions with reasonable accuracy. In carrying out the first such survey in 1978, for instance, Hartjen and Priyadarsini (1984) went to great lengths to insure that respondents understood and truthfully responded to each question. Besides instructing respondents and aiding them in completing the questionnaire, post-response interviews were held with samples of respondents to review their answers. In the 1987 survey such interviews were not conducted, but similar questionnaire construction, review, and administration procedures were followed. The somewhat more elaborate instrument used for the 1990 survey was pre-tested on small samples of high-school students and others to determine what, if any, problems were encountered in interpreting and answering questions. This led to minor adjustments in the physical design of the questionnaire but indicated that respondents would have no problem in dealing with the instrument. In the case of drug-related questions, respondents' general unfamiliarity with substances such as hashish or cocaine led them to ask interviewers what these questions pertained to. In effect, their almost total ignorance of drug terminology serves to validate the extremely low frequencies of drug-related delinquency reported by them.

However, a more subtle problem exists in cross-national self-report research that could have an unmeasurable effect on results and that can largely go undetected. That problem involves the cultural differences in the meaning of words, something that standard reliability and validity measures may not reveal. For example, behaviors such as "joyriding," "cheating" on tests, or "strong-arming" others (translation issues notwithstanding) could produce extraneous answers depending on cultural differences in the meaning of such phrases as "driving without permission," "cheating," or "using force." It is not often clear that the behavior one may assume is being described by the terms is in fact similarly perceived by respondents in both societies. In-depth interview techniques may help minimize this problem but cannot resolve it. Indeed, is taking some stranger's car and driving around in it for a few hours equivalent to using a motorscooter belonging to someone in the village or an acquaintance without asking their permission? Very misleading interpretations could result from identical responses to questionnaire items tapping these different orders of behavior. This is especially the case if one is ignorant of the cultural context in which the acts occur. In drawing conclusions from our findings, therefore, we have actively sought to be culturally sensitive to what the numbers recorded in the self-report tables may actually mean. Were the authors not well versed in both the Indian and American sociocultural settings in which the self-report surveys were conducted, such sensitivity would be effectively impossible.

Finally, a rather obvious difference exists in what is recognized as "offense" behavior for juveniles in India and the United States, especially given the differences in legal codes between the two societies. Conspicuously absent in Indian definitions of delinquency are the host of "status" offense to which American juveniles could be subject (if even only rarely so in recent years) to legal/correctional treatment. Yet the self-report survey we used (as with most others) is made up of a substantial number of such activities. We, however, disagree with Klein's (1989: 37) suggestion that in comparative research we should try to construct measures of delinquency identical to official measures (e.g., arrest statistics) used in a country. Unless laws were identical across societies, comparative self-report research would be greatly hampered following this strategy. Instead, we feel that comparative research should focus on "behavior" and not necessarily its legal status as delinquent or criminal, as is our concern here. Thus, while truancy, for instance, may not be an "offense" under Indian law, but is a "status offense" in many American jurisdictions, the question "Have you skipped classes without a legitimate reason?" is legal-status neutral for all intents and purposes. Indeed, it is doubtful if many American juveniles contemplate that skipping classes could get them into legal trouble, any more or less than Indian truants contemplate that similar conduct could subject them to the wrath of school officials and family members if not official agents of legal control.

As such, even though the legal/illegal status of the act in question could affect the behavior of juveniles in either country, it is unlikely that this would influence responses to "have you ever" questions to any great extent. Obviously, legal status could influence commission rates, and this could be one factor in accounting for any differences in rates of behavior or even why children do or do not engage in the act at all (e.g., It's wrong! It's against the law!). But this concerns the issue of explanation, not inclusion or exclusion of particular behaviors from a self-report questionnaire. Whether or not the "offense item" is of interest to the researcher or whether the cost and effort justify including it in a self-report questionnaire are, of course, totally different matters.

CONCLUSION

The findings and conclusions presented in this volume are based on multiple data sources as well as the cross-national ethnographic experiences of the authors. Prominent among these are official arrest statistics and several self-reported delinquency surveys. Our principal interest in this undertaking is to compare and attempt to explain delinquency rates among Indian and American juveniles. This kind of inquiry should enhance both the descriptive and explanatory ability of criminological research and enable us to draw more exact conclusions about the epidemiology and etiology of delinquent behavior than single-society inquiries allow.

In a pure sense, this is not a "comparative" or even a "cross-national" investigation since the research was not explicitly designed with such an analysis in mind. While conducting the initial analysis of the data collected in the 1987 India survey, however, we realized that any conclusions we could draw from that data would have wider implications if we could somehow compare our findings in a somewhat systematic way with similar findings in the United States and/or other countries. Having a considerable body of information about delinquency in the United States upon which to draw, we decided to restrict the direct comparative analysis to an Indian/American comparison. Since the NYS offense categories were used as the model for constructing the 1987 survey, it seemed to be the appropriate survey for our comparisons. In so doing, we quickly realized that many of the questions we wanted to answer could not be addressed given the limitations of the 1987 survey. Consequently, another survey using a more elaborate instrument also modeled after the NYS instrument was conducted in 1990. Given the contingencies of funding for research in India, that inquiry was largely financed at the authors' own expense, necessitating our limiting it to a reasonable size. A survey using a sample drawn from the same high schools studied in 1987 (and mostly in 1978) became the strategy we followed. This allowed us to assess the data from both inquiries more fully, both with regard to offense behavior as well as the effects of using somewhat different survey instruments on samples drawn from similar population groups and at different times. If, however, this rather ad hoc approach to comparative research opens us up to accusations of comparing apples and oranges, we have but one response to make. Even if their taste is somewhat different, at least they are both fruits! It is therefore in that spirit that we begin our exploration in cross-national criminological research.

CHAPTER THREE

Law and Judicial Processing

To some extent, the juvenile justice system found in any country both reflects and helps to shape the nature of the delinquency problem that country exhibits. Laws and systems of justice specifically pertaining to juveniles are extremely diverse throughout the world, ranging from virtually none to highly complex (Shoemaker, in press). India's system of juvenile justice seems to fall somewhere between the extremes of systems found in other countries. This chapter is devoted to a comparison of India's law and system of justice for juveniles with those found in the United States and several other countries.

INDIA DELINQUENCY LAW

India's legal system is a combination of state and central government agencies (Mitra, 1988). A national penal code defines criminal acts for the entire country. In addition, a variety of "special" and "local" laws also define criminal acts, some of which apply nationally while others apply only to the specific state in which they have been enacted. Similarly, while law enforcement, judicial, and correctional activities are largely carried out at the state or local level, criminal justice agencies are under the supervisory authority of national administrative bodies (Bayley, 1969). For juveniles, this national/state system of law and justice produced a diverse (and in many places basically a non-existent) body of law and judicial procedures in India until 1986 when a national law passed by the Indian Parliament set up uniform definitions and procedures for the entire country.

Legal History

The first law to recognize a special status for juveniles in India took the form of the *Apprentice Act 1850* (Central Bureau of Correctional Services, 1970). *The Indian Penal Code 1860* set age limitations for criminal culpability, and *The Code of Criminal Procedure 1861* contained three sections (298, 399, and 562) that, in effect, allowed the separate trial of persons under age fifteen and their confinement in reformatories or placement on probation. This separate treatment of juveniles was bolstered by *The Reformatory Schools Act 1897* which provided that boys under fifteen who had been sentenced to transportation or imprisonment should instead be placed in reformatories. The period of incarceration was stipulated as not less than three or more than seven years (Natt & Malik, 1973; Ranchhoddas & Thakore, 1953). *The Madras Children Act 1920*, enacted in what is now the state of Tamil Nadu, was the first "delinquency" law in India. The law did not employ the term "delinquent" but instead defined a "child" as anyone under the age of fourteen, a "young person" as someone from age fourteen to eighteen; and a "youthful offender" as anyone under age eighteen convicted of an offense under the Penal Code or any special and local laws for which an offender could be imprisoned. This law was also significant in that it included within its provisions various "non-criminal" acts for juveniles (typically referred to as status offenders in the United States) and dependent/neglected children. As such, the law allowed for state control of children and young persons who are uncontrollable, homeless, dependent, neglected, destitute, frequent the company of reputed thieves, or are in moral danger, although they may not have been guilty of any offense.

Following the Madras example, several other provinces, such as Bengal (1922) and Bombay (1924), enacted similar legislation and various other states followed suit in the years following independence. Although quite varied in scope, definitions, and procedural requirements, by the 1960s many states had established separate bodies of law and systems of justice for juveniles. But the extent to which these laws were actually implemented and enforced varied widely. In 1960 *The Children's Act 1960* was passed. This law was applicable to union territories (jurisdictions directly administered by the central government) and was intended to serve as a model for state legislation and became the basis for the national law enacted in 1986.

Contemporary Juvenile Law in India

Prior to 1986, each of the Indian states was free to enact its own legislation and to establish separate systems of justice regarding juveniles. However, with the exception of several states and the union territories, few states either enacted special delinquency legislation, or, if such laws existed, did little to implement or enforce them. Where laws were in force, definitions of delinquency and procedures for dealing with youthful offenders varied widely from state to state. Thus, while the idea that juveniles enjoyed a distinctive legal status had been well established in India since 1920, it is likely that relatively few juveniles were subjected to or benefited from the legal processing this status accorded them. However, with passage of *The Juvenile Justice Act 1986* the patchwork situation of juvenile justice that characterized India changed dramatically (see Sharda, 1988; Hartjen & Kethineni, in press).

The importance of the 1986 legislation is that it not only requires uniform definitions and judicial procedures for delinquent and neglected children in India but that it also heralds a growing national recognition of youth crime and the special needs of children throughout India. It also foretells a growing nationalization of government in India that seeks to counterbalance the divisiveness of regional and "community" differences that have plagued the country since Independence.

Basically a modification and elaboration of *The Children's Act 1960*, the preamble to the 1986 legislation specifically sets forth the purpose of the law.

An act to provide for the care, protection, treatment, development and rehabilitation of neglected or delinquent juveniles and for the adjudication of certain matters relating to, and disposition of, delinquent juveniles (*The Juvenile Justice Act 1986*, 1988: 2).

This law defines a "juvenile" as a boy under the age of sixteen and a girl under age eighteen. "Delinquent" juveniles are those who have committed an "offense" (thus, basically restricting the definition to persons accused of crimes). "Neglected" juveniles, on the other hand, are defined as those juveniles who are either begging, without homes, destitute, whose parents are unfit or unable to exercise control over them, live in a brothel, lead an immoral, drunken, or depraved life, and/or who are likely to be abused or exploited for immoral purposes or unconscionable gain (*The Juvenile Justice Act 1986*, 1988: 4–5).

Both neglected and delinquent juveniles can be housed together in "observation" (detention) homes prior to adjudication of the case. Juveniles found to be neglected are subsequently to be housed in "juvenile homes" while those judged delinquent may be placed in "special homes."

Proceedings with regard to neglected juveniles are handled by special "welfare boards," which are ostensibly nonpunitive and nonjudicial in character. Juveniles found to be neglected can be dealt with in any manner the welfare board deems necessary for the well-being of the juvenile. Normally such persons are placed under the custody of some "fit person" or "fit institution" or are housed in so-called "juvenile homes" until they are no longer juveniles, or, if circumstances warrant, up to the age of eighteen (for boys) and twenty (for girls).

Delinquency proceedings are judicial in character and are governed by *The Code of Criminal Procedure 1973* (Krishnamurti & Alagamalai, 1975). However, as in other countries, juveniles are to be processed by separate "juvenile courts." The exact composition of these courts is left to the determination of individual states. But the law specifies that persons appointed to them must have special knowledge of child psychology and welfare. In addition, each court must be assisted by a panel of two honorary (unsalaried) social workers, at least one of whom must be a woman. Where no special court is appointed, the local magistrate is empowered to act with the authority of the juvenile court.

As detailed by the law, adjudicated delinquents can be disposed of by the court in the following ways (*The Juvenile Justice Act 1986*, pp. 18–21):

a. be sent home with admonition;

b. be released on probation on good conduct under the care of a "fit person";

c. be released on probation on good conduct under the care of a "fit institution";

d. be sent to a "special home" (training school) for not less than three years if a boy is over age fourteen and a girl is over age sixteen, or for both until such time as the individual ceases to be a juvenile;

e. be fined if over fourteen years of age and earns money;

f. and, if fined or sentenced to probation, be placed under the jurisdiction of a probation officer for a period not to exceed three years.

No juvenile may be sentenced to death or imprisonment or be committed to prison for default.

The law imposes some procedural restrictions in cases involving juveniles. Such proceedings, for example, must be held in a structure different from (or time apart from) that given to criminal matters. They should be concluded within three months. Trials are not open to the general public. While the juvenile and his or her parents are normally required to attend the proceedings, such attendance can be dispensed with by the court. Proceedings are to be kept confidential and reports to news and other media are prohibited, except if it is deemed to be in the interest of the juvenile. Finally, any order issued by the court or welfare board can be appealed to the court of session.

In short, under the 1986 law juvenile delinquents in India are persons below specific ages who commit acts that would be crimes if committed by adults. Such persons are to be processed by special courts following the due process rules applied to adults with the exception that the proceedings are private, confidential, and as "nonjudicial" as possible. Persons convicted as delinquents can be fined, incarcerated, or placed under supervision for up to three years but may not be executed or imprisoned.

DELINQUENCY LAW IN OTHER COUNTRIES

Compared to other countries, the Indian approach to juvenile justice is unique in its apparent simplicity and combined punitive/rehabilitative focus, but at the same time it is reminiscent of laws and procedures found elsewhere (see e.g., Hackler, 1991). Some sense of the international dimensions of juvenile justice (and India's place in the world picture) can be gained by a brief look at juvenile laws and systems of justice around the world. For this purpose, the United

States, Canada, and New Zealand have been selected to illustrate the similarity as well as diversity in how countries deal with young offenders and needy youth.

Delinquency Law in the United States

Since it has been extensively described and analyzed in a host of publications and undoubtedly well known to most readers of this volume, lengthy discussion of the juvenile justice approach taken by the United States is not required here except to contrast it with the post-1986 India system (see: Bernard, 1992; Champion, 1992; Roberts, 1989; Schwartz, 1989). Similar to pre-1986 India, the United States does not have a single system of juvenile justice. Rather it has fifty separate systems created by the various states. Supreme Court decisions of recent decades do provide some national coherence as far as due process rules are concerned, but essentially each state has its unique body of law and judicial/correctional approach. In some ways these systems are similar to one another, although they differ greatly as far as specific laws and approaches are concerned.

Founded as a legal-social-welfare mechanism to deal with needy and misbehaving youths at the turn of the century, disillusionment with rehabilitation, an apparent growth in crime generally and youth crime specifically, and a general social discontent over the past several decades has caused the juvenile justice systems of many states to first be transformed into benevolent "kiddie courts" and more recently into punitive legal systems aimed at young people (Bensinger, 1991; Corrado & Turnbull, 1992; Krisberg, 1988; Kratcoski & Kratcoski, 1991; Stapleton, 1982). Today, basically two separate philosophies ("justice" versus "welfare") guide the operation of juvenile justice in the various states. To some extent both philosophies can be found operating in individual states. But each jurisdiction can be categorized as emphasizing one approach over the other. In this respect, the term schizophrenic, as described by Empey and Stafford (1991:465–487), can be used to characterize the contemporary American approach to juvenile justice both across and within its numerous jurisdictions.

Many states have largely abandoned the idea that a special court and "correctional" system can handle both "criminal" as well as dependent and neglected youths so that the original idea that the juvenile court would act as a superparent responding to the needs, rather than the behavior, of young people has been eroded. Increasingly, the court is being reserved to handle "delinquent" youths (those accused of criminal-like behavior) while alternative ways of dealing with status offenders and needy children are being devised, either in the form of alternative courts (e.g, family courts) or various diversion programs. Liberalization of waiver laws has also meant that youths accused of serious offenses are increasingly being treated as adults and subject to "adult" proceedings and punishments. Thus, those handled by the juvenile court are basically processed in a "juvenile-criminal court" in which their legal rights are to some extent protected, but their dispositions are increasingly punitive in tone and intent. In this regard, an extensive patchwork of procedures and agencies exists throughout the country to respond to the needs of youths basically defined as "neglected." But, those that would be defined as "delinquent" are, in effect, subject to judicial processing similar to that adults receive and many (if not the same severity) of the sanctions received by adults.

To this extent, the approaches of India and the United States are similar— i.e., the separate definitions of "need" and "delinquent" youths and mechanisms for responding to youths defined as one or the other type. The approaches differ, however, in that India now has a nationalized (if not truly national) system, whereas the United States has preserved the legal autonomy of states. In addition, India's law, while treating offenders in a legal manner similar to that of adults, is explicitly non-punitive in nature (if not necessarily so in actual practice). Conversely, in the United States the orientations of specific states may be highly divergent, although a distinct trend toward a more punitive and less-benevolent handling of youths accused of "crimes" is clear throughout the country.

Delinquency Law in Canada

Compared to the United States and some western European countries, Canada, with a population of slightly less than 25 million people, has had a delinquency problem of rather inconsequential proportions, until recently (Hatch & Griffiths, 1992). Still low in terms of rates, in the past decade or so youth crime (especially violent youth crime) has become increasingly noticeable throughout the provinces. To some extent this apparent growth of a "delinquency problem" justified, if not directly produced, a rather substantial change in Canada's delinquency law in the early 1980s (Corrado et al., 1992).

In 1982 the Canadian Parliament enacted the *Young Offenders Act* (YOA) which went into force in 1984. This law replaced the *Juvenile Delinquency Act* (JDA) in force since 1908. The earlier law rested on the philosophy of positive criminology and was decidedly non-punitive and rehabilitative in nature. By contrast, the YOA is largely based on the idea that youths willfully engage in their behavior and thus can be held responsible for their actions (Leschied, 1991). As Bala (1992: 25) notes "... the YOA is unmistakably criminal law, not child welfare legislation." As such, the juvenile justice system of Canada was redesigned as a modified adult criminal justice system focusing on the "offense" rather than the "offender," with procedural fairness and determinate sentencing based on the offense and juvenile's prior record being the priority. Bala (1992:25) describes the act as follows:

... the *YOA* is not simply a "'Kiddie' Criminal Code." Rather, the act establishes a youth justice system which is separate from the adult criminal justice system and distinctive in several critical respects. First, while it recognizes that young persons must be held accountable for criminal acts, they need not always be held accountable in the same manner or to the same extent as adults. Secondly, the *YOA* extends rights and safeguards to youth that go beyond those enjoyed by adults. Perhaps most importantly, the Act recognizes that youth, by virtue of their adolescence, have special needs and circumstances which must be considered when any decision is made pursuant to the *YOA*.

Although provisions under the YOA allow for mitigating both the degree of accountability and the severity of sanctions received by juveniles found guilty of crimes under this law, both the length and number of custodial sanctions received by juveniles increased substantially shortly after implementation of the law. According to Markwart (1992) this increase cannot be readily accounted for by any other factors so that the law has probably resulted in more punitive reactions to young offenders than had previously been the practice under the JDA (also see Leschied et al., 1993; Sentencing in Youth Courts, 1990). On the other hand, much like the various "diversion" programs found in many American jurisdictions, the YOA also has provisions allowing offenders to be dealt with outside the formal court by means of "alternative measures." And the law provides formal endorsement for the common and traditional practice by Canadian police (as probably with police everywhere) to take no official actions against juveniles at their discretion.

The Young Offenders Act is a national law applying to persons between ages twelve and eighteen. Like India, Canada gives each province the responsibility of establishing its own administrative structure to enforce the law, undoubtedly resulting in rather wide disparities of how the law is enforced and interpreted throughout the country. Youths apprehended under the YOA are guaranteed the due process rights accorded to all persons accused of crimes in Canada. In addition, however, the law details a number of special rights to be accorded youths from the point of apprehension through disposition.

The specific form youth courts are to take is left to the discretion of the individual provinces, but they must hold hearings apart from those accorded adults. Proceedings in the youth court involve "summary" procedures, similar to those governing "summary conviction offenses." No preliminary inquiries are held. All trials are before a single judge. And, as in the United States, no jury trials are allowed. Except for a jury, during the trial a juvenile is accorded all the due process rights an adult would receive in a summary case. Assuming a not guilty plea, the determination of guilt is based on the "beyond a reasonable doubt" standard. If acquitted, a child could still be dealt with under provincial child welfare or mental health legislation. Unless special permission is received, the media cannot publish identifying information about a youth.

Youths convicted under the YOA can receive any of the following dispositions:

1. absolute discharge;
2. fine up to $1,000;
3. restitution or compensation;
4. up to 240 hours of community service;
5. up to two years' probation;
6. detention for purposes of treatment up to two years;
7. open or secure custody up to three years;
8. in the case of murder, custody up to five years.

If a custody disposition, the court can subsequently hold a disposition review hearing and consequently reduce or modify (but not increase) the disposition.

Under certain conditions, both the accused and the Crown attorney can request transfer (waiver) of a case to an adult criminal court. If granted, a youth could be tried as an adult and receive whatever criminal sanctions an adult could receive in a similar case.

Except for the explicit provision pertaining to "neglected" juveniles, the Canadian and Indian laws are quite similar both in orientation and substance. Unlike laws in the United States, both provide a fairly uniform, national scheme for dealing with young people accused of violations of criminal laws. India more explicitly suggests a child welfare approach in dealing with juveniles, but both laws are clearly oriented to treating young offenders in a legalistic, pseudo-criminal manner, allowing for the protection of due process rights. While emphasizing a legalistic approach, both reflect the same ambivalence toward the treatment of young offenders exhibited by American authorities in the diverse and often contradictory approaches taken by American jurisdictions.

Delinquency Law in New Zealand

Perhaps because it has neither a serious crime or delinquency problem, New Zealand, with a population of slightly more than three million people, recently enacted *The Children, Young Persons and Their Families Act 1989* (Moffitt & Silva, 1988; Morris & Maxwell, 1993). This law is clearly social welfare legislation geared to the care, well-being, and protection of young people. As listed by Maxwell and Morris (1993:1–2), the objectives of the legislation are to promote the well-being of young people and their families by assisting families to care for their young and to repair disruptive relationships when such occur. In addition, the law seeks to protect youths from harm, abuse, and neglect. At the same time, young people are to be held accountable for their actions, but the state is to deal with them in a way that acknowledges their needs and enhances their development.

As far as "offenders" are concerned, criminal proceedings are not to be used if any alternative means exist. If employed, criminal proceedings should not be used for welfare purposes. However, whatever measures are used, they should seek to strengthen the family or group and foster their ability to deal with the offender. In that regard, young offenders are to be kept in the community and sanctions are to be the least restrictive possible. Accused are entitled to special protection during any legal proceedings. While age is a mitigating factor, due regard is also to be given to the interests of any victim.

In brief, India, Canada, and most United States jurisdictions have emphasized the offense behavior of and adopted a legalistic approach to juvenile offenders. New Zealand, on the other hand, has done the reverse, focusing instead on a social welfare, family-bonding approach. Nevertheless, the New Zealand law also conceals a justice ideology that, while lessening or mitigating the accountability of young people, holds them responsible for their actions. This dual-purpose philosophy is reflected in the design and operation of the country's juvenile justice system.

In New Zealand the age of criminal responsibility starts at age ten. However, except in the case of murder or manslaughter, children under age fourteen cannot be prosecuted. Otherwise, children up to seventeen whose behavior causes concern can be dealt with by a warning, police diversion to a Family Group Conference (FGC), if in need of care or protection, referred to the Department of Social Welfare (DSW), or dealt with by the family court. Persons over sixteen can be treated as adults in either district or high courts. Youth courts automatically transfer cases involving murder to the high court and can also transfer cases involving other serious offenses to this court.

As is true in the United States and other countries, police in New Zealand can essentially handle a delinquency case in three ways: informally, formal arrest, or diversion to some agency (in this case the Youth Aid Section). Then the case is either dealt with in a legal fashion with formal charges and court hearing, or a semi-formal procedure involving the Family Group Conference is followed.

What is distinctive about the New Zealand approach is the importance of the Family Group Conference (FGC) regardless of the particular route followed in the disposition of the case. In the FGC procedure, the matter is discussed among all participating parties with the state acting as a kind of arbitrator to facilitate and give force to the resolution reached. In the youth court procedure, trial proceedings similar to those followed in adult criminal courts are carried out, but both before and after the hearing FGC's are held to either make placement or disposition recommendations which the court is obliged to follow.

In this respect, even though formal court proceedings are reserved for only a minority of young offenders, Family Group Conferences are at the heart of the process, either as an alternative way of dealing with cases or as an integral feature of the formal apparatus. Those cases that appear before the court are accorded due process, legal representation, and are to receive sanctions appropriate to the gravity of the offense. Proceedings are closed and confidential. Legal representation is provided youths who do not have attorneys, and all youths are allowed a "lay advocate" to insure that the court is aware of cultural matters relevant to the proceedings.

Youths who admit to or are found guilty of offenses in the youth court can receive a variety of dispositions. Among these are supervision with residence, other supervision, fine, reparation, restitution, or forfeiture. More lenient dispositions include a kind of conditional discharge, admonition, discharge, or withdrawal of the information. Court orders are determinate and supervision with residence can involve any person or organization so nominated, thereby allowing cultural or tribal elders to work with the offender directly.

PROCESSING AND DISPOSITION OF CASES IN INDIAN JUVENILE JUSTICE

National data on the judicial processing and dispositions of juvenile offenders throughout India are difficult to come by and of questionable validity. Official crime and arrest statistics report the dispositions of juveniles sent to court. But no age or gender breakdowns are provided, and the disposition categories are often vague and seemingly overlapping. Moreover, until 1988 (the year the 1986 national law went into effect) the category "juvenile" included persons up to twenty-one. Thus, it is neither clear which offenders were treated as "juveniles" or the extent to which persons below eighteen were treated differently from their eighteen- to twenty-one-year-old counterparts.

Data on the processing of juveniles by "juvenile courts" and the handling of juveniles sent to and discharged from "children's homes" and "fit person" institutions as designated by various state Children Acts are also available. However, the extent to which these data pertain to all juveniles arrested and processed by the judicial/correctional system is not known. In spite of the rather severe limitations of official court/corrections data in India, some estimates of how youthful offenders are handled by Indian authorities can be gleaned from this information, and rough comparisons to similar types of information provided by authorities in other countries can be made.

Dispositions

Table 3.1 depicts the numbers and treatment of juveniles processed by juvenile courts in India the first two years following implementation of *The Juvenile Justice Act 1986.* Two things should be noted from this table. First is the extremely small number of cases processed. For a country the size of India, 20,000 cases is a miniscule number. Undoubtedly, a larger number of persons under eighteen are actually dealt with by India's system of criminal justice. But, even then, it is clear that very few young people experience formal judicial processing in India. Second, of those processed, only 4 to 5 percent receive "confinement" as a disposition. Instead "probation," fines, and simple release to parents/guardians appear to be the common fate of juveniles appearing before Indian magistrates. Indeed, almost one third of those disposed were acquitted or sent home with a warning.

The data in Table 3.1 only apply to juveniles convicted of some "offense." But many non-delinquent youngsters may also receive processing by authorities in India. Unfortunately, post-1986 data on these cases are not yet available. However, information on how cases were processed under the various Children Acts by juvenile or children's courts throughout the country in the early 1980s provides clues as to how "neglected" youths are probably handled by the recently established welfare boards. Indeed, the similarities in the dispositions "delinquents" received in both time periods suggest that in spite of major changes in law, major changes have not occurred in how the Indian equivalent of "JINS" cases are dealt with.

The figures in Table 3.2 are based on a survey of juvenile/children courts covering 10 states and 3 union territories and should, thus, be viewed as relative rather than exhaustive. In the jurisdictions surveyed, 64,147 cases were pending or received during the year. Of these 40,707 (63.4 percent) were disposed. A slight majority of the disposed cases (53.5 percent) were "non-delinquents" involving destitute, neglected, uncontrollable, and victimized children. The vast majority (total of 88 percent) of either delinquent or non-delinquent cases involved boys with boy:girl ratios of 2:1 to 12:1 depending upon type of case.

Table 3.1
Dispositions Received by Juveniles Arrested and Sent to Court for Violations of the Indian Penal Code and Special and Local Laws, India, 1988 and 1989

	1988		1989	
Disposition	#	%	#	%
Sent Home After Admonition	4,009	17	3,253	14
Released on Probation Under:				
Parent/Guardian	7,380	32	9,402	41
Fit Institution	2,229	10	1,809	8
Sent to Special Home	920	4	1,082	5
Fined	4,841	21	3,772	17
Acquitted/Other	3,849	17	3,458	15
Total Disposed	23,228	100	22,776	100

Source: Based on *Crime in India 1988* (New Delhi: National Crime Records Bureau, 1989), p. 149 and *Crime in India 1989* (New Delhi: National Crime Records Bureau, 1990), p. 158.

Table 3.2
Dispositions Received by Boys and Girls from Juvenile/Children's Courts,
India, 1982–1983

Dispositions	% Receiving Disposition	
	Boys	Girls
Restored to Parent/Guardian Unconditionally	30	28
Sent to Children's Home	5	9
Discharged/Acquitted	10	13
Released on Admonition	23	18
Released on Supervision	7	4
Sent to Approved/Certified School	6	8
Placed in Care of Fit Person/Institution	5	8
Discharged/Other	14	12
Total Disposed	35,861	4,846

Source: *Statistical Abstracts India 1989* (New Delhi: Central Statistical
Organization, Department of Statistics, Ministry of Planning, Government of
India, 1992), Table 4.

In spite of the numeric disparity by gender, overall remarkably similar
dispositions were received by both boys and girls. Much like the dispositions of
delinquency cases in 1988, almost a third of the cases were resolved by
restoring children to their parents unconditionally. Also, rather large
proportions were acquitted, discharged, or released after admonition, or some
other discharge action was taken. In this respect, for youngsters (delinquent or
non-delinquent) who appear before courts dealing with juveniles in India, only
about 11 percent of the boys and 17 percent of the girls receive some kind of
institutionalization (not necessarily "correctional" in nature), and a very small
number are placed on formal probation.

Institutions

Reliable information on institutions for juveniles in India is extremely difficult
to come by and provides a somewhat obtuse picture when available.
Preliminary information made available to the authors by Indian officials shows
that as of 1987 some 626 institutions of all types (e.g., observation homes,
juvenile homes, after care) were in operation throughout India with a total
capacity of 41,351 wards. But information on the exact number of juveniles
housed in these institutions was not yet available.

Two surveys (see Table 3.3) conducted in the early to mid-1980s of
children's homes/fit person institutions and approved/certified schools
(correctional facilities) cast some light on the nature and extent of the
institutional treatment delinquent and other youths receive in India. A total of
232 homes and 106 schools (of which 92 provided data) were investigated
throughout the country in the two surveys. This number was roughly equivalent

to the number of institutions of similar types in 1987. Thus, it appears that under *The Juvenile Justice Act 1986,* the names of existing institutions were simply changed, but no significant change in the number or types of institutions to which delinquent and neglected children could be sent probably took place.

Table 3.3
Children Homes/Fit Person Institutions and Approved/Certified Schools, India, 1981–1985

Institutions and Wards	Homes		Schools	
	#	%	#	%
Institution Characteristics				
School Classification	232	100	92	100
Government	64	55	79	86
Voluntary Agency	52	45	13	14
Male	51	44	N/A	
Female	28	24	N/A	
Co-Sex	37	32	N/A	
Expenditures in 100,000 Rs	253.8	100	337.1	100
Establishment	109.7	43	163.9	50
Children	137.8	54	154.7	46
After Care/Other	6.3	3	2.1	14
Characteristics of Wards	13,001	100	11,916	100
Age				
< 12	5,661	43	7,059	41
12–16	5,172	40	8,115	47
16 >	2,168	17	1,912	12
Religion				
Christian	1,709	13	971	6
Hindu	9,048	70	14,133	82
Muslim	903	7	1,461	9
Sikh	38	<1	N/A	
Other	1,303	10	521	3
Reason for Custody				
Delinquent	1,159	9	1,807	22
Destitute/Neglected/Orphaned	11,067	85	6,167	74
Victimized	775	6	340	4

Source: Based on "Statistical Survey: Children Homes/Fit Persons Institutions," *Social Defence* #96 April 1989, pp. 43–54 and "Statistical Survey: Approved/Certified Schools," *Social Defence* #81 July 1985, pp. 43–57.
Note: For school data, number of wards is equal to end of year totals, age and religion based on N of 17,086, reason for custody based on N of 8,314.

More than half the facilities were government run although a large number of voluntary (or private) facilities were also found. Only about a quarter of the homes were exclusively for females, although almost one third were co-sex institutions. The various states and union territories surveyed spent almost 60 million rupees on these institutions. While this is a substantial sum in India, compared to the United States, India does not devote sizable resources to housing needy and delinquent youths.

Only about 25,000 youths were housed in these various institutions on any given day, with about half that number being admitted and discharged during the course of a year. A surprisingly large percentage of the wards were under twelve years of age. Hindus are somewhat underrepresented and Christians decidedly overrepresented in homes although not so in (correctional) schools. But of most significance is the fact that fewer than 10 percent of those housed in homes were delinquents and only 22 percent of the youths in schools were delinquents. Instead, almost 80 percent of all institutionalized youths in India were not convicted of any offense. Given that disposition data for delinquents processed both before and after the 1986 law indicate that very few delinquents are actually sentenced to incarceration, these figures are reasonably reflective of the reasons for which youths are confined in institutions throughout India. Indeed, both from the authors' observations and the comments of correctional authorities in India, it appears that institutions in India (while housing delinquents) are often primarily facilities to provide care and housing for children who otherwise have little or no alternative recourse. In this regard, they are more like places of "refuge" than "correctional" institutions—a situation quite unlike that found in the United States and Canada.

PROCESSING YOUTHFUL OFFENDERS IN OTHER COUNTRIES
Due to lack of available data and differences in recording and categorizing practices (among other things), direct comparisons of India's court and corrections data can not be made with that of any other country. However a brief survey of similar kinds of information (while often wanting) published by authorities in the United States, Canada, and New Zealand helps place the Indian figures in perspective and allows us to gain a broader comparative sense of the international dimensions of and societal responses to needy and delinquent youths.

Delinquency Processing in the United States
Table 3.4 presents disposition data for delinquent and status offenders processed by American juvenile courts in 1988. Corrections data for 1985 are presented in Table 3.5. In contrast to India, vast numbers of young people in the United States experience juvenile justice processing in any given year. Indeed, even when neglected and destitute children are counted, the number of cases

handled by Indian juvenile courts equal less than 1 percent of the numbers processed through American courts.

Similarly, whereas only small numbers of (even delinquency) cases are institutionalized in India, institutionalization (even of status offenders) is a much more popular disposition in the American system. However, like India, the bulk of the cases disposed in 1988 by juvenile courts in the United States were either dismissed or placed on probation.

In 1985 more than six times as many American compared to Indian youths were housed in some kind of correctional institution and almost an equal disparity existed in the number of such facilities found in the two countries. In terms of national currency, the jurisdictions in the United States collectively spend about 33 times more on confining their youths than do Indian jurisdictions.

Table 3.4
Dispositions Received by Petitioned Delinquency and Status Offense Cases in United States Juvenile Courts, 1988

Dispositions	Delinquency #	Delinquency %	Status #	Status %
Petitioned	559,000	48	82,000	100
Waived	12,000	2	—	—
Adjudicated	324,000	58	50,000	61
Placement	97,000	30	9,000	18
Probation	185,000	57	30,000	60
Other	25,000	8	7,000	15
Dismissed	16,000	5	3,000	7
Nonadjudicated	223,000	40	32,000	39
Placement	4,000	2	< 1,000	1
Probation	59,000	26	6,000	18
Other	31,000	14	6,000	19
Dismissed	130,000	56	20,000	62

Source: *Juvenile Court Statistics 1988* (Washington, DC: U.S. Department of Justice, May 1990), pp. 14 & 38.

Like in India, most wards in the United States are males, but most are between fourteen and seventeen years of age with only a small proportion under fourteen and less than 10 percent over seventeen. While whites make up the bulk of the institutional population, unlike the slight overrepresentation of religious minorities in Indian facilities, racial minorities disproportionately appear in the ranks of American wards. Finally, almost all youths in correctional facilities in the United States are delinquents, whereas less than 20 percent of those in comparable institutions in India are so categorized. Facilities other than "correctional" ones house dependent, neglected, and similar youths throughout the United States so that their numbers do not appear in Table 3.5. Including them would only serve to swell the ranks of those youths coming under some kind of state control in the United States, thereby increasing the disparity between the two countries.

Table 3.5
Private and Public Correctional Facilities, United States, 1985

Institutions and Wards	#	%
Institution Characteristics		
Institution Classification	3,036	100
Detention Centers	428	14
Shelters	297	10
Reception/Diagnostic Centers	39	1
Training Schools	263	9
Ranches/Farms/Camps	260	9
Halfway Houses/Group Homes	1,749	57
Expenditures (1984) Millions $	205.2	100
Characteristics of Wards	83,404	100
Gender		
Male	66,393	80
Female	17,011	20
Age		
9 Years And Younger	732	1
10–13 Years	9,043	11
14–17 Years	66,898	80
18–20 Years	6,652	8
21 Years and Older	77	<1
Race		
White	53,968	65
Black	27,473	33
Other	1,961	2
Reason for Custody		
Delinquent	57,743	69
Status Offender	9,019	11
Dependent/Neglected/Abused	7,348	9
Disturbed/Retarded	1,932	2
Other	208	<1
Voluntary Admission	7,119	9

Source: Based on *Children in Custody, 1975–1985* (Washington, DC: U.S. Department of Justice, May 1989), Tables 14, 19, & 31.

Clearly, we are not dealing with matched data sets here so any conclusions we might draw from these comparisons are at best highly speculative. However, it does seem clear that tremendous differences exist between India and the United States in both the absolute and relative numbers of youths handled by agencies of justice and the relative types of dispositions they received (e.g., proportions institutionalized). Thus, while the United States would appear to have a delinquency problem of mega proportions, India either has few delinquent/needy youths to deal with or has devoted few resources to so doing.

Delinquency Processing in Canada

Court data for Canada indicate that a small (but sizable for the nation's population) number of children appear on delinquency petitions before juvenile courts. Of these, about 80 percent are found guilty. However, as with the United States and India, relatively few offenders are institutionalized in Canada—even though the relative proportion appears to have increased since passage of the more punitive law in 1985. Nevertheless, insofar as the "most

Table 3.6
Dispositions Received by Young Persons Appearing in Youth Courts, Canada, 1988–1989

Action & Dispositions	#	%
Total Appearing	35,094	100
Action Taken		
Transfer to Adult	50	< 1
Guilty	28,228	80
Not Guilty/Dismissed	1,534	4
Stay/Withdrawn	5,187	15
Other	95	< 1
Dispositions of Guilty		
Secure Custody	2,921	10
Detain for Treatment	28	< 1
Open Custody	2,741	10
Probation	14,472	51
Fine	4,391	16
Community Service	1,865	7
Other	376	1
Absolute Discharge	1,0931	4

Source: Based on Canadian Center for Justice Statistics. Sentencing in Youth Courts, 1984–85 to 1988–89. *Juristat Service Bulletin 10* (No. 1) Ottawa, Ontario (Canada): Statistics Canada, Tables 2 & 3.

severe" disposition is concerned, confinement is reserved for only about 20 percent of those found guilty of crimes in Canadian juvenile courts. Probation remains the single most frequent disposition.

In 1986–87 a daily average of 4,013 youths in Canada were in confinement. Of these, about 40 percent were in secure facilities with most of the rest in open custody confinement and a small number in detention awaiting trial or disposition. Approximately 86 percent of confined youths were males. In contrast to India, only about 3 percent are under twelve with about 30 percent being seventeen years of age and almost 75 percent between fifteen and seventeen. These figures only deal with persons convicted of offenses in juvenile courts, so dependent, neglected, and other needy youths are not included. Undoubtedly both the numbers of "confined" youths in Canada would increase and their demographic characteristics change were such cases recorded in official disposition data. In any case, available data suggests that in spite of Canada's enactment of a "modified justice" law, in reality relatively few youths are subjected to formal judicial processing as delinquents and, of these, only a select few are actually accorded the most severe dispositions available to Canadian juvenile courts (Canadian Center for Justice Statistics, 1990; 1994).

Delinquency Processing in New Zealand

According to Dr. Gabrielle Maxwell (personal communication) of the Office of the Commissioner for Children in New Zealand, no reliable annual national statistics on youth court outcomes are available for New Zealand following enactment of the new youth law because: (a) published 1990 statistics used old disposition categories that are not reminiscent of those employed in the new system, and (b) after 1990 no such information is being collected. Thus, any comparative comments we might make about societal reactions in New Zealand to young offenders are speculative. That caveat notwithstanding, enough information is available in diverse sources to put together a picture of official delinquency in New Zealand for rough comparative analysis (Department of Corrections, 1992).

Table 3.7 shows the numbers and outcomes of cases processed in youth courts the year following enactment of the new law in 1989. Several observations can be made regarding the data provided in this table. For one, even granted that New Zealand has a relatively small population compared to the other three countries discussed here, a total of only 7,378 youth court cases suggests that judicial processing is an infrequent response to New Zealand's offending youth. More than 68 percent of these cases involved property offenses with violent crimes totaling about 10 percent and various public order crimes about 20 percent—a pattern found routinely in courts throughout the world. Similarly about 88 percent of the charges involved males. However, only minor gender-related differences exist in the actual results of youth court processing. While age-based breakdowns are not provided, only youths fourteen, fifteen, and sixteen years of age can be charged so that a relatively small age spectrum is reflected in these data.

Table 3.7

Total Charges and Results of Hearings in Youth Courts, by Gender, New Zealand, 1990

Results	Boys #	Boys %	Girls #	Girls %
Total Charges	6,484	100	894	100
Not Proved/Withdrawn	1,855	29	306	34
Proved but Discharged	1,323	20	216	24
Imprisonment	747	12	38	4
Community Based				
Periodic Detention	153	2	14	2
Adult Supervision	133	2	18	2
Community Care/Service	84	1	13	2
Fined	66	1	7	1
Care D.S.W.	17	< 1	0	0
Supervision Social Worker	1,626	25	182	20
Other	480	7	100	11

Source: Based on *Justice Statistics 1990* (Wellington, New Zealand: Statistics New Zealand, 1991), pp. 43–44.

Similar to American juvenile courts, about 30 percent of the charges were withdrawn or not proved, and about 20 percent of those proved were still dismissed. Thus, about 50 percent of the cases that involve formal charges result in no disposition. Of those not withdrawn or discharged, about 23 percent of the boys and 10 percent of the girls are "imprisoned for corrective training" (respectively, 12 percent and 4 percent of those charged). Equal proportions of the cases disposed (about 14 percent) receive some kind of community disposition or fines, and almost half are placed under the supervision of a social worker. According to Maxwell this supervision could involve "residence orders" (such as detention in a youth facility), but the category does not delineate between detention and non-detention statuses. In any case, the actual number of dispositions with confinement is probably somewhat higher than the table discloses. The category "other" involves a variety of dispositions including many of those referred to as "alternative sentences" in the United States (e.g., reparation, forfeiture, etc.).

In spite of its unique law, when compared to other countries, in practice those cases that do appear in New Zealand youth courts are disposed of in ways not radically different from the dispositions youths receive in American, Indian, or Canadian courts. However, many of the New Zealand cases are in effect "dropped" from further processing, even if proved guilty, and very few potential youth court cases actually receive formal judicial processing in the first place.

According to an early analysis by Hassall and Maxwell (1991), about 74 percent of the youth justice cases coming to the attention of authorities receive a police warning or diversion. Twenty percent are referred to the Department of Social Welfare, and only 6 percent are sent to the youth court. Most of these (about 73 percent of all referrals) are screened by the Family Group Conference procedure. Of these cases, 15 percent are subsequently sent to youth courts for formal hearings, and only a small minority (about 4 percent) of the cases that were first dealt with by Family Group Conferences wound up receiving some type of custodial disposition. In short, the Family Group Conference acts as a kind of pre-court screening device. Only those cases not agreeing to a conference or for which no settlement could be reached actually receive full youth court processing and disposition. In that regard, most of the "informal" results of the youth court cases are the product of FGC's.

About 12,000 "care and protection" cases (similar to neglect or in some ways "status offense" cases in India and the United States) were also handled by juvenile authorities in New Zealand in 1990 (Maxwell & Robertson, 1991). Of these, only 31 percent were referred to the "Care and Protection Co-coordinator" and 28 percent resulted in FGC's. Official action occurred in only 14 percent of the actual cases brought to the attention of authorities. Why this rather substantial shrinkage occurred is not known. However, under the law the principle of "minimal intervention" undoubtedly has some impact, and in other instances informal resolution of the case may have sufficed to deal with the matter. Of the cases handled by FGC's about 66 percent receive Department of Social Welfare or other service provision outcomes. No further action was taken in 15 percent of the cases, and 10 percent were returned to the court to resolve the matter. In effect, rather than using the authority of the court to handle most non-criminal matters in New Zealand, informal procedures along with the FGC approach are employed (but see Department of Justice, 1992).

The use of a kind of community body rather than judicial authority to deal with matters of need and misconduct (as the New Zealand FGC experiment envisions) is yet to be fully tested or assessed, although as discussed in Chapter Seven, informal ways of responding to misbehaving and needy children have been practiced in countries like India for centuries. Available data for New Zealand suggest that many cases that would have received formal judicial processing prior to the new law are now being diverted, either before formal proceedings begin, or even prior to their resolution once notices of need or charges of offenses have been filed.

Yet, New Zealand's system of institutionalized informality does not appear to produce dramatically different outcomes than those received by youths in other countries who exhibit similar behavior or are in similar life situations. In New Zealand few young offenders are incarcerated, as is the case for all the juvenile justice systems discussed here. And, even then, the proportions of those that are confined are remarkably similar. Most youths who could be processed formally are "diverted" from the system (either extralegally or by legal mandate). And most of those who are subjected to "processing" escape the full wrath or benefit of the "system" in any country. In that respect, the specific approach any people take in dealing with their needy or misbehaving youths may be more of a symbolic statement reflecting the culture, socioeconomic circumstances, and political forces that govern the lives of a nation's inhabitants rather than matters of justice, need, reason, or scientific wisdom.

CONCLUSION

The rather limited comparative analysis of law and official handling presented in this chapter highlights a number of things about how youthful misconduct is viewed and reacted to by legal authorities around the world. As represented by the countries focused on here, tremendous diversity (if, perhaps, only superficial) exists in the formal ways countries define delinquency, the philosophies guiding their responses to it, and the structures and mechanisms societies establish to deal with offenders. For example, India's new juvenile justice law might be called a "benevolent-legalistic" approach. The United States, on the other hand, is characterized by a schizophrenic mixture ranging from states with extreme punitive-justice models to traditional rehabilitative-social welfare jurisdictions. Canada has adapted a national "modified-justice" approach tempered by discretion on the part of provincial authorities as to how "modified" the local system may be. And New Zealand represents an explicit "welfare-family-control" non-system with a hint of punitive handling for extreme cases. Other countries have developed approaches that both resemble and deviate from the four systems discussed here (see, e.g., Feld, 1994; Hackler, 1991a).

However, all four societies exhibit considerable ambivalence as to what to include in formal reactions, who should be handled in formal-institutional versus informal-welfare ways, and just what the objective of juvenile justice is to be in the first place. In many respects this ambivalence represents the underlying dilemma of child rearing as such—the unending conflict between nurturing and disciplining our young.

This is perhaps no better reflected than in the dispositional statistics available for the countries examined. The overriding similarities across the composite disposition categories used in this analysis suggest that, regardless of law, societies respond in very similar ways to those youths caught up in their judicial/correctional machinery. Institutional confinement, for example, is reserved for a small minority of those youths processed in every country, although the frequency with which this sanction is used may vary across jurisdictions. India, in this respect, appears to be at the low end of the punitive spectrum, with the United States being at the high end. But, some kind of supervised release ("probation") is singularly most favored by all, and simply dismissing offenders or imposing some kind of "alternative" sanction (e.g., restitution, apology, community service) on them is a common practice in any country.

To some extent this may reflect a desire on the part of people to, in effect, "give kids a break" before imposing harsh punishment. It could also reflect the comparatively infrequent occurrence of serious offense behavior on the part of most youths in every society. This, however, cannot be determined either from a scrutiny of law, the numbers of young people responded to by juvenile justice authorities, or the manner in which they are dealt with.

Obviously, given the tremendous amount of pre-judicial screening (both official and informal) that goes into the juvenile justice processing of youths in all societies, it is impossible to draw any but the most vague conclusions about the extent, nature, and distribution of delinquent behavior from analyses of law and/or judicial processing—and, therefore, the need for or appropriateness of either in the first place. One could assume that a welfare-oriented legal system with negligible rates of institutional confinement would reflect low rates of offense behavior. Conversely, a justice-model approach with high incarceration rates would indicate that a society is beset by a serious delinquency problem. But, of course, neither may be true.

The law and judicial system of a country can, in this regard, only offer clues as to the nature and scope of a country's delinquency problem. But as far as describing and explaining the actual behavior of its young people is concerned, they can provide us with little more. Law and judicial practices are barometers of societal reaction more than measures of the behavior being reacted to (Hartjen, 1978:5–15; Turk, 1969:10). Of interest in their own right, they can only serve as crude indicators of the extent and nature of the delinquent behavior to be found in any society. As such, the next two chapters seek to more directly map the extent and distribution of delinquency on the part of India's youth and compare it with the behavior of American youth and juveniles in societies around the world.

Chapter Four

Arrests

The disposition data presented in Chapter Three suggest that youth crime and delinquency in India are practically nonexistent, given the numbers of juveniles processed by courts or confined in various facilities especially when compared to the rather sizable number of youths similarly handled in the United States. But legislation and court dispositions are far removed from the actual behavior we seek to understand and deal with. Special laws may or may not suggest that youthful misconduct is a matter worthy of concern. Disposition data can tell us little about those offenders/offenses not detected or processed to the full extent by legal authorities. Thus, even though suggestive, they can not tell us how extensive delinquency is among the youth of a country. Nor can they tell us where it is located and among whom what forms of conduct comprise it and how the youth of this country compare to those of some other. It is the purpose of this chapter to begin to more fully address these questions.

As far as available data sources are concerned, arrest statistics are generally recognized as being as close to measuring the "real thing" as we are likely to get, save for direct observation and self-reported surveys (see Grove et al., 1985; Hindelang et al., 1981). Therefore, this chapter reports arrest data in India and attempts to compare arrest frequencies for India with similar data pertaining to juveniles in the United States and elsewhere.

General Patterns in India

Table 4.1 summarizes the numbers of arrests recorded in India and the proportion of arrests attributed to juveniles for 1987 (the year of the 1987 self-report survey). Offenses are grouped into two broad categories: Indian Penal Code offenses (IPC) and special and local law violations (SLL). IPC offenses are violations of the criminal code that applies throughout India. *Crime in India* lists the number of arrests for specific IPC offenses and provides a "total" category for all arrests of all kinds. However, the "total" number of arrests is almost twice the number of arrests for the specific crimes. The total number of arrests for specific crimes, in short, does not add up to the "total" number of arrests. Thus, the difference between the "total" arrests and those for specified crimes was computed and is shown here as "other" (even though an "other" category is not utilized in *Crime in India*). On the other hand, about a third of all SLL arrests are categorized in the report as "other." These are so reported here. Most of the specifically listed offense categories under the SLL title are

Table 4.1

Total and Juvenile Arrests for Indian Penal Code and Special and Local Law Violations, 1987

Offense	Total Arrests	Juvenile Arrests	Percent Juvenile of Total
Indian Penal Code Offenses			
Murder	65,008	532	.82
Criminal Homicide	8,446	41	.48
Rape	11,430	216	1.89
Kidnapping & Abduction	20,799	138	.66
Dacoity*	35,070	94	.27
Robbery	28,917	164	.57
Burglary	91,557	2,538	2.77
Thefts	203,744	5,581	2.74
Riots	557,327	3,175	.57
Criminal Breach of Trust	15,705	45	.29
Cheating	20,579	51	.25
Counterfeiting	825	21	2.54
Other Offenses (Computed)	1,125,938	8,223	.73
Total I.P.C. Offenses	2,185,345	20,819	.95
Special And Local Laws			
Arms Act	56,905	177	.31
N.D.P.S. Act**	10,428	56	.54
Gambling Act	311,785	2,472	.79
Excise Act	97,611	568	.58
Prohibition Act	501,523	5,663	1.13
Explosives Act	3,816	7	.18
S.I.T. Act***	16,064	234	1.46
Motor Vehicles Act	1,450,548	155	.01
Prevention of Corruption Act	341	0	0
Customs Act	245	0	0
Railways Act	29,265	249	.85
Other Special and Local	1,220,812	7,475	.61
Total Special and Local	3,699,343	17,056	.46
Total Arrests	5,884,688	37,875	.64

*Gang armed robbery, **Narcotic Drugs and Psychotropic Substances Act, ***Immoral Trafficking Act.

Source: *Crime in India 1987* (National Crime Records Bureau, Ministry of Home Affairs, 1992), pp. 77, 88, 108–109.

nationally applicable. But it is impossible to determine the national generalizability of the offenses contained in the "other" category or even what is contained in it. Thus, although about 40 percent of all recorded arrests in India are for unspecified offenses, Table 4.1 does offer considerable clues as to the extent and nature of crime in India and the contributions juveniles make to it.

Several things can be concluded from the figures presented in Table 4.1. First, for a country the size of India (over 800 million people) an arrest total of fewer than 6 million (rate of about 500 per 100,000 population) appears to be exceedingly small. Either people in India are extremely law abiding, the police are exceptionally inefficient, and/or other than formal mechanisms of social control are relied upon by the Indian populous to deal with "offense" behavior. Any, or all three, of these possibilities could, in fact, be the case. While we cannot precisely document it, our research and experiences in India suggest that the "all-three" conclusion is probably correct, as is discussed later in this volume. What is clear, is that even though numerous arrests are made for criminal offenses in India each year, the relative use of formal-legal control is actually infrequent.

As is universally true, the bulk of the criminality recorded in India consists of property crimes (excluding the category "other"). This is especially true of the non-violent variety such as burglary and theft, which alone constitute more than a third of the IPC offenses. Violent personal crime, although not infrequent, makes up a relatively small proportion of overall criminality. Less than 6 percent of the IPC offenses consist of what might be called "ordinary personal" crimes, although riots which may involve interpersonal violence alone equal about 8 percent of recorded crime. The violent property crimes of robbery and dacoity (gang armed robbery) comprise less than three percent of IPC arrests. In short, as far as "Index" type offenses are concerned, crime in India, as elsewhere, is property crime.

Similarly, where special and local laws are concerned, a sizable number of arrests involve economic activity, especially gambling and tax irregularities, as well as theft associated with the national railroads. In contrast to similar data published in other countries, drug abuse offenses make up a very small portion of India's official criminality. Alcohol does appear to be a problem in that about 13 percent of the SLL arrests were for violations of prohibition laws in force in various states.

The single largest category of SLL arrests was for violations of the Motor Vehicles Act. This law covers a host of activities relating to motor vehicles so that the specific crime people were being arrested for is by no means clear.

In general, as determinable from arrest figures, crime in India is relatively infrequent. But, with some idiosyncrasies, of course, it looks very much like crime reported for countries throughout the world.

JUVENILE ARRESTS IN INDIA

Of particular interest for present purposes are the number of these arrests for juveniles. Keeping in mind that persons under eighteen constitute about one third of India's population (about 300 million people in 1987), the extremely small numbers of arrests for persons between seven and eighteen are striking. Overall, less than 1 percent of all arrests involved persons under eighteen. When eighteen- to twenty-one-year-olds are added to these figures, the numbers more than double. About 5 juveniles are arrested per 100,000 total population, or approximately 13 arrests per 100,000 juveniles each year. Regardless of how one looks at it, the arrest figures for juveniles in India suggest that young people make up a miniscule portion of the country's official criminal population. Identical conclusions could be drawn from official statistics regarding the contributions juveniles make to the numbers of criminal cases recorded (i.e., "known to the police") for the country.

Arrest proportions vary somewhat by type of crime. But generally the pattern of criminal involvement exhibited by India's juveniles does not depart dramatically from the overall pattern in the country or from that found among juveniles elsewhere. Clearly, both the rate and proportionate contribution are small for juveniles for such crimes as cheating (fraud), criminal breach of trust (embezzlement), and various other acts since juveniles are likely to have little if any opportunity to engage in such conduct. By contrast, gambling and violations of prohibition laws contribute a sizable proportion of juvenile arrests for SLL violations. These arrests, however, do not necessarily mean the juveniles were actually gambling or consuming prohibited beverages. Often, juveniles are used by adults to transport illegal alcohol or may simply be in the vicinity of (children of) persons engaged in illegal gambling activities. Very few young people are apprehended for motor vehicle violations of any kind, and drug-abuse activities make up a very small portion of the total SLL arrests.

Both numerically and proportionate to their contribution to total arrests (excluding "other") Indian juveniles are frequently arrested for the property crimes of burglary and theft. Over 3,000 arrests were made for riots (many of which involve political demonstrations), but proportionally juveniles are not frequently involved in that behavior. Conversely, even though only a handful were arrested, juveniles represent a comparatively high proportion of persons arrested for counterfeiting (again often employed as accessories to adults engaged in food adulteration and the like). However, with the exception of drug abuse offenses, the general pattern of illegal conduct on the part of juveniles in India is not unlike that to be found just about anywhere.

Regional Variations

Considerable variability exists in India in the number of juvenile arrests recorded in various localities (e.g. states, union territories, and major cities).

For lack of reliable age-specific data, computing age-specific arrest rates is a haphazard undertaking. However, it does appear that a fairly close association exists between a state's population rank and the relative number of juveniles arrested in the various states since a Spearman rank order coefficient computed for population and arrest ranks yields a value of .75. Nevertheless, some states have arrest frequencies totally inconsistent with their population size. Uttar Pradesh, for example, with a population of over 100 million people records only 361 juvenile arrests in 1987, mostly for SLL violations. Conversely, of the 63 million people of Maharashtra 22,000 juvenile arrests occurred, mostly for IPC violations. Andra Pradesh with a slightly smaller population of 54 million only registered 1,577 juvenile arrests, almost all for IPC violations. In short, state by state (if not necessarily regional) differences in arrest frequencies as well as the general types of activity (e.g., IPC vs. SLL) for which youths are subject to legal action are as numerous in India as is the case for any other large, diverse society. What accounts for these variations in India, however, remains largely unexplored (see Sandhu, 1987; Verma, 1993).

The several union territories (recognized in 1987) have somewhat more consistent population sizes and arrest rates. One of these, the union territory of Delhi, which contains the major city of New Delhi, has both an exceptionally large population (being comprised almost exclusively of an urban settlement) and a correspondingly large rate of juvenile arrests. On the other hand, the major cities in India have extremely diverse juvenile arrest frequencies, not always corresponding to the city's size. As in other countries, the largest number of arrests tend to occur in the largest cities, such as Bombay, Madras, and New Delhi. However, the largest city of Calcutta registered only 34 juvenile arrests in 1987, and some smaller cities (notably Ahmedabad) have disproportionately high rates. Clearly the variations in city arrest frequencies presented in Table 4.2 need to be explained—a task unfortunately far beyond the scope (and available data) of this report. Nevertheless, even though delinquency is correlated with urban residence, as in other countries, the arrest frequencies reported by Indian cities strongly suggest that youth crime is not a matter for serious social concern in India, even in the supposedly crime-producing environments of urban places.

Table 4.2

Juveniles (7-18) Apprehended for Indian Penal Code and Special and Local Law
Violations, by State, Union Territory, and City, India, 1987

Region	Population (Millions)	Total Arrests	IPC	SLL
State				
Andra Pradesh	53.55	1577	1292	285
Arumachal Pradesh	.63	56	56	0
Assam	19.89	1385	1274	111
Bihar	69.91	1447	1326	121
Gujarat	34.09	5093	2373	2720
Haryana	12.92	998	736	262
Himachal Pradesh	4.28	1412	240	174
Jammu & Kashmire	5.99	163	161	2
Karnataka	37.14	557	496	61
Kerala	25.45	111	106	5
Madhya Pradesh	52.18	4519	3243	1276
Maharashtra	62.78	22049	18668	3381
Manipur	1.42	211	211	0
Meghalaya	1.34	26	26	0
Mizoram	.49	99	34	65
Nagaland	.77	124	120	4
Orissa	26.37	207	204	3
Punjab	16.79	96	24	72
Rajasthan	34.26	782	740	42
Sikkim	.32	7	7	0
Tamil Nadu	48.41	8904	1156	7748
Tripura	2.05	109	106	3
Uttar Pradesh	110.86	361	77	284
West Bengal	54.58	552	408	144
Union Territory				
A & N Islands	.19	4	4	0
Chandigarh	.45	96	52	44
D & N Haveli	.10	12	11	1
Goa, Daman & Diu	1.08	147	129	18
Delhi	6.22	1232	1002	230
Laksh Dweep	.04	2	2	0
Pondicherry	.60	62	62	0
City				
Ahmedabad	2.52	1344	469	875
Bangalore	2.91	137	121	16
Bombay	8.23	1951	435	1516
Calcutta	9.17	31	29	2

Region	Population (Millions)	Total Arrests	IPC	SLL
City (cont.)				
New Delhi	4.88	999	785	214
Hyyderabad	2.53	354	59	295
Jaipur	1.00	102	102	0
Kanpur	1.69	81	28	53
Lucknow	1.01	3	3	0
Madras	4.28	1023	88	581
Nagpur	1.30	831	269	562
Pune	1.69	573	429	144

Source: Computed from *Crime in India 1987* (National Crime Records Bureau, Ministry of Home Affairs, Government of India, New Delhi, 1992, pp. 122–123) and Census Data.

Age & Gender

Of all the variables criminologists have investigated as contributors to relative involvement in crime and delinquency, the two that most consistently and most dramatically discriminate among persons are age and gender (Empey & Stafford, 1991; Thornton & Voigt, 1992). Typically rates of virtually any kind show that boys are far more often arrested for (and apparently involved in) crime and delinquent behavior. Comparisons of official and self-report data indicate that the often extreme differences in arrest rates between boys and girls are smaller insofar as self-reported delinquency is concerned (Berger, 1989; Chesney-Lind & Shelden, 1992). But nowhere are girls recognized as being more (or apparently actually) involved in delinquency than boys and, regardless of how they are measured, crime and delinquency are decidedly male-dominated activities (see Hagan & Kay, 1990; Osgood et al., 1989; Steffensmeier & Steffensmeier, 1980). This is definitely so also as far as arrests in India are concerned.

As indicated in Table 4.3, boys are arrested more frequently than girls at all ages and for virtually every offense category. Indeed, as one would expect, arrests of girls only outnumber those of boys for violations of the S.I.T. Act (prostitution). But a total of 234 juvenile arrests for this offense could hardly be called substantial. Overall boys are arrested at a ratio of about 10:1 compared to girls, although this varies somewhat by offense category and age. For IPC offenses, a consistently larger disparity occurs with increasing age (ratios = 9, 11, & 14 per age category) while for SLL violations a slight dip in arrests of twelve- to sixteen-year-old boys occurs and a steady increase in arrests for girls (due largely to prohibition law violations) produce a slight curvilinear trend in ratios. This pattern is replicated in overall age-category related ratios.

Table 4.3
Arrests for Indian Penal Code and Special and Local Law Violations, by Age
and Gender, India, 1987

| Offenses | Age & Gender | | | | | |
| | 7–12 | | 12–16 | | 16–18 | |
	Boys	Girls	Boys	Girls	Boys	Girls
Indian Penal Code						
Murder	21	1	127	17	290	76
Criminal Homicide	0	0	9	1	29	2
Rape	9	0	68	0	137	2
Kidnapping & Abduction	3	1	19	18	82	15
Dacoity*	1	0	3	1	87	2
Robbery	5	0	33	3	114	9
Burglary	193	17	1,080	10	1,186	52
Thefts	487	57	2,118	133	2,650	136
Riots	151	15	620	60	2,189	140
Criminal Breach of Trust	2	0	17	0	19	7
Cheating (Fraud)	3	2	11	0	32	3
Counterfeiting	1	0	2	0	18	0
Other Offenses (Computed)	465	48	1,596	285	5,421	408
Total Indian Penal Code	1,341	141	5,703	528	12,254	852
Special And Local Laws						
Arms Act	1	0	22	0	154	0
N.D.P.S. Act**	0	0	16	0	38	2
Gambling Act	84	0	486	0	1,901	1
Excise Act	12	1	92	2	390	71
Prohibition Act	589	322	1,266	96	2,125	1,265
Explosives Act	0	0	2	0	5	0
S.I.T. Act***	0	3	0	5	0	226
Motor Vehicles Act	0	0	15	0	140	0
Prevent. of Corruption Act	0	0	0	0	0	0
Customs Act	0	0	0	0	0	0
Railways Act	10	0	60	0	178	1
Other Special & Local	2,717	58	2,018	76	2,499	107
Total Special & Local Law	3,413	384	3,977	179	7,430	1,673
Total Arrests	4,754	525	9,680	707	19,684	2,525

*Gang armed robbery, **Narcotic Drugs and Psychotropic Substances Act,
***Immoral Trafficking Act.
Source: *Crime in India 1987* (New Delhi: National Crime Records Bureau,
Ministry of Home Affairs, 1992), pp. 108–109.

The large number of arrests in 1987 of girls in the sixteen to eighteen age bracket for prohibition offenses in 1987 is decidedly unusual and could be misleading. No such relatively large proportion of arrests can be found both before or after this particular year. We suspect that this anomaly is the result of either a recording discrepancy or some unusual change in police arrest practices. Indeed, much of this departure from other years appears to be the result of activities taking place in the state of Tamil Nadu during 1987. This state has enacted and variously enforced prohibition legislation for many years. Between 1986 and 1987 prohibition arrests in Tamil Nadu jumped by over 186 percent overall. Among juveniles, however, the increase was more than 248 percent. Since the arrest frequency tables in *Crime in India* do not provide the necessary age/gender breakdowns per offense by state, it is impossible to determine whether these changes apply to both genders equally at all ages or to what extent they are responsible for the national numbers. However, it seems quite likely that the offense categories used to designate crimes for which many females (probably of all ages) were previously arrested in Tamil Nadu were altered for some unknown reason. And, given the large number of arrests for prohibition offenses recorded for this state, this change probably affected the national totals. As such, based on data from pre- and post-1987 reports, we believe that the likely arrest pattern for seven- to eighteen-year-old boys and girls in India is actually one of a continuously increasing gender gap by age, due basically to progressively larger increases in arrests for boys.

In spite of proportionate differences in overall arrest frequencies, the patterns of arrest by offense types are extremely similar for boys and girls (see Hartjen & Kethineni, 1993). And this is largely consistent for each age category. As indicated in Table 4.3, with a couple of exceptions, for IPC arrests burglary and thefts are the largest single categories for both genders regardless of age. Prohibition violations dominate the arrests for SLL offenses, both by age and gender, although gambling and various property crimes begin to gain prominence among boys as they mature, while prostitution becomes a sizable arrest category for girls in the sixteen- to eighteen-year-old category. Similarly arrests for riots make a substantial jump for sixteen- to eighteen-year-old boys over the arrests of twelve- to sixteen-year-olds, undoubtedly because of the increased political activism of youths in the older age range. Violent crime remains the purview of boys at every age, especially with regard to rape in the older age categories. Murder arrests are low for both gender groups, and while increasing for both with age, make up a small portion of overall arrest rates.

In these regards, the gender and age configuration of arrests in India (except for the very large gender gap in arrests) is not widely different from those likely to be found in virtually every country of the world.

Arrest Trends in India

The figures in Table 4.4 show a rather remarkable and fairly consistent decrease in the number of youths arrested in India between 1977 and 1987. This decline is especially noticeable among the younger age groups. Indeed, during this decade, a decrease of almost 10,000 arrests for youths aged seven to twelve and twelve to sixteen occurred. A much smaller decrease occurred for sixteen- to eighteen-year-olds, and a slight increase (not shown) occurred for eighteen- to twenty-one-year-olds, resulting in an overall small net increase in arrests for persons under twenty-one in India. These figures are even more dramatic given that India has had substantial population increases over the past several decades.

Table 4.4
Trends in Juvenile Arrests by Age, India, 1977–1987

			Age			
Year	7–12	% Total	12–16	% Total	16–18	% Total
1977	15,113	25.0	21,291	35.2	24,011	39.7
1978	11,955	21.2	18,954	33.6	25,488	45.2
1979	10,539	19.1	18,315	33.3	26,226	47.6
1980	10,457	15.6	20,048	29.7	36,899	54.7
1981	9,485	15.5	17,649	28.9	33,969	55.6
1982	8,272	16.8	15,218	31.0	25,618	52.2
1983	8,290	16.1	16,949	33.0	26,153	50.9
1984	5,846	13.5	12,472	28.8	25,054	57.7
1985	5,991	15.5	11,516	29.8	21,172	54.7
1986	5,138	12.5	12,163	29.5	23,940	58.0
1987	5,279	13.9	10,387	27.5	22,209	58.6
% Change						
1977–1987		−65.1		−51.4		−7.5

Source: *Crime in India 1987* (National Crime Records Bureau, Ministry of Home Affairs, Government of India, New Delhi: 1992), p. 112.

On the average, seven- to twelve-year-olds make up about 15 percent of the total number of juvenile arrests, twelve- to sixteen-year-olds 30 percent, and sixteen- to eighteen-year-olds about 55 percent. As with the decline in actual arrest frequencies between 1977–1987, the proportionate contribution made by seven to twelve and twelve- to sixteen-year-olds to overall juvenile arrests similarly declined while that of sixteen- to eighteen-year-olds increased slightly. Thus, even though the actual number of arrests for this age group have decreased, they have come to make up a persistently greater proportion of juveniles arrested in India during the 1980s. Whether this age group made up a correspondingly larger proportion of the juvenile population is doubtful. In any case, arrest rates in India suggest that whatever youth-crime problem the country may have, it has been a steadily declining one. Why this might be the case is unknown. To some extent, alternative ways (e.g., child welfare boards) of dealing with offenders and potential offenders have been developed since the 1980s throughout India, reducing the ranks of those young people who would otherwise have been handled by the criminal justice system. Yet India is still an impoverished country with high rates of unemployment and underemployment. The population is also experiencing the effects of modernization and urban growth, as well as the unsettling consequences of ethnic and religious strife. However, the hordes of beggars one confronted in India during the late 1970s seem to have largely disappeared by the late 1980s. Persons who gained meager employment as servants or indentured laborers are increasingly opting for employment in factories or other industries providing steady incomes and benefits formally beyond the reach of many Indians. Literacy rates have increased steadily, and an Indian middle class is becoming increasingly visible. Hard data to document change, much less any association it may have to criminality, are not available. But the kind of economic situations engendered by poverty that may have been responsible for much of India's youth crime in the past (e.g., theft and burglary) appear to have decreased. At the same time, the possible crime-inducing effects of affluence apparent in western countries have not yet taken hold. Thus, the decline in arrest rates for juveniles may, in fact, indicate an actual change in behavior. On the other hand, given the often inexplicable anomalies that seem to appear in Indian crime statistics, it is possible that these figures reveal nothing more than changes in police or Crime Records Bureau recording procedures. Whatever the case, the data presented in Table 4.4 simply beg for focused inquiry by Indian criminologists.

UNITED STATES AND INDIA COMPARISONS

The Indian arrest statistics discussed above are significant. But for persons not especially interested in India, these findings may not necessarily be particularly interesting. To contextualize this data, we have attempted to compare features of arrests in India with similar data reported by other countries. Of course, the wide disparity in legal definitions, laws, age ranges, data forms and collection methods as well as virtually anything else that relates to research methodology renders impossible direct comparisons of Indian arrest statistics with official statistics from other countries. Thus, the following is not to be construed as a comparative analysis of matched data sets. Instead, we hope to highlight some apparent similarities as well as differences in the relative forms and frequencies of delinquent behavior found in India compared to what similar data seem to reveal about the conduct of juveniles in other socioeconomic environments during the past few decades. To do so, data from Indian and United States arrest reports are discussed in this section. This is followed by brief summaries of published accounts of arrest reports (or other official information) that criminologists have obtained from countries throughout the world.

Based on data in *Crime in India 1987* and *Crime in the United States 1987*, Tables 4.5 and 4.6 highlight some similarities and some dramatic differences between the official delinquency of Indian and American youths. In Table 4.5, the number, rate, and respective proportions of juvenile arrests in the two countries are reported for the broad age categories used in the Indian report. For Americans, these categories are computed from the individual year-age categories reported.

Table 4.5

Comparison of Indian and United States Arrest Rates and Proportions, by Age, 1987

Age	India	U.S.
Below Age 12		
Number of Arrests	5,279	189,371
Rate per 100,000 Population	.71	94.50
% of Juvenile Arrests	13.94	8.43
% of Total Arrests	.08	1.84
Age 12–16		
Number of Arrests	10,387	681,421
Rate per 100,000 Population	1.42	340.50
% of Juvenile Arrests	27.42	30.35
% of Total Arrests	.18	6.63
Age 16–18		
Number of Arrests	22,209	1,374,351
Rate per 100,000 Population	3.14	687.00
% of Juvenile Arrests	58.64	61.21
% of Total Arrests	.38	13.36
Total Juvenile Arrests	37,875	2,245,143
Total Arrests	5,884,688	10,287,309

Source: Based on *Crime in India 1987* (New Delhi: National Crime Records Bureau, Ministry of Home Affairs, 1992), pp. 108–109 and *Crime in the United States 1987* (Washington, D.C.: U.S. Department of Justice, 1988), p. 179.

What is clear from this table is that both the total number of arrests as well as the number of juvenile arrests in India for all offenses are dramatically less than that of the United States. Given that India has a population four times that of the United States, these differences are even more pronounced than the absolute frequencies imply. Overall, the number of American arrests is about twice the number of Indian. But for juveniles the ratio is more on the order of 60 American arrests for every juvenile arrest in India. The ratio is about half (36:1) for persons under age twelve, and most disparate (66:1) for twelve- to sixteen-year-olds with a slight drop (62:1) for the sixteen- to eighteen-year-olds.

When rates per 100,000 population are compared, the differences in the extent to which American youths are subject to arrest compared to Indian youths is simply mindboggling. Clearly, regardless of all the possible problems we might find in comparing these data, something is distinctively different about India and the United States. Whether American youths are 60 times more delinquent than Indian youths or American law enforcement agencies are 60 times more efficient, effective, repressive, or concerned (depending upon how one might choose to interpret these statistics) is unclear. We suspect that both factors are involved. However, since arrest rates tend to rise dramatically in India for the eighteen- and twenty-one-year-old age category (although still substantially below the American frequency), what is probably revealed in these figures is not only differences in behavior and overall arrest proclivities on the part of officials in the two countries but also differences in the age-arrest curve (e.g., Greenberg, 1978). Whereas a rather steady increase in arrests takes place for American youths from adolescence to young adulthood, it is in early adulthood that fairly substantial increases in the likelihood that Indians will experience arrest begin to take place. Unfortunately, the lack of yearly age data for India makes it difficult to accurately graph the two trends.

The issue, however, is by no means a straightforward matter of frequencies. Differences in these numbers notwithstanding, the figures in Table 4.5 also point to some important similarities in juvenile arrests between the two countries. For one, a rather progressive (although not equally so) increase in arrests occurs by age for both countries. For India, rates almost double by each age category. For the United States a kind of reverse geometric increase occurs, tripling and then doubling between age groups. Although the patterns of increase may differ, it is clear that older juveniles in both countries are more likely to experience arrest than are young ones. Also, except for persons under twelve, roughly similar proportions of the juveniles arrested in each country are accounted for by their respective age category, with sixteen- to eighteen year-olds representing around 60 percent of all juveniles arrested in both countries.

These similarities and differences in juvenile arrests are also revealed in Table 4.6. In this analysis, offenses are grouped into broad categories (see

Appendix C), roughly corresponding to distinctive offense types of interest to criminologists. Frequencies for each offense category are reported by gender for each country. Two important results are revealed in the figures presented in this table.

Table 4.6
Comparison of Indian and United States Arrests, by Gender, 1987

	U.S.		Ratio	India		Ratio
Offense Category	Boys	Girls	B:G	Boys	Girls	B:G
Personal	132,059	28,504	5:1	1,192	148	8:1
Property	476,055	125,069	4:1	8,561	492	17:1
Public Order	186,263	28,717	6:1	5,615	450	12:1
Substance Abuse	183,070	47,668	4:1	4,034	1,685	2:1
Other*	202,543	53,285	4:1	14,716	982	15:1
Total Arrests	1,179,990	283,243	4:1	34,118	3,757	9:1

*Suspicion, Curfew & Loitering, and Runaway excluded for U.S. This category computed for India.
Source: Based on *Crime in India 1987* (New Delhi: National Crime Records Bureau, Ministry of Home Affairs, 1992), pp. 108–109, and *Crime in the United States 1987* (Washington, D.C.: Federal Bureau of Investigation, 1988), p. 171.

One, the differences in arrest frequencies and rates for total arrests also occur for all types of offense behavior. Thus, American juveniles are not overwhelmingly more often involved in some type of illegal activity and Indian youths in some other although frequencies are not distributed proportionately across offenses and country either. Instead, Americans are more often arrested for virtually every kind of criminality. And this is true regardless of gender.

Two, the often-found gender gap in crime/delinquency rates also occurs for both countries regardless of offense type. Significant, however, is the fact that this gap is considerably greater for Indian youths compared to Americans. Indeed, for Americans the proportion of boys and girls arrested for various offense types is quite similar and the ratios quite uniform (basically 4:1) regardless of offense type. In short, while American boys are more "delinquent" than American girls, they are not dramatically so (relatively speaking that is), nor is there an extreme discrepancy in the types of offense behaviors for which they are more or less often arrested. In contrast, disregarding the anomaly in substance-abuse (prohibition) arrests for girls that occurred in 1987, not only are Indian boys dramatically more delinquent than Indian girls, it appears that more variability also exists in the kinds of activities for which each group is likely to be arrested. For example, relatively small proportions of both genders in India are arrested for personal crimes (3 and 4 percent, respectively—compared to 11 and 10 percent for Americans), but compared to Americans, boys in India are considerably more likely to be arrested for various property offenses than are girls. Undoubtedly these differences reflect more extreme differences in socialization and opportunity factors between boys and girls in India compared to the United States (see Hartjen, 1986; Hartjen & Kethineni, 1993). But these matters require considerably more research than is presently available.

In summary, what seems clear from the limited comparisons one can make using arrest statistics from India and the United States is that American youths are much more often subject to arrest than are Indian youths of similar age. Whether or to what extent this means that American youths are more involved in delinquent activities remains unclear. On the other hand, as far as offense behaviors and variables such as age and gender are concerned, a kind of universality in delinquency also seems to be found between the two countries. For both, property and (to a lesser extent in India) public disorder types of misconduct make up the bulk of offenses for which youths in both countries are arrested. And in both countries older youths and boys tend to be more delinquent than younger youths or girls although the relative proportions are not identical. Data from countries throughout the world indicate that this is by no means unusual.

ARRESTS OF JUVENILES IN OTHER COUNTRIES

Obviously, either the United States or India could be extreme examples as far as arrest rates are concerned. To what extent the picture of delinquency reported here for these countries differs or is similar to that of other countries is difficult to assess given the scant international data available. A systematic comparison of arrest data across a sampling of countries around the world using primary data is far beyond the scope of this inquiry. However, to place the India/United States comparisons into the broader context, data reported in articles in a special edition of the *International Journal of Comparative and Applied Criminal Justice* (1992) provide as complete a readily available source of information on delinquency rates and forms in other countries as we are likely to find. The following draws liberally from this resource.

Canada and Europe

According to Hatch & Griffiths (1992), 169,679 youths were charged with federal offenses in Canada during 1990. Of these about 10 percent were for crimes of violence; 62 percent, property crimes; 24 percent, various other crimes of which one-half involved "mischief," and only about 3 percent of the youths were charged for drug and narcotic offenses. These rates apparently increased fairly substantially between 1980 and 1990. Girls were charged with about 10 percent of the property crimes and almost 16 percent of the violent crimes. The country does appear to have a growing youth-gang problem, and youth in some aboriginal communities may disproportionately come to the attention of legal authorities compared to non-aboriginal youths.

Reporting on England, Farrington (1992) notes that convictions and cautions for indictable offenses for youths aged ten to sixteen increased rather steadily from 1961 to 1985 and then seemed to decline, although he speculates that real offense behavior has actually continued to increase. With delinquency rates of between 15 and 55 per 1,000 youths, it appears that official delinquency in England is also considerably more frequent than that in India. Yet, as elsewhere, males come to the attention of legal authorities about four times more often than females, and older youths (fourteen- to sixteen-year-olds) are two to three times more likely to come under legal control than are younger ones (ten- to thirteen-year-olds).

According to Kaiser (1992) conviction rates for youths and young adults in The Federal Republic of Germany appear to be historically higher than those of adults (twenty-five plus). Juveniles (fourteen to eighteen), however, have conviction rates between 1,000 and 2,000 per 100,000 juveniles, and these have shown a fluctuating increase between 1960 and 1990. Rates for older adolescents (eighteen to twenty-one) and young adults (twenty-one to twenty-five) have been consistently higher, averaging around 3,000 per 100,000 persons in each age bracket. Theft and traffic offenses are the predominant reasons for those juveniles arrested or brought to court, with illegal drugs and violent crimes together only equaling about one fifth of the total. Violent crime by young people, however, does appear to be on the increase in Germany.

In the Netherlands, rates of delinquency (persons twelve to eighteen) increased steadily between the 1960s and 1980s and then apparently stabilized and even declined somewhat (Junger-Tas, 1992). Much of the increase in overall crime rates in the Netherlands, however, is attributable to juveniles. Generally, offender rates for boys are higher than those of girls at a ratio of about seven to one. However, while the rate for boys decreased, that of girls increased. As elsewhere, the bulk of the official juvenile crime consists of property offenses and vandalism. For girls, property crimes make up almost all of the total, while for boys, public order and willful damage offenses are also a sizable number. For both genders, violent crime makes up only about five percent of the total.

Like many other European countries, Sweden also experienced a sizable growth in crime between the 1960s and 1980s, with rates apparently stabilizing by the end of that period (Friday, 1992). The majority of the known offenders are males, largely between fifteen and nineteen years of age. The rate of increase for females was greater, although girls still make up a relatively small share of all known offenders. Most youth crime involves property, with about 40 percent concerning vehicles. Much of this activity apparently is committed by a relatively small number of repeat offenders. Conversely, some 60 percent of the youths apprehended account for only 17 percent of total offenses, the remaining 83 percent being the work of fewer than one half of all youths coming to the attention of authorities.

Somewhat in contrast to western European countries, youths in the former Soviet Union appear to make up only about 10 percent of registered offenders, although the level of juvenile crime seems to have increased over the past few decades (Finckenauer & Kelly, 1992). Violent crime by juveniles equals about 5 to 10 percent of all juvenile offenses, but violence on the part of juveniles equals about 20 percent of all recorded violent crime. Females make up only about 5 percent of the offenders. Similar to the number of juvenile arrests in India and about one tenth the number recorded for the United States, juvenile arrests in 1987 totaled only 164,623 out of a population of some 200 million persons.

Asian Countries

In China juveniles (persons fourteen to eighteen) equal about 10 percent of the population but about 30 percent of the persons charged with crimes (Fu, 1992). This proportion has remained roughly the same since 1982 (with the exception of the 45 percent reported for 1985). Yet, while juvenile involvement in crime is disproportionately large, overall crime rates in China are fairly low, ranging from 49.9 to 89.4 per 100,000 persons between 1981 and 1987, with a rate of around 50 per 100,000 being normal for the latter four years. In 1987 only 570,439 crimes were reported, more than 90 percent of which were larcenies. It appears, however, that even though crime is not a serious problem in China, youth crime is beginning to become one since the offenses committed by juveniles are apparently becoming more serious and violent (Fu, 1992: 266). Similarly, the age of first arrest has declined and youth gangs are proliferating.

Vaughn and Huang (1992) report that in Japan theft and embezzlement rates among juveniles increased dramatically between 1970 and 1990. Overall arrest rates for juveniles also jumped from about 900 in 1970 to over 1,700 in 1990, peaking in 1980 at about 1,900 per 100,000 juveniles. Thus, Japan paralleled the United States and western European pattern of an increase in juvenile arrests through the 1970s-80s followed by stability or decline. Yet, as total juvenile arrests went up, felony arrests steadily declined overall. Thus, in spite of Japan being an affluent, industrialized country with a relatively miniscule crime problem, youth crime, especially involving property offenses, makes up a sizable share of it.

In Korea, delinquency also increased between the 1970s and 1990s with a jump of 35 percent between 1977–1987 (Cho and Chang, 1992). Overall juveniles have made up between 16 and 7.5 percent of total offenders over the decade with the proportion decreasing since 1987. Thus, the increase in delinquency matched that of overall crime, although at a somewhat slower rate. Even then, a juvenile offender rate of about 100,000 cases per year is neither particularly high or low. As in India, a miniscule (about 5 percent) of the offender population is female, and the age distribution of offenders increases consistently for each age bracket such that eighteen- to nineteen-year-olds constitute over 50 percent of all known juvenile offenders. However, only about 30 percent of all delinquency cases in 1987 involved property crimes (mostly larceny), and almost fifty percent were "riotous" offenses (almost all assault). As found generally, about 5 percent of juvenile crime consists of "violent" crime in Korea, about half involving rape and most of the rest robbery.

African Countries
Only 74 juvenile felony arrests took place in Egypt in 1987 according to Souryal (1992) of which 30 percent were for robbery. On the other hand 9,485 misdemeanor arrests for youths were registered, of which battery and theft make up much of the total. These figures suggest that while not unknown, juvenile crime in Egypt is neither widespread or serious. As indicated by Souryal, delinquency in Egypt basically involves urban lower-middle class males with low educational attainment and poor prospects for economic and social mobility. As elsewhere, youthful lawbreaking appears to largely consist of property offenses and, to a smaller extent, sexual offenses.

A not dissimilar picture seems to apply to Nigeria (Ebbe, 1992). In that country also juvenile crime is largely an urban phenomenon normally involving property offenses. Robbery is not a significant category of juvenile offenses, and such behavior as carrying guns and knives to school is practically unheard of. Indeed, the rate of delinquency is extremely low with only 2,044 juvenile offenses reported to the police in 1987 (about 1.35 percent of all cases) equaling about 2.42 cases per 100,000 population. About 55 percent of these cases involved theft and burglary. Serious violent crime and drug offenses make up miniscule proportions of the total.

A SUMMARY OF WORLD PATTERNS IN OFFICIAL DELINQUENCY RATES
Except in the broadest terms, it is, of course, nearly impossible to make any data-based comparative statements about delinquency in countries throughout the world. The Indian and American arrest data and individual country reports summarized here are, however, suggestive.

Specific national idiosyncrasies notwithstanding, it does appear that juveniles and young people make up a sizable, if not necessarily overwhelmingly disproportionate, segment of the crime problem found in many economically developed countries as well as among those that have been experiencing rapid development in the past few decades (e.g., China and

Korea). On the other hand, in countries such as Egypt and Nigeria both crime and, especially, youth crime are relatively inconsequential. India in 1987 appears to fall into this latter grouping of countries; the United States, into the former.

Also, many countries indicate that youth crime increased tremendously in the past few decades although in most this trend seems to have leveled off or reversed by the 1990s. Other countries, however, do not seem to have experienced any sizable growth in delinquency. Again, these appear to be among the economically disenfranchised nations of Africa and possibly elsewhere. India in 1987 also seems to fall into this grouping of nations.

What appears to be essentially universal about delinquency for countries throughout the world are some broad similarities in its relative frequencies and patterns. In virtually every country, delinquency consists largely of property and various public-order forms of misconduct. The nature of these offenses may differ depending upon the unique characteristics of specific societies. But no especially peculiar patterns seem to occur regarding the general types of misconduct on the part of youths throughout the world. Violent behavior everywhere makes up a small portion of total official crime. However, the proportionate share of this behavior attributed to young people does vary cross-nationally. Boys also appear to be considerably more delinquent than girls, and rates of involvement in offense behavior seem to increase with age. Again, however, wide disparities in these rates can be found across countries. Finally, some evidence indicates that official delinquency rates are higher in urban areas and that poor and otherwise disenfranchised youths are more likely than others to come to the attention of authorities universally. In these respects also, India is by no means an atypical society.

CONCLUSION

Official crime statistics offer a revealing but possibly distorted picture of the delinquent behavior of youths in any country. But with appropriate reservations such data can help us judge the degree to which one society is alike or differs from others insofar as the behavior of its young people are concerned.

This chapter analyzes arrest statistics for Indian juveniles (seven- to eighteen-year-olds) for the year 1987 and attempts to compare the epidemiological picture of delinquency in India with that of other countries based on similar types of data. What is implied by this analysis is that during the last years of the 1980s juvenile crime in India was by no means a serious matter of concern, especially in comparison to countries such as the United States. Arrest rates in India are low generally. But, what is of even greater importance is the fact that juveniles make up such a miniscule total of all official crime in India, both in total numbers and proportionate to their percentage of total population. Indeed, compared to the 15 to 30 percent or more that youths contribute to official offense/offender rates reported in other countries, the less than 1 percent contribution of Indian youths to overall arrests is dramatic for its paltriness. It is for this reason alone that the epidemiological facts of delinquency in India are of compelling criminological interest.

In other respects, juvenile crime in India looks very much like such activity everywhere in the world. Specific features of the Indian situation do, however, warrant special attention (such as very low rates for girls and the apparent age-related delay in arrests). Assuming that arrest rates reflect actual behavior to some reasonable extent, we are confronted with three issues: (1) Why are juvenile arrests in India, and apparently in Third World countries generally, so strikingly low as such and by any conceivable measure of "relative to"?, (2) Why are the offense behavior patterns of youths in these countries not unlike those reported in all manner of society?, and (3) What explains the gender and age disparities in arrests found in countries throughout the world? Comparisons of two or more decidedly different societies can help us answer these questions.

CHAPTER FIVE

Self-Reported Delinquency

From a comparative point of view, vast differences in laws, law enforcement and judicial systems, public willingness to report offense behavior, extra-legal alternative ways of dealing with young offenders as well as the more technical matters of the practices used to acquire, record, and categorize data for official reports make cross-national comparisons of official statistics highly debatable. But, it is likely that only a small, and undoubtedly non-representative, segment of total delinquency is recorded in these figures in any country. To what extent the kinds and amounts of undetected delinquency are similar or dissimilar across different societies (even if the official picture is or is not alike) simply cannot be fully determined from official statistics alone. The only other mechanism available to criminologists to make some judgments regarding the extent and nature of the "dark figure" of delinquency in various countries is by means of self-reported delinquency surveys.

Data from several self-report surveys carried out in a variety of countries have become available to criminologists in recent years. And efforts to conduct international research of this kind have begun (e.g. Junger-Tas et al., 1994). As of this writing, however, no major self-report survey has been carried out in non-western nations. While admittedly a modest undertaking, the 1987 survey of Madras and New Delhi high-school and institutionalized youths reported in this volume is perhaps one of the more extensive such studies involving Third World juveniles yet attempted. In conjunction with the arrest and other statistics reported in Chapters Three and Four, our discussion of the results of that survey in this chapter helps to flesh out the dimensions of delinquency epidemiology in India and provide a more secure basis to compare Indian rates with those of American and other youths than is possible by using official statistics alone.

GENERAL RATES AND PATTERNS IN INDIA

Our analysis of the epidemiological picture of delinquency presented by the self-reported survey conducted in 1987 begins with a discussion of the percentages of respondents admitting individual offense items and the differences and similarities in these proportions found for high-school and institutionalized respondents generally and in the two cities included in the survey.

Official/Unofficial Delinquents

A considerable body of research conducted on samples of western juveniles indicates that while delinquent behavior is probably ubiquitous, youths apprehended and/or incarcerated as offenders tend to be considerably more delinquent than the general population of young people (Cernkovich et al., 1985; Dunford & Elliott, 1984; Erickson, 1972; Erickson & Empey, 1963; Sampson, 1985; Williams & Gold, 1972). Given the exceedingly low arrest rates in India, it would be useful, therefore, to investigate the extent to which incarcerated youths in India do or do not resemble the juvenile population generally.

Table 5.1 presents prevalence rates for individual offense items reported by high-school and institutionalized respondents, respectively. Phi coefficients were computed to assess differences and similarities in the relative magnitude of these rates between the two samples. Spearman's Rank Order Correlation Coefficient (Rho) was calculated to determine the extent to which relative rates of involvement (or the pattern of offense activities) were similar or dissimilar across the two groups. A high Rho coefficient would indicate that even though the absolute proportions of high-school or institutionalized respondents may differ, respondents in the two samples are similar insofar as their relative involvement in various types of offense conduct is concerned. Conversely, a low value on this coefficient would suggest that the two groups are involved in different kinds of illegality, regardless of the actual proportional similarities or dissimilarities in their admitted offense behavior.

As suggested by Table 5.1, with the exception of their exceedingly low prevalence rates for drug-related misconduct, Indian juveniles commit the spectrum of offenses normally included in self-reported delinquency surveys. For both high-school and institutionalized respondents, the highest admission rates tend to concentrate around pilfering of various types, such as stealing from family or school, public disorder offenses such as vandalism, and various "status" offenses like truancy and cheating on school tests.

Of the high-school respondents, small percentages admit serious personal and theft crimes, and practically none was involved in sale, consumption, or public displays related to alcohol and drugs. On the average, about 10 percent of the high-school respondents admitted to each offense. Status offenses were admitted at proportions about three times the offense-rate average, while serious forms of criminality were admitted at about one half the average.

Table 5.1
Prevalence Rates and Phi Coefficients for High-School and
Institutionalized Respondents, 1987 Survey

Offense	H.S.	INS.	PHI
Assault	6	9	NS
Gang Fight	6	11	.08
Hit Parent	3	10	.14
Concealed Weapon	6	10	.07
Steal Rs 500+	6	9	.05
Steal Rs 50–500	2	12	.19
Steal Rs < 50	6	15	.13
Vehicle Theft	1	5	.11
Joy Ride	8	8	NS
Possess Stolen Property	6	15	.14
Steal from Family	16	30	.13
Steal from School	11	30	.21
Strongarm Others	6	9	.05
Break and Enter	7	16	.13
Avoid Payment	21	31	.10
Vandalism	19	15	NS
Throw Objects	12	21	.10
Disorderly Conduct	11	12	NS
Drunk in Public	2	7	.09
Beg for Money	3	12	.19
Runaway	4	33	.38
Truancy	29	30	NS
Lie About Self	28	35	.07
Cheat on School Test	47	33	−.12
Sold Hard Drugs	< 1	4	.16
Sold Soft Drugs	< 1	4	.13
Drank Alcohol	12	11	NS
Used Soft Drugs	1	7	.14
Used Hard Drugs	1	5	.16
Mean % per Offense	10	15	.08
Sample N	2077	523	

Note: percentages are rounded to nearest whole number,
NS = not significant, all others significant <.01.

Average admissions per-offense by institutionalized respondents were about 50 percent greater than the proportion for high-school respondents. For all but a handful of diverse offenses, significantly greater proportions of the institutionalized youths admitted some involvement in each offense compared to the high-school respondents. The Phi coefficients representing these differences are consistent (except for cheating on school tests), although generally quite small. Important differences, however, occur regarding some types of conduct—differences that may, in part, explain why these youths are incarcerated. These particularly involve theft and other property crimes, running away from home, and substantially more frequent admissions to drug sale and use (although the admission rates for these offenses for both groups are extremely low). In this regard, not only do somewhat greater proportions of incarcerated youths admit delinquency involvement of all kinds, they also more frequently admit serious offenses or the kinds of misconduct likely to get them into trouble with authorities. In short, as early studies in the United States found, youths officially recognized as delinquents tend to be somewhat more delinquent than those not so labeled although such conduct is by no means exclusive to them.

In spite of these differences, the moderately high Rho of .78 suggests that high-school and institutionalized students are not dramatically different as far as the pattern of their involvement in various kinds of offense behaviors is concerned. Thus, although admission patterns are not identical, official delinquents are not, for instance, heavily involved in major criminal acts to the exclusion of serious forms of lawbreaking. Instead, both groups are similarly involved in the spectrum of delinquent acts with institutional offenders somewhat more likely to be involved in all forms of delinquency, and especially in the more serious forms of criminality.

Geographic Distributions

A considerable body of official data suggests that crime/delinquency rates tend to be highest in urban areas. Yet both the magnitude and frequencies of various types of behavior are by no means identical among cities of similar size. The official statistics from India discussed in Chapter Four also suggest that urban places tend to have higher arrest rates than rural localities. But, wide disparities in these arrests occur among cities as well as geographical localities in India. The extremely sparse self-reported delinquency research utilizing samples of youths in different localities within various countries hints that these differences in arrest rates may not be reflected in the offense behaviors tapped by such surveys. Thus, while real differences in criminality may exist among the residents of various urban areas in India as well as other countries, it is likely that considerable similarity exists also insofar as the wider spectrum of misconduct included in self-report research is concerned.

Table 5.2

Prevalence Rates and Phi Coefficients for High-School and Institutionalized Respondents, by City, 1987 Survey

Offense	High School			Institution		
	Madras	Delhi	Phi	Madras	Delhi	Phi
Assault	7	6	NS	9	7	NS
Gang fight	7	5	−.05*	13	7	NS
Hit parent	4	1	−.09	12	4	−.12
Concealed weapon	6	5	NS	12	9	NS
Steal Rs 500+	2	9	.16	9	8	NS
Steal Rs 50–500	1	3	.04*	9	16	.10
Steal Rs < 50	5	8	.05	14	18	NS
Vehicle theft	1	1	NS	3	9	NS
Joy ride	2	14	.22	7	9	NS
Possess stolen prop.	10	1	−.20	15	14	NS
Steal from family	19	9	−.14	35	19	−.16
Steal from school	12	10	NS	40	8	−.33
Strongarm others	3	9	.11	9	8	NS
Break and enter	9	5	−.07	19	11	−.10*
Avoid payment	26	16	−.22	36	20	.10
Vandalism	10	29	.24	14	22	NS
Throw objects	17	7	−.14	26	11	−.17
Disorderly conduct	8	14	.10	13	9	NS
Drunk in public	1	2	NS	5	9	NS
Beg for money	4	1	−.09	15	7	−.11
Runaway	6	2	−.09	32	34	NS
Truancy	35	23	−.13	35	20	−.15
Lie about self	39	21	−.20	44	15	−.29
Cheat on school test	26	72	.46	34	32	NS
Sold hard drugs	0	0	NS	4	4	NS
Sold soft drugs	0	0	NS	4	2	NS
Drank alcohol	7	17	.17	11	12	NS
Used soft drugs	2	1	−.04*	6	9	NS
Used hard drugs	1	0	NS	6	3	NS
Mean % per offense	9	10	NS	17	12	NS
Sample N	1115	962		360	163	

NOTE: Percentages rounded to nearest whole number, NS = not significant, * significant <.05, all others significant <.01.

In the course of the 1987 survey, two major cities in India were selected as research localities. Although India is a rural society, cities were chosen as research sites in part because arrest rates tend to be higher in urban localities and for logistical reasons given the economic and time constraints faced by the investigators. The two cities chosen—Madras and New Delhi—were selected because of their geographical, cultural, and economic disparity (see Chapter Two) to assess the extent to which rates of delinquent behavior may vary by geographical regions in India. The results of this analysis are presented in Table 5.2.

Although some differences are found for individual offense items, the data presented in Table 5.2 suggest that no dramatic or patterned differences in offense behavior exist between either Madras and New Delhi high-school or institutionalized juveniles. Obviously, were more refined measures of incidence employed, it is conceivable that more substantial differences might be observed between the respondents in the two cities (see e.g., Elliott et al., 1989: 4–19; Hindelang et al., 1981; Klein, 1989; Natalino, 1981). But, we think this to be doubtful given the findings for Madras based on the 1990 survey. Moreover, were differences to exist, they would be unlikely to be profoundly meaningful. In this regard, it would probably be incorrect to conclude that either the unofficial or official delinquents of either city are fundamentally more (or less) delinquent than their counterparts in the other.

As far as high-school students are concerned, New Delhi respondents demonstrated significantly higher prevalence rates for nine of the twenty-nine offenses. Of these, substantially more New Delhi students admitted joy riding, vandalism, cheating on tests, and drinking alcohol. On the other hand, Madras respondents had higher prevalence scores for twelve offenses, of which possessing stolen property, stealing from family, throwing objects, and lying about self show substantially greater admission proportions. In neither case are higher admission rates concentrated around one or a single type of behavior, so these differences are probably random, or, at least, certainly do not reflect some patterned difference between the two samples. The moderately high Rho of .72 similarly indicates that Madras and New Delhi high-school youths are probably quite similar in, at least, the kinds of offense conduct admitted in self-report surveys.

A similar statement applies to the institutionalized respondents. These respondents are considerably more delinquent than high-school youths in both cities. But for almost two thirds of the offenses, no statistically significant differences existed between admission rates for these respondents. The Rho of .65 also indicates that relative proportions are similarly distributed across the two samples, although less so than is the case of high-school students.

In only one instance (moderate theft) were New Delhi institutionalized respondents more delinquent than Madras respondents. Otherwise, where differences are found, Madras youths produced higher prevalence rates. Since these cover the spectrum of offense behaviors contained in the survey, it is unlikely that Madras official delinquents are decidedly more delinquent than New Delhi offenders. Instead, the differences probably reflect differences in the characteristics of youths housed in the institutions of the two cities. In Madras, both male and female wards were primarily convicted offenders sentenced to long terms of incarceration. In New Delhi, the smaller number of incarcerated youths consisted of convicted offenders and (especially among girls) neglected youths not necessarily seriously involved in offense behavior. To what extent, if at all, these sample differences affect the results is not known.

Whatever the case, these data strongly imply that youths (whether officially recognized as delinquents or not) in two geographically, culturally, linguistically, and economically distinct regions of India exhibit very similar involvement in delinquent activity. While regional and other variations in crime and delinquency undoubtedly exist throughout India, as elsewhere, these findings (along with interviews and observations conducted by the authors over many years) make us confident that any conclusions we might draw regarding the epidemiological dimensions of delinquency in India based on our survey findings are probably generalizable to a much larger population of Indian youths. It is on this assumption that we proceed with an analysis of the correlates of delinquency rates in India and a comparison of India with other countries (primarily the United States).

CHARACTERISTICS OF INDIAN OFFENDERS
Debate still exists over the precise demographic distribution of delinquent behavior among western youths as well as the meaning this distribution might have (see the summaries presented in Empey & Stafford, 1991; Gibbons & Krohn, 1991). Nevertheless, criminological research throughout the world repeatedly reveals that the epidemiological distribution of delinquent conduct may vary in rather patterned ways. Primarily, males tend to be more delinquent than females, although the proportions are by no means uniform across countries (see, e.g., Hartjen & Kethineni, 1993). To a lesser extent, offense rates also tend to increase with age throughout the adolescent years, peaking in late teens or early twenties and declining thereafter. But the age at which delinquency peaks and the speed with which the peak is reached may not be uniform throughout the world (e.g., Farrington, 1986; LaGrange & White, 1985). Somewhat more controversial and decidedly less well documented, are possible associations among delinquency rates and such variables as grade in school, social class, and religious and other affiliation. Yet the data derived from research on western societies paint a rather consistent picture concerning at least the broad dimensions of offense rates by such factors as age and gender and, to a lesser extent, such variables as social class and ethnicity.

Table 5.3
Percentage of Respondents Committing an Offense on at Least One Occasion,
by Sample and Respondent Characteristics, 1987 Survey

Respondent			Sample		
Characteristics	India	Madras	Delhi	H.S.	Inst.
Gender					
Male	84	81	87	84	86
Female	64	58	71	65	65
Sample N	(2570)	(1452)	(1118)	(2051)	(510)
CHI Sq	130.20	92.59	45.33	97.90	31.85
Age					
14 Years	71	67	78	69	72
15 Years	75	71	79	74	81
16 Years	78	74	83	77	83
17 Years	77	76	78	76	82
Sample N	(2578)	(1459)	(1119)	(2067)	(510)
CHI Sq	11.11	9.29*	NS	10.98	NS
Education					
9th Grade or Less	72	70	76	69	77
10th Grade	76	76	76	74	85
11th Grade	79	71	87	80	67
12th Grade	75	69	80	75	81
Sample N	(2560)	(1288)	(1114)	(2057)	(496)
CHI Sq	9.19*	NS	12.68	17.14	NS
Guardian's Income P.M.					
Below Rs. 500	73	73	73	68	83
Rs. 500–1,499	74	72	79	72	85
Rs. 1,500 or over	78	67	82	78	100
Sample N	(2305)	(1288)	(1017)	(1959)	(316)
CHI Sq	6.95*	NS	NS	15.33	NS
Guardian's Occupation					
Unskilled	77	75	84	72	89
Skilled	75	70	81	74	86
White Collar	71	70	73	72	67
Sample N	(2599)	(1474)	(1125)	(2076)	(405)
CHI Sq	5.83*	NS	9.65	NS	32.44
Religion					
Hindu	75	70	80	73	79
Non-Hindu	78	79	74	76	81
Sample N	(2478)	(1412)	(1066)	(1989)	(486)
CHI Sq	NS	6.60	NS	NS	NS
Total Sample N	(2600)	(1475)	(1125)	(2077)	(523)

Note: all percentages are rounded to nearest whole number. Sample N's are
number of persons providing responses to each respondent characteristic,
excluding missing cases. NS = not significant, * = significant, <.05, all others
significant <.01.

But from an international perspective, given the extreme diversity in economic and social conditions related to these seemingly standard variables, drawing conclusions about the worldwide demographic distribution of delinquent conduct would be pure speculation at this point. Most of the research regarding these dimensions is based on official statistics of questionable credibility. Only a limited number of scattered self-report surveys, typically involving small samples, are available to provide information on the extent and distribution of hidden or unrecorded delinquent conduct in Third World or non-western societies so that it is simply not known if, or to what extent, relative rates of delinquent conduct are similarly or dissimilarly distributed among juveniles throughout the world. Whatever the case, the implications for criminological theory are profound.

To assess the demographic patterns of delinquent behavior in India, prevalence rates for the total sample and those in each of the sub-samples were computed in terms of respondents' demographic characteristics. These proportions are summarized in Table 5.3 along with corresponding Chi Square statistics.

The percentages presented in Table 5.3 suggest that substantial majorities of all respondent-samples report at least some involvement in delinquent forms of behavior (although for Madras girls the proportion is comparatively small). A slight, but not pronounced increase in admission rates occurs by age and, to a lesser extent, by grade in school. The small decline observed among 12th-grade respondents probably reflects the fact that relatively few institutionalized respondents had reached this grade level, thereby inflating the proportions at lower grades.

Interestingly, a sizable increase in admission rates occurs on the basis of income among New Delhi respondents, but the reverse is found for Madras respondents, although for the total sample prevalence rates are positively associated with income. The reverse, however, is found for parent's occupation. Religion seems to make no difference as far as prevalence is concerned in India. Of the factors investigated by criminologists, the three that have received the most attention and appear to have the greatest policy and theoretical relevance are age, gender, and social class.

Age

Self-report research on western populations suggests that while rates of involvement in the more serious criminal offenses tend to decline through the adolescent years, relative involvement (both prevalence and incidence) in less serious, more "adult," forms of misconduct (e.g., drinking, disorderly conduct, etc.) tend to increase (see Elliott et al., 1983: 95–101; Loeber, 1987). Conversely, arrests for criminal offenses actually increase substantially from

Table 5.4
Prevalence Rates and Chi Squares for High-School Respondents, by Age, 1987
Survey

Offense	Age				X^2
	14	15	16	17	
Assault	5	6	7	9	9.0*
Gang Fight	4	6	7	7	NS
Hit Parent	3	3	3	2	NS
Concealed Weapon	4	7	4	8	9.1*
Steal Rs 500+	1	1	1	2	8.2*
Steal Rs 50–500	1	3	2	2	NS
Steal Rs < 50	4	7	9	7	13.8
Vehicle Theft	1	1	0	1	NS
Joy Ride	6	8	10	9	7.2*
Possess Stolen Property	1	2	2	1	NS
Steal from Family	12	16	19	18	10.9
Steal from School	10	13	13	9	NS
Strongarm Others	5	6	7	7	NS
Break and Enter	6	7	8	8	NS
Avoid Payment	16	19	26	23	19.8
Vandalism	17	20	19	19	NS
Throw Objects	12	11	13	12	NS
Disorderly Conduct	8	10	12	13	8.7*
Drunk in Public	0	1	1	4	29.2
Beg for Money	2	3	3	2	NS
Runaway	6	4	4	5	NS
Truancy	24	26	31	38	28.7
Lie About Self	23	28	33	26	12.8
Cheat on School Test	39	49	52	51	22.2
Sold Hard Drugs	0	0	0	0	NS
Sold Soft Drugs	0	0	0	0	NS
Drank Alcohol	9	11	15	15	15.6
Used Soft Drugs	1	1	2	2	NS
Used Hard Drugs	0	1	1	1	NS
Mean % per Offense	8	9	10	10	NS
Sample N	610	503	526	428	

Note: percentages rounded to nearest whole number, NS = not significant, * = significant <.05, all others significant <.01.

Table 5.5
Prevalence Rates and Chi Squares for Institutionalized Respondents, by Age,
1987 Survey

Offense	14	15	Age 16	17	X^2
Assault	7	7	5	17	11.5
Gang Fight	11	9	10	14	NS
Hit Parent	8	9	14	12	NS
Concealed Weapon	8	10	9	15	4.0*
Steal Rs 50+	6	7	12	11	NS
Steal Rs 5–50	9	13	13	15	NS
Steal Rs < 5	11	18	16	22	6.5
Vehicle Theft	4	4	5	6	NS
Joy Ride	7	9	7	7	NS
Possess Stolen Property	10	12	20	21	8.5
Steal from Family	21	22	40	46	28.2
Steal from School	30	23	27	40	7.4
Strongarm Others	9	8	8	12	NS
Break and Enter	12	14	15	30	15.9
Avoid Payment	24	26	38	47	18.5
Vandalism	11	12	20	22	8.1
Throw Objects	21	18	19	25	NS
Disorderly Conduct	10	11	15	17	NS
Drunk in Public	4	9	6	11	5.6*
Beg for Money	7	11	11	24	19.0
Runaway	24	29	39	49	20.8
Truancy	24	27	33	44	13.4
Lie About Self	33	24	43	45	12.4
Cheat on School Test	28	31	34	45	9.2
Sold Hard Drugs	4	3	2	7	4.0*
Sold Soft Drugs	5	3	2	3	NS
Drank Alcohol	7	12	8	19	10.7
Used Soft Drugs	4	5	10	13	10.5
Used Hard Drugs	4	5	4	10	4.1*
Mean % per Offense	13	13	17	22	4.9*
Sample N	224	101	90	95	

Note: Percentages rounded to nearest whole number, NS = not significant,
* = significant <.05, all others significant <.01.

about age ten to eighteen, followed by a steady decline as people age (Empey & Stafford, 1991: 106; Farrington, 1986; Loeber & Snyder, 1990).

Arrest rates for juveniles and young adults in India (while not as precisely measured as UCR data) indicate a similar trend but with a much later age-peak in the arrest-rate curve (see Chapter Four). At least for the age range of respondents (fourteen to seventeen) included in this survey, our self-report data suggest that only a very weak association between age and delinquency may exist. However, as Tables 5.4 and 5.5 indicate, for both high-school and institutionalized respondents respectively, the age/delinquency association among Indian youth may also vary considerably by specific types of offenses.

Table 5.6
Prevalence and Incidence Rates for the Total Sample, by Age, 1987 Survey

Offense Category	Age				
	14	15	16	17	
	Prevalence				X^2
	%	%	%	%	
Total Delinq.	71	76	78	77	11.11
Status Offenses	55	58	63	66	16.50
Property Crimes	21	27	28	29	7.26
Personal Crimes	15	14	16	16	6.01
Substance Abuse	10	14	16	18	19.88

	Incidence								
	Mean	SD	Mean	SD	Mean	SD	Mean	SD	F
Total Delinq.	3.17	4.16	3.57	4.66	3.96	4.73	4.50	5.75	11.23
Status Offenses	.61	.79	.63	.82	.73	.83	.82	.92	8.28
Property Crimes	.38	.90	.55	1.31	.56	1.27	.66	1.55	6.03
Personal Crimes	.19	.46	.17	.45	.19	.48	.24	.54	NS
Substance Abuse	.11	.37	.14	.41	.19	.48	.22	.53	8.06
Sample N	825		609		618		526		

Note: Coefficients computed with missing cases excluded, therefore, offense category N's may differ from sample N's. NS = not significant, all others significant <.01

For both groups remarkably similar age-related increases in prevalence rates are found for individual offenses. Significant Chi Squares are found throughout the spectrum of offense types. But rather pronounced increases by age tend to center around status and some public-disorder offenses as well as the use of alcohol. Some property crimes also tend to be significantly related to age, but the pattern of association is less consistent in that no apparent linear increase in serious criminality occurs throughout adolescence among either official or unofficial delinquents in India.

The findings for individual offenses suggest that the age-related involvement of Indian youth might vary depending upon the general type of offense behavior in question. To explore this possibility, responses to individual offense items were summed into total and several offense-type categories similar to those used in the NYS (see Appendix D). Prevalence and incidence rates with appropriate association measures regarding these offense-types are presented in Table 5.6.

The data in Table 5.6 highlight and expand the findings from the offense-specific tables. Specifically, insofar as personal offenses are concerned, prevalence and incidence rates show a mixed pattern with slight decreases and then small increases over the four age categories. For all other offense types small, but consistent, increases occur at each age bracket for both prevalence and incidence rates; and this is especially noticeable among incidence means. In this regard, as youths age in India, it is not necessarily the case that more of them become involved in various kinds of delinquency, but that the frequency increases somewhat for those who are involved—especially for status and substance abuse types of misconduct. This finding does not appear to be unique to this sample population.

Gender

The 10:1 difference in arrest ratios between boys and girls in India reported in Chapter Four is not duplicated for either high-school or institutionalized respondents. Indeed, on the average, prevalence ratios of about 2:1 and 3:1 are respectively reported for the two samples. Of course, arrest statistics reflect a rather distinctive order of illegal activity. Thus, for the kinds of offense activity for which boys and girls are likely to be subject to arrest, real gender-related differences may exist. However, even for relatively serious offenses, admission ratios of 3:1 or more are not often found for either sample. In this regard, as in other countries, the gender gap in India for crime and delinquency is much less pronounced in self-report findings than for arrest rates. Clearly the gender gap in arrests reflects more than real differences in behavior on the part of boys and girls in India as is probably true in most, if not all, countries (see Canter, 1982; Shoemaker, 1994).

This is also true when patterns of involvement are considered. Spearman Rho's of .91 for high-school boys and girls and .72 for institutionalized boys and girls suggest that even though identical relative proportions of boys and girls do not admit involvement in each delinquent act, they are alike insofar as the types of misconduct they are more or less likely to admit. In fact, with a few exceptions, the Phi coefficients are of very similar magnitude across offenses for the two samples, suggesting that one gender group does not engage in one kind of delinquent behavior while the other is engaged in totally different kinds of misconduct.

Table 5.7

Prevalence Rates and Phi Coefficients for High-School and Institutionalized
Respondents, by Gender, 1987 Survey

Offense	High School			Institution		
	Boys	Girls	Phi	Boys	Girls	Phi
Assault	11	2	.20	13	2	.18
Gang Fight	7	3	.15	16	3	.20
Hit Parent	2	3	NS	13	5	.13
Concealed Weapon	9	3	.14	13	5	.13
Steal Rs 50+	8	3	.10	10	6	NS
Steal Rs 5–50	3	1	.08	18	2	.23
Steal Rs < 5	10	3	.14	22	5	.23
Vehicle Theft	8	4	.08	13	2	.19
Joy Ride	10	5	.10	21	9	.16
Possess Stolen Prop.	1	1	NS	5	4	NS
Steal from Family	13	2	.21	11	2	.18
Steal from School	23	10	.18	42	11	.33
Strongarm Others	15	7	.13	36	21	.17
Break and Enter	10	2	.17	22	3	.26
Avoid Payment	32	10	.27	10	45	.37
Vandalism	27	11	.21	18	10	.10*
Throw Objects	19	6	.19	29	10	.22
Disorderly Conduct	16	5	.18	15	8	.10*
Drunk in Public	2	1	.08	10	2	.16
Beg for Money	3	2	NS	17	4	.20
Runaway	7	2	.12	46	9	.39
Truancy	38	21	.19	37	19	.19
Lie about Self	34	21	.15	40	26	.15
Cheat on School Test	54	40	.14	35	31	NS
Sold Hard Drugs	0	0	NS	6	1	.14
Sold Soft Drugs	0	0	NS	5	2	.09*
Drank Alcohol	19	6	.20	18	1	.27
Used Soft Drugs	2	1	.05*	10	1	.18
Used Hard Drugs	1	1	NS	8	1	.15
Mean % per Offense	13	6	.12	20	7	.15
Sample N	1013	1038		195	315	

NOTE: Percentages rounded to nearest whole number, NS = not
significant, * = significant <.05, all others significant <.01.

Nevertheless, what is also clear is that boys are distinctively more delinquent than girls, regardless of whether or not they have been officially recognized as such. This is somewhat more true of institutionalized respondents compared to high-school youths. But, even then, major distinctions in this regard do not appear. Among high-school respondents, the most substantial differences are for assault, stealing from family, avoiding payment, and drinking alcohol. Among institutionalized respondents boys and girls are most disparate for engaging in gang fights and moderate and petty theft, breaking and entering, avoiding payment, throwing objects, begging, running away, and drinking alcohol. While one might consider these to be "masculine" types of offense activities, the fact that fairly small Phi coefficients were found for similar types of activity could render a "masculine/feminine form of delinquency" hypothesis quite doubtful.

Table 5.8
Prevalence and Incidence Rates for the Total Sample, by Gender and Offense Category, 1987 Survey

Offense Category	Gender				
	Boys		Girls		
	Prevalence				
	%		%		PHI
Total Delinquency	84		64		.22
Status Offenses	66		51		.15
Property Crimes	37		12		.29
Personal Crimes	23		7		.22
Substance Abuse	20		6		.19
	Incidence				
	Mean	SD	Mean	SD	ETA
Total Delinquency	5.55	5.55	1.91	2.67	.33
Status Offenses	1.23	1.22	.69	.81	.24
Property Crimes	.77	1.42	.20	.72	.29
Personal Crimes	.35	.78	.09	.35	.33
Substance Abuse	.31	.79	.07	.33	.19
Sample N	1446		1124		

Note: Coefficients computed with missing cases excluded, therefore, offense category N's may differ from sample N's. All coefficients significant <.01.

The fairly small admission percentages for individual offenses, however, make it difficult to detect broad similarities or differences in types of offense behaviors. The figures in Table 5.8 may partly explain why such substantial gender-related disparities in arrests are found for India. Except for substance abuse and status offenses, rather sizable Phi coefficients are found for prevalence rates for total delinquency, and property and personal crimes. This is particularly true for incidence frequencies as suggested by the Eta coefficients for these offenses. Thus, more Indian boys are more often engaged in delinquency than are girls, and they are especially more so engaged in the broad kinds of conduct of interest to legal authorities. Thus, to some extent, their greater frequencies of arrests reflect these differences in behavior.

In short, as measured by self-reported behavior, Indian boys are more delinquent than are Indian girls. But the size of the disparity is not as great as that indicated by official statistics, and boys and girls are generally not widely different as far as individual offenses are concerned (see Steffensmeier & Steffensmeier, 1980).

SES

Much of the theory and research on delinquency in western criminology has centered around the seeming association between poverty and delinquency. Since most of the persons arrested, prosecuted, and sanctioned as criminals/delinquents are poor, the idea that delinquent behavior is somehow a function of low socioeconomic position seems reasonable. Self-report research, however, has cast considerable doubt on theories based on this assumption even though the class-crime association is by no means a settled matter (Braithwaite, 1981; Brownfield, 1986; Edwards, 1992; Elliott & Ageton, 1980; Elliott & Huizinga, 1983; Hagan, 1993; Hindelang et al., 1981; Patterson, 1991; Tittle & Meier, 1990).

In Third World countries where people are steeped in traditionalism and experience widespread poverty, high levels of unemployment, and little if any social mobility, the issues of social class and its effects on delinquent behavior take on a whole new dimension. If, in itself, poverty is a breeding ground for crime, such societies should exhibit comparatively high rates of delinquency. The available evidence, however, suggests just the opposite. That is, if societies are compared in terms of their relative economic position, it is economic affluence rather than poverty that is correlated with high rates of crime and delinquency (see e.g., Adler, 1983; Shelley, 1981).

But poverty, of course, is relative. Perhaps, therefore, within Third World societies, even where overall crime rates are low, it is the poor who are predominantly responsible for such behavior. Indeed, even through data on the socioeconomic status of persons processed by legal authorities is either lacking or highly unreliable, it would be readily apparent to any observer that the ranks of those appearing in courts and housed in correctional facilities are overwhelmingly poor. Conceivably, in more affluent western societies delinquency is more homogeneous among the juvenile population (as suggested by self-report studies), while in the Third World, a closer link between poverty and delinquency is discernable. If so, the class-crime association is relative to the overall socioeconomic situation of a country. Conversely, of course, if impoverished societies, such as India, exhibit offense rates based on class similar to those found in the United States and other affluent countries, then the etiological effect, or lack thereof, of social class must be taken as a universal.

The Chi square findings presented in Table 5.3 regarding the income and occupation of respondents' parents/guardians suggest that any association between social class and delinquency in India is probably quite complex. To more fully assess this relationship, a simple socioeconomic status measure (SES) was computed based on responses to the income and occupation questions. This produced a five category scale with scores coded from one (low SES) to five (high SES). Obviously social class is a much more complex phenomenon than we can possibly assess by such a measure. Indeed, the extent to which "social class" (as that concept is traditionally used in western social science) can even be applied to the Indian context is highly debatable, especially given the problem of caste and the unmeasurable effects of an agrarian, tradition-bound economic structure. In that respect, the SES scale used here is relative to this inquiry. Our purpose here is not to test class-based hypotheses. Rather we seek to make some judgments about relative socioeconomic position and self-admitted involvement in general delinquency or delinquency of various kinds.

Prevalence proportions for individual offense items by SES rank reported by high-school and institutionalized respondents are presented in Tables 5.9 and 5.10. It should be noted that separate tables are presented here primarily for the sake of consistency since the large number of missing cases for institutionalized respondents make any statistical analysis of prevalence rates by SES questionable. Analyses using raw as well as collapsed SES categories were conducted. The discussion presented here is a summary of these analyses. What is implied by the figures contained in these tables is that no pronounced association between SES and delinquency appears to exist among Indian youths. In that respect, SES is probably no more important as an explanatory variable in accounting for delinquency in India (at least that tapped by self-report surveys) than it has been found to be elsewhere.

Prevalence rates for virtually every offense are higher for institutionalized respondents than for high school students. And institutionalized youths as a group generally register lower SES scores than do high-school youths. Thus, one might conclude that their delinquency, if not just the fact of their incarceration, is a function of their SES standing. Indeed, when institutionalized and high-school respondents are compared in terms of SES rank, the incarcerated respondents still register higher offense proportions. In short, the bulk of the youths who wind up in correctional facilities for juveniles in India are not only poorer on average than Indians generally, but they are also somewhat more delinquent regardless of SES standing.

Table 5.9

Prevalence Rates and Chi Squares for High-School Respondents, by SES, 1987 Survey

| | SES Rank | | | | | |
| | Low | | | | High | Chi |
Offense	1	2	3	4	5	Square
Assault	6	8	5	6	9	NS
Gang Fight	8	6	7	6	9	NS
Hit Parent	2	2	3	2	2	NS
Concealed Weapon	8	5	5	5	9	NS
Steal Rs 500+	5	2	4	7	9	18.59
Steal Rs 50–500	0	2	2	3	2	NS
Steal Rs < 50	6	2	5	8	12	23.39
Vehicle Theft	2	1	1	1	2	NS
Joy Ride	5	2	4	12	14	46.91
Possess Stolen Prop.	9	11	7	3	3	28.23
Steal from Family	18	20	17	14	17	NS
Steal from School	16	11	11	10	11	NS
Strongarm Others	4	5	4	8	8	12.56*
Break and Enter	9	10	7	6	5	NS
Avoid Payment	14	22	23	20	24	NS
Vandalism	5	11	14	25	26	63.39
Throw Objects	12	17	14	9	13	13.82
Disorderly Conduct	13	9	8	12	14	NS
Drunk in Public	1	0	2	2	2	NS
Beg for Money	4	5	2	2	2	NS
Runaway	11	7	4	3	4	21.80
Truancy	29	28	32	27	32	NS
Lie about Self	30	31	30	23	32	15.56
Cheat on School Test	21	31	43	59	53	111.21
Sold Hard Drugs	0	0	0	0	0	NS
Sold Soft Drugs	0	0	1	0	0	NS
Drank Alcohol	5	8	10	16	15	27.07
Used Soft Drugs	3	2	1	1	2	9.64*
Used Hard Drugs	2	0	1	0	1	NS
Mean % per Offense	9	9	9	10	11	NS
Sample N	133	246	595	777	205	

NOTE: Percentages rounded to nearest whole number. Coefficients computed with missing cases excluded, therefore, offense category N's may differ from sample N's. NS = not significant, * = significant <.05, all others significant <.01.

Table 5.10

Prevalence Rates and Chi Squares for Institutionalized Respondents, by SES, 1987 Survey

| | SES Rank | | | | |
| | Low | | | High | Chi |
Offense	1	2	3	4	Square
Assault	8	12	12	12	NS
Gang Fight	6	10	14	24	9.86*
Hit Parent	9	12	19	10	NS
Concealed Weapon	13	14	11	19	NS
Steal Rs 500+	8	10	10	17	NS
Steal Rs 50–500	16	11	17	24	NS
Steal Rs < 50	17	20	19	26	NS
Vehicle Theft	3	3	6	14	7.92*
Joy Ride	7	5	13	14	NS
Possess Stolen Property	16	20	16	24	NS
Steal from Family	34	41	38	21	NS
Steal from School	30	31	37	33	NS
Strongarm Others	7	10	16	12	NS
Break and Enter	18	19	22	21	NS
Avoid Payment	33	41	33	43	NS
Vandalism	14	20	15	29	NS
Throw Objects	24	23	24	21	NS
Disorderly Conduct	14	12	15	19	NS
Drunk in Public	5	14	9	12	NS
Beg for Money	13	16	12	7	NS
Runaway	41	43	40	43	NS
Truancy	34	41	38	33	NS
Lie about Self	34	37	41	38	NS
Cheat on School Test	28	38	38	43	NS
Sold Hard Drugs	2	5	4	12	NS
Sold Soft Drugs	0	4	5	10	NS
Drank Alcohol	10	16	12	26	NS
Used Soft Drugs	7	14	6	17	NS
Used Hard Drugs	5	5	8	12	NS
Mean % per Offense	16	19	19	22	NS
Sample N	88	74	112	42	

NOTE: Percentages rounded to nearest whole number. Coefficients computed with missing cases excluded, therefore, offense category N's may differ from sample N's. Because SES Rank # 5 has only 6 respondents, this category was collapsed with # 4. NS = not significant, * = significant <.05, all others significant <.01.

However, what is probably more important for criminological theory is the fact that where a patterned association between delinquency and SES rank is found among the samples surveyed, it is as often positive as negative in direction. This finding is particularly pronounced among institutionalized youths, although it occurs among both samples. That is, higher SES youths often report higher prevalence rates than lower SES respondents whether they are officially recognized as delinquents or not. As we would expect from "strain" theories, a slight negative association is found between SES and delinquency. But this only occurs for some offenses, and these do not seem to cluster around some problem relating to economic deprivation as strain theories would predict.

Table 5.11
Prevalence and Incidence Rates for the Total Sample, by SES and Offense Category, 1987 Survey

SES Rank	Total Delinq.		Status Offenses		Offense Category Property Crimes		Personal Crimes		Substance Abuse	
					Prevalence					
Low	%		%		%		%		%	
1	77		56		36		18		12	
2	70		51		31		17		12	
3	75		51		33		19		13	
4	78		41		38		12		17	
5	77		50		41		18		16	
High										
					Incidence					
Low	Mean	SD	Mean	SD	Mean	SD	Mean	SD	Mean	SD
1	3.36	3.66	.88	.93	.67	1.16	.24	.55	.16	.47
2	3.16	3.70	.77	.89	.53	1.00	.20	.50	.16	.47
3	3.19	3.60	.75	.86	.56	1.08	.22	.49	.15	.43
4	3.02	3.38	.55	.75	.68	1.14	.14	.41	.19	.45
5	3.48	3.77	.71	.83	.76	1.25	.22	.50	.19	.49
High										
Sample N	2408		2541		2520		2560		2552	

Note: Coefficients are computed on SES rank N's with missing cases excluded, NS = not significant, * = significant <.05, all others significant <.01. Degrees of freedom for all calculations = 4.

What is even more intriguing is that among both samples higher SES respondents often have higher delinquency scores across the spectrum of offense types. But this is particularly true for substance-use activity. Indeed, contrary to what one might expect, higher SES respondents even have higher prevalence rates for theft and other property-related activities. To the extent that these findings are generalizable, it would appear that relative economic affluence is a positive stimulant to delinquency in India rather than a deterrent. That possibility is something that has significant implications for a country striving for economic development.

The data presented in Table 5.11 showing prevalence and incidence rates for the five offense scales used in this analysis help clarify the SES/delinquency relationship among Indian juveniles. For total delinquency, no meaningful difference in SES and delinquency seems to exist. This is true also for personal offenses. On the other hand, somewhat higher percentages of lower SES respondents do (and more frequently) report status-offense behavior. But rates for substance abuse and property-related crimes are somewhat higher for higher SES respondents. In that regard, higher SES respondents appear to be more involved in relatively serious offense behavior compared to poor Indian juveniles.

Yet even though a mixed SES/delinquency association is suggested by our data, given the limitations of the SES measure used in this inquiry and the limitations of self-reported delinquency measures, any conclusions about SES and delinquency in India would, at this time, be premature. Nevertheless, based on the data reported here and the observations and interviews conducted by the authors in India, we feel it very likely that more focused and refined research in this area would indeed uncover a heightened involvement of westernized, usually more affluent, youths in various forms of delinquency compared to more traditional, usually poorer, youths. Clearly this is speculative at this point. But the matter certainly warrants further inquiry.

Correlations

The analyses of associations between demographic characteristics and rates of self-reported delinquency overall or for various offense types produced a mixed bag of findings. Moreover, the extent to which any of these variables individually or together explain delinquency rates is not clear. Pearson correlation coefficients were computed between the several respondent characteristics and incidence rates for the various offense categories. These clearly reveal that gender is the single most important variable in determining relative delinquency since correlations of .32 (total) to .17 (substance abuse) are found for this variable. Parents' income, occupation, and the combined measure of SES produced no significant correlations, while age had weak but statistically significant positive associations with various offense scales. Thus, except for gender, none of the demographic variables alone seems to be particularly important insofar as explaining delinquency rates in India is concerned.

But how predictive are these dimensions of delinquency in combination? The multiple regression analysis presented in Table 5.12 using age, gender, and

SES as independent variables and incidence rates for the various offense scales as dependent variables sheds some light on this question.

Table 5.12
Multiple Regression Analysis of Age, Gender, and SES on Offense Types, Total Sample, 1987 Survey

Offense Category	R^2	F
Total Delinquency	4	112.93
Status Offenses	09	69.13
Property Offenses	07	51.34
Personal Offenses	05	34.27
Substance Abuse	05	34.40

Note: probability of F in all cases <.0001.

Only about 14 percent of the variance in overall delinquency is explained by the combination of demographic characteristics. While not substantial, this proportion is not grossly different from that explained by similar variables in other countries. Considerably smaller proportions of the variance in other offense scales are similarly explained by the combination of demographic variables used in this analysis. Although statistically significant, demographic characteristics seem to do little to help us understand variations in relative involvement in offense activity among Indian youths. Generally very little variance in delinquency appears to exist among youths in India in any case. Thus, possibly of greater criminological relevance at the moment are the differences or similarities among the self-reported delinquency of Indian compared to youths in other countries.

COMPARISONS WITH THE UNITED STATES AND OTHER COUNTRIES
As with arrest data, interpretations of the self-report survey findings may be expedited by comparing the India findings with the results of similar data obtained in other countries. To that end, some direct comparisons of the India data with findings from the NYS are made here, followed by general discussion of the research carried out in other countries.

United States
Table 5.13 presents prevalence proportions and Phi coefficients for the individual offenses investigated in the Indian and National Youth Surveys. The Spearman Rho of .43 clearly suggests that not only do admission rates vary for

Table 5.13

Prevalence Rates and Phi Coefficients for Indian 1987 and United States 1978
High-School Samples

Offense	India	U.S.	Phi
Assault	6	4	-.04*
Gang Fight	6	8	.04*
Hit Parent	3	5	.05
Concealed Weapon	6	6	NS
Grand Theft	6	2	-.09*
Moderate Theft	2	5	.08
Petty Theft	6	15	.15
Vehicle Theft	1	1	NS
Joy Ride	8	4	-.08
Possess Stolen Property	6	9	.06
Steal from Family	16	10	-.08
Steal from School	11	5	-.10
Strongarm Others	6	2	-.09
Break and Enter	7	2	-.11
Avoid Payment	21	15	-.07
Vandalism	19	26	.08
Throw Objects	12	39	.31
Disorderly Conduct	11	29	.23
Drunk in Public	2	21	.32
Beg for Money	3	2	NS
Runaway	4	5	NS
Truancy	29	39	.10
Lie about Self	28	31	NS
Cheat on School Test	47	47	NS
Sold Hard Drugs	< 1	1	.06
Sold Soft Drugs	< 1	9	.23
Drank Alcohol	12	27	.19
Used Soft Drugs	1	31	.44
Used Hard Drugs	1	3	.10
Mean % per Offense	10	14	.08
Sample N	2077	1247	

Note: percentages are rounded to nearest whole number, NS= not significant,
*= significant <.05, all others significant <.01.

individual offenses, but as far as relative involvement in specific types of activities are concerned, overall Indian and American youths exhibit fairly dissimilar offense patterns. In terms of the percentage of respondents admitting each offense, on the average American youths are slightly more delinquent than Indian youths. Moreover, greater proportions of the American respondents admitted to about one-half of the individual offenses. For eight offenses (almost all property crimes) Indians have higher prevalence rates, although the value of Phi for the majority of these is negligible. In about one-quarter of the cases no statistically significant differences are found between American and Indian respondents.

Table 5.14
Prevalence and Incidence Rates with Association Measures for Offense Categories, Indian 1987 and United States 1978 High-School Samples

Offense Category		Sample			
		India		U.S.	
			Prevalence		
		%		%	Phi
Total Delinquency		74		81	.09
Status Offenses		44		51	.08
Property Crimes		23		22	NS
Personal Crimes		13		14	NS
Substance Abuse		13		45	.36
Theft Offenses		10		17	.10
Home Delinquency		20		16	-.04*
Public Delinquency		20		37	.27
			Incidence		
	Mean	SD	Mean	SD	ETA
General Delinquency	3.33	4.35	3.81	3.91	.07
Status Offenses	.61	.73	.75	.84	.08
Property Crimes	.44	1.10	.39	.92	NS
Personal Crimes	.18	.54	.17	.47	NS
Substance Abuse	.17	.51	.52	.69	.29
Theft Offenses	.14	.44	.24	.60	.10
Home Delinquency	.26	.73	.20	.51	.05
Public Delinquency	.26	.62	.51	.74	.18

Note: NS = not significant, * = significant <.05, all others significant <.01.

While statistically significant (to be expected given the large samples) the Phi coefficients are generally extremely small, suggesting that few meaningful differences in individual offenses-item prevalence rates exist between the two samples. However, fairly substantial (.15 or higher) Phi's are found for seven (one quarter) of the offense items. In all cases these involved higher admission rates for American respondents. Other than petty theft, these items involved public disorder types of behavior and substance abuse activities. On the other hand, the offenses for which Indians exhibited higher prevalence rates almost exclusively involved property types of activity. This suggests that, while extreme differences are not found in self-reported delinquency among Indians and Americans, real differences may exist in their relative involvement in various types of behaviors. And, to some extent, these behavioral differences may be reflected in the extremely disparate arrest rates discussed in Chapter Four although alone they would hardly suffice to explain this disparity.

The data in Table 5.14 highlight these similarities and differences. In order to more clearly tap broad cross-national similarities and differences, this table adds three offense categories (theft, home and public delinquency) to the "within-India" comparisons made in similar tables earlier in this chapter (see Appendix D). Since an "institutionalized" sample cannot be identified for the NYS sample, this analysis focuses on respondents attending high schools in both countries at the time of the survey.

No differences are found in prevalence or incidence rates for property and personal crimes. Indians exhibit small but significantly higher "home delinquency" rates consisting of such offenses as striking a parent, running away from home, or stealing from one's family. Overall, and for all other offense types, Americans have higher Phi and Eta coefficients. For total delinquency, status offenses, and theft offenses these differences are extremely small, suggesting that meaningful differences probably do not exist between Americans and Indians (except, perhaps, in the frequency with which American youths engage in status offenses). On the other hand, pronounced differences in both prevalence and incidence rates are found for substance abuse offenses and public forms of delinquency. Americans are two or three times more delinquent compared to Indians for these offenses. Such conduct may not involve serious types of criminality. But it is the kind of behavior likely to be easily noticed by authorities and the public and, consequently, likely to fuel a perception of youths as rowdy and dangerous. This, in turn, could contribute to a climate of fear favoring official reaction to misbehaving youths, and consequently increase the probabilities that some of these offenders will experience arrest.

In short, major differences in offense rates are not revealed between American and Indian youths in the self-reported delinquency data investigated here. Yet, these figures may indicate that differences could exist in the relative numbers and frequencies with which youths in these two countries engage in various kinds of offense behaviors. And these differences may be reflected in such measures of societal reaction, as rates of arrest.

Other Countries

The international youth survey of thirteen western countries has done much to enhance our understanding of the extent and nature of delinquency among youths in the populations surveyed (Junger-Tas et al., 1994). As summarized by Junger-Tas (1994), findings from this research suggest that, at least among western youth, both the extent and distribution of self-reported delinquency are remarkably similar, idiosyncratic anomalies in individual surveys notwithstanding. However, other than for the samples of western youth surveyed, systematic self-reported delinquency data using a common survey instrument based on similar samples drawn among youth throughout the world are not available and are unlikely to be so in the foreseeable future. This is especially true for those societies in Asia, Africa, and Latin America about which we have the least amount of information on delinquency and youth crime. Instead, a hodgepodge of more or less sophisticated and extensive inquiries are reported in the criminological literature. Drawing any kind of comparative conclusions from these would require a substantial leap in methodological faith. Nevertheless, a brief review of a convenience sampling of these studies can help us to more fully contextualize the Indian survey findings reported here and their similarities and differences compared to the NYS data.

Of the few self-reported delinquency surveys published in the English-language literature from countries outside western Europe or North America, fewer still can reasonably be directly compared to the findings from the NYS or IYS reported here—either because of extreme differences in samples and/or the offense items investigated in the surveys. Of the smattering of studies available, perhaps the research carried out in New Zealand by Moffitt and Silva (1988) offers the most comparable such study. In that inquiry, Moffitt and Silva sampled a cohort of 1,139 persons born in Dunedin, New Zealand, between April 1, 1972, and March 31, 1973. From this cohort, responses to self-report questionnaires were obtained from 742 youths, then thirteen years of age. With a population of 120,000 residents, Dunedin does not offer a sampling universe comparable to the cities of Madras and New Delhi or the national sample used in the NYS. But the substantial size of the sample and the inclusiveness of the 58 offense item survey instrument used in the inquiry allows us to make some meaningful comparisons of that study with the present inquiry.

Of the 58 items (29 illegal acts and 29 "norm violations") investigated, 21 items correspond to those queried in the IYS and NYS studies. Prevalence rates for boys and girls reported by Moffitt and Silva for New Zealand youths show remarkable similarities with those found for Indian and American respondents. Probably due to the youth of the respondents sampled, prevalence rates are generally lower for the New Zealand respondents. But when compared to persons of similar age responding to the IYS and NYS, these differences are greatly reduced, and extreme differences are not found as far as general offense types or patterns are concerned. As with the Indian and American surveys, boys are almost always more delinquent than girls, and admission rates to the more serious offense items are typically lower than rates for minor or status-like behavior. Data reported specifically for the eighteen-year-olds surveyed in this study do not alter these observations (Moffitt et al., 1995).

In this regard, the New Zealand findings highlight the apparent universality in delinquency suggested by the two-sample comparison of India and the United States. Findings from self-report research in diverse regions of the world would probably not seriously challenge this conclusion, although such data could lead to its refinement or qualification.

For example, Gomme et al., (1987) sampled 428 senior elementary and junior-high-school students in South Ontario, Canada. Reporting the responses of males and females to a 12-offense-item instrument, this investigation found that admission rates, especially for serious criminal offenses, are generally quite low for both genders although almost always higher for males. Yet, while more boys than girls report delinquency involvement, the types and patterns of delinquency found were quite similar. According to Gomme et al., the Canada findings are very similar to those reported in a number of studies from the United States. Compared to India, however, overall offense rates are somewhat higher for similar offenses, and the average male/female ratios of less than 2:1 are more reminiscent of the American than the Indian gender gap in delinquency.

Research by Sheu (1988) on a sample of 3,717 senior- and junior-high-school students in the Republic of China using a questionnaire investigating 17 offense items also found that boys are more delinquent than girls for all behaviors, especially the more serious assaultive crimes. However, the differences between genders are somewhat greater than for either Canada or the United States and are more reminiscent of those found for India. Similarly, prevalence rates are remarkably like those reported by Indian youths, being somewhat lower than those found for either Canada or the United States. As with self-report research findings reported by almost every study in almost every country, SES is not related to self-reported delinquency in Taiwan either.

According to William Skinner (1986), youths in Iceland tend to be somewhat less involved in drug-use behavior and property crimes compared to findings from studies of youths in various northern European countries. In general, however, prevalence rates for a list of 17 offenses do not reveal any particularly unusual patterns for Icelandic respondents. As is also typically the case, wherever such figures are reported, incidence means cluster around the lower end of the frequency scale. Icelandic boys are also more delinquent than girls with the smallest differences involving the consumption of alcoholic beverages and the largest associated with major property crimes. While measures of SES (e.g., father's occupation) and other demographic variables have only negligible associations with delinquency, variables relating to school and peer-group involvement are more strongly related. With the exception of alcohol consumption and public drunkenness, rates for Iceland tend to more closely resemble those of India than America or Canada.

Other research conducted in Korea (Shim, 1987), Hong Kong (Cheung & Ng, 1988), and the Netherlands (Junger-Tas & Block, 1988) reflect the kinds of findings produced by the research sampled above. Thus, the overall magnitude of prevalence and incidence rates of self-reported delinquency vary somewhat from society to society, as do rates for individual offenses. These differences are undoubtedly partly due to real differences in behavior as well as due to a host of measurement, sampling, instrumentation, and various factors. But self-report findings from around the world are more striking for their similarities than their differences. Indeed, prevalence rates for respondents in the 13 western nations study are so similar that, unless more sophisticated analyses of these findings demonstrate otherwise, it would be correct to say that "delinquency" is common to youths everywhere. Moreover, universally the most pronounced involvement in such conduct seems to center on milder, status-like, substance use and petty criminal types of behavior while the more serious, personal offenses are least often reported. Whether this is reflective of the inherent limitations of self-report research techniques or of the true nature of delinquency epidemiology is, of course, a matter for dispute.

Similarly, gender appears to be an important correlate of self-reported delinquency everywhere while SES and age appear to be unrelated to delinquency, although they may be associated with variations in some types of activities. Nevertheless, while similar, important differences exist across countries in specific forms of misconduct, the overall magnitude of rates, and the variations in these rates by gender, age, SES, and other variables. In this regard, delinquency may be universal but is not universally identical. To what extent, if at all, the rather small differences in self-reported delinquency, both within and across specific societies, are reflected in or help explain the rather gross differences in the official rates reported for various countries is not known. But the issue should (we would think) occasion massive expenditures of energy in criminological research.

CONCLUSION

The data reviewed in this chapter indicate that, as far as self-reported delinquency is concerned, Indian juveniles are probably not unlike youths in the rest of the world. Almost all of them admit to having committed at least one "delinquent" act, although few appear to be multiple or chronic offenders. Most of this conduct seems to center around relatively mild property offenses, various public-disorder types of conduct, and what in some societies constitute status offenses. Youths incarcerated in correctional facilities tend to be somewhat more delinquent in that they exhibit higher prevalence rates for almost all offenses, especially the more serious crimes and other activity likely to bring them to the attention of authorities.

As elsewhere, considerable differences in admission rates are found by gender, although no dramatic disparities exist in the relative types of delinquency committed by males and females. Age and (largely associated with it) year in school are both positively associated with delinquency, although not consistently or to any strong degree. Similarly, various measures of socioeconomic status suggest that delinquency is actually positively related, if only weakly so, to SES. This casts considerable doubt on the applicability of strain theories as explanations of delinquency among Indian youths and suggests that new class-linked explanations of delinquency may be needed for international inquiry. Taken together, the various demographic characteristics of respondents explain significant, if small, amounts of the variance in overall delinquency and delinquency of various kinds.

Compared to self-reported delinquency findings obtained from countries throughout the world, India does not appear to be particularly distinctive in having either exceptionally low or high rates, or rates reflecting some unusual pattern or type of delinquency involvement. To the extent that such information is available, Indian youth do appear to resemble those in other Third World countries more than American and western European juveniles. However, worldwide reports of survey findings do not produce the extreme disparities in offense rates that one finds when comparing various official measures. In this regard, studies of self-reported delinquency surely seem to suggest that, at least as far as the kind of misconduct they measure is concerned, a certain universality in delinquent behavior exists.

But, while similar, youths in various societies are also not apparently identical either in the relative prevalence and incidence of offense activity generally or for various kinds. Some Indian juveniles are undoubtedly involved in serious criminality and may be frequently so engaged. For the bulk of Indian youths, however, such conduct is relatively rare. Even for what appears to be serious criminality (in an offense category contained in a self-report table), informal interviews with many Indian youths lead us to believe that very little of their delinquency can be called "serious." Stealing from school can often mean taking a pencil or similar item from the grounds. Stealing from family can easily be translated into taking a sibling's change or other possession. Avoiding payment consists of not paying the bus conductor, who often is physically prevented from collecting fares anyway due to the chronically overcrowded conditions of Indian buses. Drinking alcohol usually involves tasting some relative's beer or whisky. In part, this may be why this activity is more frequent among wealthier youths whose family members are not only more able to afford but, emulating western society, are more likely to have such substances available in their homes, encouraging experimentation. For purposes of analysis we must, of course, take the answers of survey respondents literally; but we must also be careful in interpreting the nature and severity of the offense behaviors they appear to reveal. This would necessitate a considerable refining of self-report survey techniques before they can be realistically used as barometers of actual rates of delinquency internationally.

CHAPTER SIX

Etiology: Explaining Delinquent Behavior in the United States and India

Data presented in previous chapters describe the relative frequencies and distributions of delinquent behavior among Indian juveniles in comparison to youths in other countries. But analyses of rates cannot reveal the extent to which the causal dimensions behind Indian delinquency are similar or dissimilar to those believed to generate such conduct among youths in other countries. Major causal theories of delinquent behavior have largely focused on western (mainly, American) youths. Few efforts to test these theories on youths in Third World or non-western societies can be found in the literature so that it is not known if, or to what extent, concepts such as differential association theory or bond theory have universal explanatory relevance. Thus, before attempting to make sense out of delinquency rates in countries with diverse socioeconomic characteristics, it would be beneficial to investigate the etiology of the behavior responsible for these rates in some depth.

The 1990 survey of Madras high-school students was designed to assess the extent to which explanatory dimensions derived from major etiological theories apply cross-nationally. Rather than assessing aspects of one, another, or even several causal theories, it was decided that the causal model developed by Elliott and his colleagues incorporating measures from the three major theoretical perspectives in contemporary criminology (i.e., strain, control, learning) would be most productive for a comparative inquiry. In doing so, we sought to evaluate the relative explanatory merits of each theory as well as their combined ability to account for delinquent behavior in diverse socioeconomic environments. The survey instrument used in this inquiry was based on the one employed in the 1978 sampling wave of the National Youth Survey, and a modified version of the integrated theory model developed by Elliott et al. (1985) was chosen as the model for this inquiry.

A variety of statistical procedures similar to those employed by Elliott et al. (1985) were followed to assess the individual and combined cross-national explanatory ability of the etiological theories investigated in the NYS study. Each procedure was applied to the Indian as well as the subsample of NYS respondents for comparative purposes.

Several of the scales developed by Elliott et al. (1985) to test aspects of each of the three theoretical dimensions they investigated were employed in the present analysis also. Four scales measured aspects of strain theory. Four tapped dimensions of control theory relating to family and school involvement and normlessness. Three learning theory scales measuring peer involvement and attitudes toward deviance were also employed, along with an index developed to assess respondents' relative involvement with delinquent and other peers. Four offense scales (general delinquency, index offenses, minor offenses, and a substance abuse scale) were used as dependent variables (see Appendix D).

Table 6.1 compares the mean scores of Indian and American respondents on the four offense scales. As found in the discussion of the 1987 India survey findings (see Chapter 5), except for index offenses, on all measures Americans have substantially larger incidence scores than Indians. Indeed, for substance-related behavior, mean scores for Indians are practically nil, whereas among Americans high frequencies of involvement in substance abuse were found, surpassing their involvement in even minor forms of non-substance-related delinquency.

Table 6.1
Comparison of Mean Scores of United States 1978 and Indian 1990
Respondents on Delinquency Scales

Scale	Mean	SD	t
General Delinquency			
U.S. Sample	15.02	70.84	3.91
Indian Sample	4.32	11.70	
Index Offenses			
U.S. Sample	.90	5.90	NS
Indian Sample	1.21	4.52	
Minor Offenses			
U.S. Sample	4.54	21.39	3.70
Indian Sample	1.48	3.76	
Substance Abuse			
U.S. Sample	4.82	7.33	15.12
Indian Sample	.39	1.96	

NOTE: NS = Not Significant, all others significant < .01.

Table 6.2
Pearson Correlations between Theory and Offense Scales for United States
1978 and Indian 1990 Respondents

Theory Scale	Gdl	Offense Scale Index	Mdl	Sab
Strain				
Family Strain				
U.S.	.11	.09*	NS	.16
India	.24	.22	.21	NS
School Strain				
U.S.	NS	NS	NS	.15
India	.21	.20	.17	.17
Control				
Invfamily				
U.S.	−.18	NS	−.16	−.27
India	NS	NS	NS	NS
Invschool				
U.S.	−.17	−.10	−.12	−.19
India	−.14	−.12	−.15	−.10
Nrmfamily				
U.S.	−.17	−.11	−.13	−.25
India	−.15	−.13	−.16	−.12
Nrmschool				
U.S.	−.19	−.15	−.12	−.24
India	−.23	−.16	−.26	−.22
Soc. Learning				
Peerinv				
U.S.	.15	NS	.09*	.18
India	.34	.31	.34	.25
Exdp				
U.S.	.27	.19	.23	.49
India	.30	.32	.28	.20
Idpindx				
U.S.	.35	.20	.26	.49
India	.32	.33	.29	.10
Att.Deviance				
U.S.	−.24	−.12	−.21	−.45
India	−.31	−.23	−.30	−.17

NOTE: Number of cases for U.S. sample = 701, for Indian sample = 428 except
for Idpindx = 159 due to missing cases. NS = not significant, all others
significant <.01.

CORRELATION ANALYSIS

To assess the cross-national relationship between the various theoretical
dimensions explored and forms of delinquent behavior, the various explanatory
dimensions were first individually correlated with each of the offense scales.
The results of this procedure are presented in Table 6.2.

The coefficients presented in Table 6.2 indicate that many of the scales used to measure dimensions derived from strain, control, and learning theories are significantly correlated with almost all of the offense scales for both Indian and American respondents. As far as the individual causal dimensions are concerned, family strain is consistently associated with offense behavior for both samples. School strain appears important for Indians but not Americans. In short, the two dimensions relating to "strain" investigated here appear to have some, but not pronounced, association with delinquency, and these appear to vary somewhat cross-nationally. Indeed, whereas disjunction between school aspirations and expectations appears to be substantially correlated with all forms of delinquency for Indian respondents, except for school strain this form of strain is virtually unrelated to the delinquency of the American sample. In part, this could reflect the differences in the impact "doing well" at school could have for Indian compared to American youths. Indeed, in India anything other than outstanding school performance virtually insures that one will be closed out of higher occupations in the future, which does not appear to be the case in the United States.

Dimensions relating to social control produced significant correlations for almost all offense types for both samples also, with some noteworthy exceptions. Interestingly, while family normlessness is substantially correlated with most offense scales for Indians, family involvement is not significantly related to any offense activity. In part, this probably reflects cultural variations in how respondents interpreted questions assessing this dimension. Asking Indians, for example, to respond to the question "How many hours after school did you spend with family?" surely elicits truthful answers. However, the phrase "spend time with" could have a different meaning for Indians compared to Americans, since in Indian society "spending time" with anyone other than "family" members is rare outside the school or work context. More likely, the measure is probably not sensitive enough to distinguish among youths varying in terms of offense behaviors and this aspect of social control in Indian society (see Winfree et al., 1989).

Practically every study directed to testing learning theory by assessing the association between involvement with delinquent peers and self-reported delinquent behavior supports the theory (Agnew, 1991; Manard & Elliott, 1994; Matsueda, 1988; Winfree et al., 1994). The present study is no exception. Among both Americans and Indians, substantial correlations are found between the various measures of learning theory and all offense scales (except between attitudes toward deviance and substance abuse among Indians and peer involvement and index offenses among Americans). As such, it is clear that in India, as in the United States, youths heavily involved with peers engaged in delinquent forms of behavior are likely also to be so engaged. And those whose peers are relatively uninvolved also seem to refrain from such conduct.

Of the theory-based scales tested here, the ones that seem to have the most pronounced association with most forms of delinquency among both Americans and Indians are family strain, involvement in school, school and family normlessness, and all measures relating to learning theory. In short, this analysis indicates that aspects of major causal theories developed in western societies seem to be related to all forms of delinquency among youths in the highly divergent socio-cultural environments of India and the United States. As such, these findings strongly suggest that the etiology of both Indian and American delinquent behavior might be explained by similar, if not identical, causal dimensions.

Yet, individual theory/offense-scale analysis is more suggestive than conclusive of the kinds of causal dimensions that may be related to specific types of offense behaviors among respondents in various societies. Integrating these dimensions in a more comprehensive theoretical formula may help show their combined causal impact as well as unravel whatever interrelationships may exist among them.

THE INTEGRATED THEORY MODEL

Studies testing a variety of integrated theoretical models employing variables derived from the theoretical dimensions investigated here demonstrate that these notions in combination can better predict delinquency than any one can alone (Krohn et al., 1984; Marcos et al., 1986; Massey & Krohn, 1986). More importantly, such a model may reveal the undoubtedly complex causal sequence and interrelations of the forces or facilitating conditions that are responsible for variations in delinquent behavior among young people generally.

Of the various models developed in this regard, one of the most tested and successful in explaining a wide range of delinquency and "deviant" conduct among juveniles was that developed by Elliott et al. (1985) using data obtained from the NYS (see also Elliott et al., 1989). This model was chosen for our inquiry largely because it offers a way to assess the universality of major theoretical concepts in explaining delinquent behavior while, at the same time, providing an opportunity to test the prospect of developing a causal model that may apply to diverse societies.

Thus, our concern here is not so much to account for large portions of the variance in delinquency among Indian youths as it is to assess the extent to which models based on existing etiological theories oriented to the crime/delinquent behavior of western youths can be employed in explaining the delinquency of youths in such culturally and economically different societies as India. To the extent that the model (or, as here, a modified version of it) can account for similar proportions of the variance in the dependent variables and do so in similar ways (i.e., various dimensions being related to the dependent variables in like manner), it suggests that the dimensions tapped are part of a universal (or general) explanation of delinquency. As such, we could argue that delinquent behavior arises from similar causal (or facilitating) forces regardless of the culture or social system in which it is found. Such a finding would be a major advance in the development of an explanation of delinquency that is truly universal in its applicability and explanatory power.

The complete integrated model developed by Elliott et al. (1985) employed four causal paths combining various elements of strain, control, and learning theories. Integrating these ideas into a causal argument, Elliott and his colleagues argue that while bonding to delinquent peers is the proximate cause of delinquency and drug use, this relationship is specified by levels of bonding to conventional persons, norms, and institutions. Thus, weak conventional bonds, plus strong bonds to delinquent peers, act as additional reinforcements for delinquency and drug use behavior. And both forms of bonding (conventional versus delinquent) can independently be affected by levels of home or school strain. In this regard, the theoretical argument specified in the model suggests that strain serves to reduce one's conventional bonds and heighten one's bonds to delinquent peers while independently having some possible direct impact on delinquent activity also. In turn, weak conventional bonds not only heighten one's likely involvement in delinquent activity but also would lead to increased bonding with delinquent peers, and this bonding to delinquent peers would directly increase one's likely involvement in various forms of misconduct.

Whether this model constitutes a valid specification of the causal sequence leading to delinquency has been a matter of dispute (Gibbons, 1994:183–188; Hirschi, 1987; Manard & Elliott, 1994; Shoemaker, 1990: 303–315). But that is not a central issue here. However, other causal models have suggested similar ideas, and the model certainly seems to be a plausible (if possibly overly simplified) causal ordering of the major theoretical arguments available in criminology.

Of particular importance to the present inquiry is the fact that this model incorporates these major theoretical ideas in a logical temporal ordering. By doing so it provides an opportunity to directly test the relative and combined ability of dimensions pertaining to strain, bonding, and learning theories to explain the etiology of delinquent behavior in two highly divergent social/cultural localities.

To that end, given both our purpose and the limitations of our data, a reduced model was tested on both the Indian and American self-report samples in order to assess (1) the overall explanatory ability of the model for delinquency or delinquency of various forms and (2) the extent to which its component dimensions are associated with one another in similar or dissimilar ways across the two countries. Thus, while the model may have equal explanatory power cross-culturally in the sense that similar amounts of variance are explained in the dependent variables for each, the relationship among the various components within the model could, logically, differ from society to society. This would indicate that the interrelationship (or causal effects) of the various underlying forces represented in the model are not universal insofar as they operate differently in different social/cultural environments. Thus, for example, strain may (or may not) have the same impact on conventional bonding in various societies, even though strain may (or may not) independently affect one's involvement in delinquent behavior. Similarly, the presumed association between conventional and delinquent bonding may be quite diverse, even if the combination of these forces may have a similar cumulative effect on delinquent conduct. In this respect, the components of the individual theories may indeed help explain the etiology of delinquency everywhere. However, how these components affect one another or the behavior of individuals could vary. Conversely, of course, the various elements of the model could operate in near-identical fashion in different societies but, nevertheless, have greater or lesser ability to explain delinquency in one society compared to another. In short, given the lack of cross-cultural comparative research, we have no reason to assume that any etiological theory or combination of theories presently available in criminology will work, or work in the same way, in different social, cultural, or economic systems.

Given this possibility, multiple regression and path analyses applied to the integrated theory model allow us to test the extent to which a logical combination of causal theory arguments can explain delinquency etiology in both the United States and India. Moreover, examination of path coefficients helps us to determine how (or in what ways) the elements employed in the model interact to, directly or indirectly, affect involvement in delinquent activity.

Path coefficients and standard errors were estimated for both samples using the full path model individually for the general delinquency, index offenses, minor offenses, and substance abuse scales. If the contribution of particular paths to the model's explained variance was insignificant for either or both samples, they were dropped from the model. The path coefficients for each sample were then recalculated for the reduced model. The final path models used for the various offense scales and samples are depicted in Figure 6.1.

Figure 6.1

Path Models for Offense Scales, Indian 1990 and United States 1978 Respondents

INDIA

General Delinquency

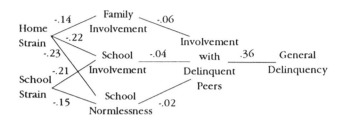

Index Offenses

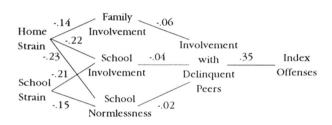

Minor Delinquency

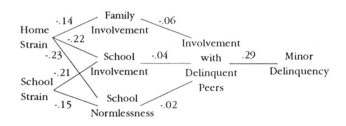

Substance Abuse

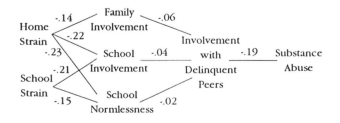

U.S.

General Delinquency

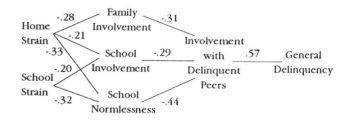

Index Offenses

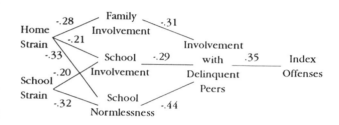

Minor Delinquency

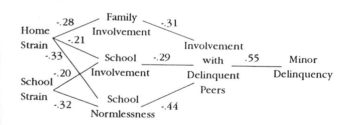

Substance Abuse

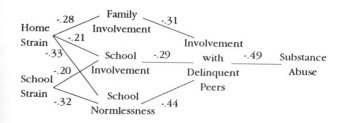

As indicated by the path models, the relationships among the theoretical variables for both American and Indian respondents are clearly those specified by Elliott et al. in their integrated theory model. For both groups of respondents, increases in strain at home led to decreases in family and school involvement and to increases in school normlessness. Similarly, increases in school strain led to decreased school involvement and increased school normlessness. Decreases in conventional bonding also led to increases in delinquent-peer involvement, and this, in turn, is directly related to increased levels of delinquency for all measures.

It should be noted, however, that the size of the coefficients between theoretical dimensions is by no means uniform across the two samples. The strength of the association between home and school strain and the various measures of social control is fairly consistent for both Indians and Americans. However, the associations are weaker between home and school strain and family involvement and school normlessness for the Indian compared to the American sample, but these differences are not substantial. However, considerable differences exist in the magnitude of the associations between control dimensions and respondents' involvement with delinquent peers. Indeed, the coefficients for these paths are four to ten times larger for American respondents compared to Indians. Quite clearly, as a theory that explains the delinquency of youths in diverse societies, something seems to be missing from existing ideas of social control. Arguably, the effect of strong social controls to reduce or inhibit delinquency, insofar as those controls may affect one's association with delinquent or nondelinquent peers, is not universally the same. Before this idea can be fully pursued in cross-national research, it is clear that considerable work needs to be done to specify how such controls could impact on the behavior of young people differently in different socio-cultural settings (see Agnew, 1985; Matsueda & Heimer, 1987; Lyerly & Skipper, 1981; Sheu, 1988).

On the other hand, the relative impact of involvement with delinquent peers on delinquency or delinquency of various forms is remarkably consistent across the two samples. For Indians, the strength of the associations is usually smaller than for Americans. But, even then, strong to moderate positive coefficients are found in all models. That is, even if the effect of social controls may not be consistently related to one's relative involvement with delinquent peers across the two samples or various offense types, the effect of that involvement on delinquent behavior is clear.

In short, although the strength of the path coefficients (among the variables retained in the model) varies cross-culturally and (to a lesser extent) by offense type, the hypothesized associations among these dimensions are similar for both Indian and American youths. The model, very simply, seems to offer an explanatory formula that may very well be useful for understanding delinquency etiology in very diverse societies.

The explained variance figures presented in Table 6.3 also suggest that the model may similarly explain both overall delinquency as well as delinquency of various forms among both American and Indian youths. Similar proportions of explained variance were found for the general delinquency scale. However, the R^2's for index offenses among Indians are about double those for Americans. Conversely, the model explains about three times the variance in substance-abuse behavior among Americans compared to Indians. And among Americans a somewhat larger proportion of the variance in minor delinquency is accounted for by the model.

Table 6.3
Multiple Regression Analysis of Predictor Variables on Offense Scales for United States 1978 and Indian 1990 Respondents

| Offense Scale | Sample | | | |
| | U.S. | | India | |
	R^2	F	R^2	F
General Delinquency	.26	24.39	.22	7.10
Index Offenses	.09	6.64	.18	5.55
Minor Offenses	.24	22.37	.18	5.50
Substance Abuse	.26	40.64	.08	4.65

NOTE: Probability of F for all offense scales = <.01.

Whether or not these differences reflect real sociocultural differences in the genesis of some types of delinquency among various societies remains a matter for future research. It is conceivable that, while the dimensions in the model similarly explain delinquent conduct everywhere, specific types of offense behavior are more or less sensitive to social controls, peer influences, and the like in different cultures. Findings from research in western countries imply this possibility (Agnew, 1991; Jackson et al., 1986). Cross-national research may be useful in more clearly specifying how different kinds of delinquent behavior are differently influenced by dimensions such as those included in the model.

It might be noted that while the R^2 values found in this analysis are lower than those found by Elliott et al. (1985), all are statistically significant and well within the range found by other researchers using similar causal models (Conger, 1976; Hackler, 1970; Marcos et al., 1986; Massey & Krohn, 1986; Rankin, 1977; Reid, 1989; Thornberry et al., 1994). Moreover, Elliott et al.'s (1985) longitudinal study allowed the use of prior delinquency as an endogenous variable and employed a more elaborate model. Adding these other variables to the present model could have resulted in increased R^2 values also. Nevertheless, of considerably greater importance than the actual amount of explained variance is our finding that the expected causal relationships among the model's dimensions (i.e., *increases in strain* ———> *weak conventional bonds* ———> *increased delinquent bonding* ———> *delinquent behavior*) occur for both Indian and American samples. And the causal ordering and effect of these variables seem to be similar for both groups. In part, where differences exist in either the overall variance explained or the relative strength of particular path coefficients, these differences are partly a statistical artifact of the comparative involvement of youths in the two countries in one or the other form of misconduct or differences in the strength of the association between one or another causal dimension and delinquent behavior. However, such differences undoubtedly also capture culturally-related differences in the relative effects strain, conventional bonding, or delinquent-peer bonding have on the delinquent behavior of youths in various countries. Some forms of delinquency undoubtedly are affected more by strain or by the constraining forces of conventional social bonds. Others are probably more open to the delinquency promoting impact of associating with peers similarly engaged in such conduct. Thus, as these variables vary in one way or another from group to group (e.g., "hanging out" with a group of drug-using friends compared to associating with peers engaged in diverse forms of illegality), the ability of a causal model to similarly account for different types of delinquent behavior among youths from quite different sociocultural settings will also vary. Until we have more refined ways to measure things like delinquent-peer association and the nature of conventional bonds, explaining differences in the ability of some model to similarly explain delinquency among various groups of youths will remain problematic.

Generally, however, the present analysis strongly suggests that research using more refined measures of theoretical dimensions and offense behaviors as well as employing wider and more representative samples of juveniles would likely produce very similar results in quite divergent societies. At minimum, we have good grounds to argue that contemporary theories of delinquency, particularly when integrated in a broader theoretical formula, do seem to have cross-national explanatory relevance. This is especially implied by the elaboration discussed below testing the combined effects of conventional/delinquent bonding on various delinquent forms of behavior.

CONVENTIONAL / DELINQUENT BONDING

The path models analyzed above show that the only variable with any significant direct effect on delinquency is bonding to delinquent peers (differential association). However, according to Elliott et al. (1985)

involvement with delinquent peers, as well as involvement in delinquency itself, is conditioned by one's bonding to conventional groups, norms, and institutions. In effect one's bonding to delinquent peers and/or the delinquency-inducing effect such bonding may have are mediated by one's bonding to conventional others. To examine the extent and nature of this presumed conditional relationship among both Indian and American respondents a procedure employed by Elliott et al. (1985:120–121) was applied to both samples.

Table 6.4
Means and Standard Deviations of the Conventional Bonding Measures for the Two Clusters, United States 1978 and Indian 1990 Respondents

Cluster and Sample	Measure	Scales			
		Invfam	Nrmfam	Invscl	Nrmscl
U.S.					
Cluster 1	Mean	8.43	13.91	4.65	17.32
Low Bonds	Sd	3.17	2.30	2.65	2.35
N = 345					
Cluster 2	Mean	11.74	16.67	8.96	20.39
High Bonds	Sd	2.62	2.10	2.40	2.52
N = 356					
Total	Mean	10.11	15.31	6.84	18.88
Sample	Sd	3.34	2.59	3.40	2.88
N = 701					
India					
Cluster 1	Mean	6.61	11.51	6.45	15.80
Low Bonds	Sd	3.74	2.92	3.83	4.00
N = 159					
Cluster 2	Mean	10.55	14.33	11.18	19.28
High Bonds	Sd	3.83	2.96	3.37	3.09
N = 269					
Total	Mean	9.09	12.75	9.43	16.57
Sample	Sd	3.93	3.53	3.63	4.58
N = 428					

Specifically, each of the samples was first divided into two groups, (1) those with strong conventional bonds and (2) those with weak conventional bonds. Since the conventional bonding dimension is composed of several variables, this was accomplished by using cluster analysis in order to locate respondents with different patterns of bonding to conventional groups. The four conventional bonding scales (family involvement, family normlessness, school involvement, and school normlessness) were entered into the equation. The cluster algorithm terminated on a two-cluster pattern for both samples of respondents. Table 6.4 presents values for the two clusters on each scale by sample. Cluster means below the sample means on the family and school involvement scales represent low involvement in conventional activities. Above-average means are equal to higher involvement. Conversely, a lower-than-average score on the two normlessness scales indicates high normlessness on each scale, whereas an above-average score equals low normlessness.

Respondents in both samples were also grouped in terms of high or low levels of involvement with delinquent peers. The median value of the Involvement with Delinquent Peers Index (IDPINDX) was used as a cutting point to divide the samples into two groups on this dimension, i.e., (1) those with high and (2) those with low bonding to delinquent peers. A cross-tabulation of the two groups with high/low conventional bonds and the two groups with high/low delinquent-peer bonds produced four groups as depicted in Table 6.5 below.

Table 6.5
Conventional and Delinquent-Peer Bond Combinations to Form Comparison Groups

| | Measure | |
| | Conventional | Delinquent |
Group	Bonds	Bonds
One	High	Low
Two	High	High
Three	Low	Low
Four	Low	High

To the extent that conventional bonding reduces delinquency and delinquent-peer bonding promotes it, we would expect the highest levels of delinquency to occur for Group Four respondents and the lowest for Group One respondents. Groups Two and Three should have intermediate levels of delinquency. It is by no means clear which of these latter two variable combinations would have the greatest delinquency promoting effect. However, given the fact that most studies investigating the relative explanatory power of bond versus learning theory, it is likely that Group Two respondents (high delinquent-peer bonding) would be somewhat more delinquent than Group Three respondents (low delinquent-peer bonding) regardless of level of conventional bonding. And this effect should hold regardless of form of delinquency and sample group. If so, it would support the generally accepted conclusion that the most immediate "cause" of delinquency is association with delinquent peers, not one's conventional social bonds (Dull, 1983; Gingsberg & Greenley, 1978; Kandel, 1973; Matsueda, 1988; Marcos et al., 1986; Warr & Stafford, 1991). However, to the extent that levels of conventional bonding increase or decrease one's level of delinquent behavior in association with delinquent-peer bonding, an important specification of the connection between delinquent-peer involvement and delinquent behavior suggested by learning theory is revealed by this procedure and its possible generalizability to delinquent promoting/reducing contingencies worldwide.

To test these hypotheses, the differences in delinquency scores between combinations of bonding groups were examined using unequal variance t-tests for both the American and Indian samples separately. The results of this analysis (along with the mean delinquency scores exhibited by the four groups for both samples) are presented in Tables 6.6 and 6.7.

As expected, the highest levels of delinquency for both American and Indian respondents on all offense scales occurs for Group Four respondents. Clearly, low conventional bonds coupled with high bonding to delinquent peers, in no matter what society a juvenile is found, result in comparatively high levels of delinquency. Conversely, Group One respondents tend to have the lowest delinquency rates. Regardless of sample and type of offense behavior, the differences between Group One and Group Four respondents are statistically significant for all offense scales. On the other hand, differences between Group One and Group Three respondents are not statistically significant (except for substance abuse among Americans). That is, youths categorizable as low in terms of delinquent-peer bonding are no different in average levels of delinquency regardless of their level of conventional bonding, although those with low conventional bonds do produce higher offense means, if not statistically significant compared to Group One respondents. Similarly, Group Three compared to Group Four respondents registered significant differences on all scales (except among Indian respondents for index offenses). However, that conventional bonding could operate to inhibit delinquency even when youths are highly involved with delinquent peers is implied by the fact that significant differences are frequently found between the delinquency of Group Two and Group Four respondents, both of which groups are high in delinquent-peer bonds but vary in terms of level of conventional bonding.

Yet the apparent overriding effect of delinquent-peer bonding on delinquency is implied by the finding that, regardless of level of conventional bonding, respondents in both countries with high levels of delinquency-peer bonding tend to have higher delinquency levels as well. But the extent of this difference could vary cross-culturally. Indeed, as we saw in the path models, social control measures did not have a very powerful effect on involvement with delinquent peers for the Indian sample, while the coefficients were fairly substantial for the American respondents. For example, among the Indian sample the differences between delinquency scores for Group Two respondents

Table 6.6
Means of Offense Category Scale Scores for Groups Defined by Levels of Conventional Bonding and Involvement with Delinquent Peers, United States 1978 Respondents

Offense Scale			Groups		Significance of Group Differences Group	Sig.
			Del. Peer Involve.		1/2	NS
			Low	High	1/3	NS
					1/4	.00
General	Conv.	High	2.80	6.52	2/3	NS
Delinq.	Bonding	Low	6.63	35.74	2/4	.00
					3/4	.00
			Del. Peer Involve.		1/2	NS
			Low	High	1/3	NS
					1/4	.00
Index	Conv.	High	.05	.42	2/3	NS
Offenses	Bonding	Low	.22	2.32	2/4	.00
					3/4	
			Del. Peer Involve.		1/2	.02
			Low	High	1/3	NS
					1/4	.00
Minor	Conv.	High	.79	4.11	2/3	NS
Offenses	Bonding	Low	3.76	19.31	2/4	.03
					3/4	.01
			Del. Peer Involve.		1/2	.00
			Low	High	1/3	.03
					1/4	.00
Substance	Conv.	High	1.35	5.94	2/3	.00
Abuse	Bonding	Low	8.43	8.96	2/4	.00
					3/4	.00

NOTE: Significance determined by unequal variance t-tests.

Table 6.7
Means of Offense Category Scale Scores for Groups Defined by Levels of
Conventional Bonding and Involvement with Delinquent Peers, Indian 1990
Respondents

Offense Scale			Groups		Significance of Group Differences	
					Group	Sig.
			Del. Peer Involve.		1/2	NS
			Low	High	1/3	.03
					1/4	.00
General	Conv.	High	2.73	4.02	2/3	NS
Delinq.	Bonding	Low	5 07	12.41	2/4	.03
					3/4	.01
			Del. Peer Involve.		1/2	NS
			Low	High	1/3	NS
					1/4	.00
Index	Conv.	High	.71	1.14	2/3	NS
Offenses	Bonding	Low	1.32	4.48	2/4	.24
					3/4	NS
			Del. Peer Involve.		1/2	NS
			Low	High	1/3	.03
					1/4	.00
Minor	Conv.	High	1.15	1.28	2/3	NS
Offenses	Bonding	Low	2.16	4.38	2/4	.02
					3/4	.05
			Del. Peer Involve.		1/2	.03
			Low	High	1/3	.04
					1/4	.03
Substance	Conv.	High	.17	.76	2/3	NS
Abuse	Bonding	Low	.54	.77	2/4	NS
					3/4	NS

NOTE: Significance determined by unequal variance t-tests.

are not statistically different from those of either Groups One or Three. For Americans, however, the effect of delinquent-peer bonding appears to be more consistent. Thus, while it is clear that high delinquent-peer and low conventional bonding produce high levels of delinquency and low delinquent-peer and high conventional bonding seem to inhibit this activity, the interrelationships of these dimensions with delinquent behavior are quite complex and undoubtedly culturally variable (Matsueda & Heimer, 1987).

It is beyond our ability in this study to specify the culturally-related complexity of the interrelated effects of conventional versus delinquency bonding on delinquent activity. Our findings, however, imply that future research may more clearly demonstrate how these two important causal dimensions combine to influence the delinquency involvement of any country's youth.

CONCLUSION

A number of inquiries have been conducted in India to test aspects of various delinquency theories (mostly psychological) developed in western countries (see Chapter One). These studies have invariably produced results similar to inquiries investigating the same dimensions in western societies. Also, the results of a handful of investigations from countries around the world have been published exploring the explanatory relevance of notions like social control and/or differential association (e.g., Cheung & Ng, 1988; Sheu, 1988; Shukla, 1979). Invariably these studies have also found results reminiscent of those produced from inquiries of American and western European youths. Findings from these studies imply that there may indeed be a universal explanation for the etiology of delinquent behavior.

But, while promising, these studies have either been too limited in scope and/or suffer from various methodological problems to base any conclusions about the cross-national etiology of delinquent behavior on them. Although cross-national etiological research is beginning to accumulate, to date no explicitly designed and executed cross-national test of general etiological theory has been completed in criminology so that any conclusions about the universality (or cross-cultural applicability) of any theory of crime/delinquent behavior is at best speculative. The present analysis, while far from a methodologically ideal inquiry of this kind, is the only systematic attempt to test causal theories on two reasonably comparable samples drawn from two highly divergent socioeconomic settings, using similar measures to assess the same behaviors and the same explanatory dimensions. The findings reported here, at very minimum, strongly suggest that major contemporary etiological theory in criminology can indeed be employed to explain delinquency in different societies and may be able to do so with about the same explanatory ability.

For some criminologists the observation that a causal model based on major theories developed to explain the crime/delinquency behavior of individuals in American society can serve to similarly explain the behavior of individuals in a country such as India is of no particular interest. We find such a pedestrian view to be somewhat amazing. Not only does this and other cross-national research allow us to test the extent to which causal theory might be used to generalize beyond the socio-cultural audience to which it was addressed, such inquiry also allows us to more reasonably assess the explanatory merits of these ideas. Equally important, cross-national etiological research holds promise of providing a broader foundation upon which explanatory theory might be developed in the future. Thus, the findings of our inquiry, in this regard, are highly intriguing.

Our data suggest a number of things possibly relevant to future formulations of strain, control, or learning theories of delinquency. Strain theory has generally been found to have relatively little direct explanatory value in most etiological research. However, as this inquiry suggests, at least as an indirect promoter of delinquency, the idea of "strain" cannot yet be discounted in causal analysis (Allan & Steffensmeier, 1989; Bernard, 1984; Bursik, 1988; Reinarman & Fagan, 1988; Warner & Pierce, 1993). Perhaps the recent reformulations of this concept produced by Robert Agnew (Agnew, 1990; Agnew & White, 1992) might better apply as explanatory dimensions and/or as more relevant to our understanding of delinquent behavior cross-nationally. Further cross-national research incorporating measures of these new concepts should be revealing.

Although control theory has found moderate support in most studies carried out in the United States, the cross-national effects of control appear to be quite variable. While measures relating to school control (as well as strain) seem to have some association with delinquency (although somewhat differently) among both American and Indian respondents, family control measures seem to be less important and consistent as explanatory variables (see Patterson & Dishion, 1985; Poole & Regoli, 1979; Singh & Agrawal, 1986; Wells & Rankin, 1988). Surprisingly, none of the scales measuring this dimension either discriminate among the delinquency of Indian youths or are strongly correlated with offense activity. Given the extremely close bonds to family exhibited by Indians (and about which a mountain of research has been published), we would have expected this to be a major variable as far as Indian delinquency is concerned. A number of possible explanations may account for our findings relating to measurement techniques and the like. However, even then, the effect of family social control on delinquency is undoubtedly culturally variable also. That is, in a country such as the United States, strong family social control may be needed to offset the numerous delinquency promoting forces in an affluent, individualistic society. Those youths subjected to such control may, as a consequence, be either less exposed to or affected by conditions that stimulate involvement in delinquent behavior. Such effects are likely to be readily apparent in etiological research on American subjects using existing measures of control. However, where strong family bonds (controls ?) are pervasive throughout the society, their effect (or lack thereof) as inhibitors of delinquency is less readily detectable. Thus, if family involvement, for example, has only a negligible negative impact on involvement with delinquent peers, it is not necessarily the case that such involvement does not impede delinquency but rather that the delinquent peers with whom Indian youths associate are likely to be one's own siblings or kin. In this regard, future versions of social control theory (e.g., Hirschi's bond formulation) must be more sensitive to the cultural variability in the nature and effects of family relationships and controls.

Finally, what is clear from this data is that involvement with peers who are, or are not, engaged in delinquent activity is closely associated with an individual's similar involvement/non-involvement, regardless of cultural setting. Assuming that the influence of delinquent/non-delinquent peers is indeed the primary, direct cause of an individual's similar behavior, a universal theory of delinquency would be one that accounts for the kinds of conditions wherein juveniles do, or do not, become involved with, and consequently influenced by, delinquent peers. Undoubtedly factors relating to strain (as possible motivating sources) and social controls (as possible inhibiting sources) are important in this regard. To that end, theories and theory models developed to explain "western" delinquency may be translatable into truly universal explanations of the etiology of delinquent behavior. As such, explaining the variations in the relative frequency, types, and distributions of delinquency (as opposed to its etiology) found both within and across different societies requires us to account for the differential operation or existence of those conditions across societies.

CHAPTER SEVEN

Explaining Delinquency Rates: A Cross-National Analysis

In this chapter we seek to draw some conclusions and make several generalizations about the epidemiological dimensions of youthful misconduct in general and in India specifically. Clearly, the limited data on which this discussion is based require that any observations be viewed as tentative. The commentary in this chapter should be taken as a set of working hypotheses for continued cross-national inquiry.

SUMMARY OF FINDINGS

The primary empirical analysis of this book has focused on India and how young people in that country compare to youths in other societies, primarily in the United States. Before attempting to explain cross-national variations and similarities in delinquency rates, a brief recap of our main findings would be in order.

Overall Rates

Juvenile court, corrections, and especially arrest statistics dealing with juvenile offenders in India suggest that the occurrence of delinquent and criminal forms of conduct on the part of Indian youths is extremely infrequent. Given both the size of the Indian population and the proportion of juveniles in it, the exceedingly small numbers recorded by the agencies of criminal justice in India could lead one to conclude that juvenile delinquency is (1) either practically nonexistent in India or (2) the figures somehow dramatically under count the true volume of offense behavior. Undoubtedly the reality of delinquency in India falls somewhere between the two. Without alternative ways of assessing it, we would have little by which to determine just where this "in between" might be located. Our best judgment is that the actual frequency of serious (or, repetitive) criminal activity on the part of Indian juveniles is in fact extremely low—both absolutely and relatively. Nothing we encounter in the form of hard data, observations, interviews, and the like encourages us to think otherwise. Conversely, a host of indicators all sustain this conclusion.

Yet the self-report data clearly suggest that young people in India are by no means immune to delinquency. While generally lower overall, rates of misconduct (both prevalence and incidence) on the part of our respondents are substantial and in many ways comparable to those of American youths and offense rates reported for juveniles in other countries.

The extreme disparity between official rates and the findings of our self-report surveys presents a paradox. Differences in official and self-reported delinquency are by no means unique to India. Rather, it is the apparent extreme difference (practically none to just about everyone) that would strike anyone trying to grasp the reality of delinquency in India as strange. Therefore, before proceeding with our summary, it is necessary to address this paradox.

A large number of factors (still to be explored) could account for the disparity in official and self-report findings and the extent to which this disparity may depart from that in other societies. Four possibilities appear to be most relevant. Either (1) our self-report data overestimate the actual involvement of Indian youths in delinquent forms of behavior; (2) law enforcement agencies are exceptionally ineffectual or reluctant to treat juvenile misconduct in an official way; and/or (3) the kinds of misconduct Indian juveniles most frequently commit are unlikely to be brought to the attention of authorities by victims or witnesses; or (4) if brought, are considered unworthy of official action. Given that nothing substantiates an "overestimate" conclusion, either or all three of the alternatives are plausible. The following elaborates these possibilities.

On the one hand, official rates reflect the practices of formal agencies of control as well as the relative reliance of societal members on formal, as opposed to informal, agencies of control. The kind of aggressive patrol and peace-keeping activities common among American police are not found in India (Bayley, 1969; Black & Reiss, 1970; Shane, 1980). Thus, a goodly amount of the rather petty (if still illegal) misconduct Indian youths report in self-report surveys is simply not brought to the attention of authorities and, therefore, is unlikely to be handled in an official manner. In short, not only do official and self-report data sources tap different orders of behavior in India, as elsewhere, in India even relatively serious offense behavior has a comparatively small chance of being detected by or reacted to by authorities.

On the other hand, official (as well as self-report) data reflect (1) actual differences in the prevalence and incidence of offense behavior between Indian youths and those of other countries and (2) differences in the kinds of offense behaviors Indian youths commit compared to those by juveniles in other societies. Thus, while self-report findings indicate that Indian and American youths (for example) are involved in "delinquent" behaviors in about equal proportions, their relative involvement in various forms of such conduct is not identical. Much of the behavior revealed by self-report surveys is unlikely to be a matter for formal social control in either country. However, if a sizable proportion of the juvenile population engages in acts of interest to and/or likely to be noticed by legal authorities, official rates could be greatly inflated. Thus, self-reported behavior among American youths reveals a substantial amount of "public" delinquency and activities best classed as "rowdy." These are precisely the kinds of things the public is likely to get upset about (although, of course, not necessarily fear the most) and the police to take notice of (Bordua, 1967; Reiss, 1971; Smith, 1986). On the other hand, Indian youths may skip school, cheat on tests, or engage in petty theft at frequencies equal to or greater than their American counterparts. But that behavior is unlikely to be recorded in official rates in either society. Thus, rather than indicating an extreme data-source disparity in the measurement of delinquent behavior in India, the self-report and official statistics discussed in this volume complement one another. In that regard, all available data suggest that Indian youths are indeed less delinquent, and less serious delinquents, than their age-category counterparts in the United States and, apparently, other western countries as well.

Distribution Patterns: Self-Reported and Official Rates
While overall exhibiting the lower rates of serious offense behavior seemingly characteristic of people in economically developing societies (Shelley, 1981), with a few exceptions, the distribution patterns of delinquent behavior on the part of Indian youths closely resemble those found almost everywhere. Specifically, self-report data show that the bulk of their delinquency consists of status-like misconduct and relatively petty forms of criminality. But as self-report surveys have found everywhere, serious crimes are by no means absent from the offenses reported by Indian youths. Official statistics record different kinds of offense behavior. But these rates also show that property crimes and various miscellaneous (probably relatively mild offenses) dominate the list. Major crimes and serious personal assaults are comparatively rare. This again is common to official statistics universally.

In India, as in other countries, arrest rates seem to vary by urban/rural locality (but see Verma, 1993). Yet, as elsewhere, self-report behavior does not show such a pattern. In this regard, the likelihood of being officially recognized as delinquent (as opposed to engaging in delinquency) is not equally distributed among the juvenile population in India as is probably true in countries throughout the world. Given that about 80 percent of India's youth reside in villages or rural areas, this may be one reason why official rates are so low.

Demographically, Indian youth exhibit offense rate patterns more or less reminiscent of those of youths everywhere. Boys, for instance, are much more subject to arrest in India than girls. This gender gap in delinquency is apparently universal. But, as with other Third World countries, the size of the gap in India is considerably larger than in western countries. Youths arrested and incarcerated in India are predominantly poor and (based on self-reports) more seriously delinquent than non-official delinquents. Yet as self-report studies in the United States and elsewhere have also found, no strong relationship between socioeconomic status and delinquent behavior was found in our data. Finally, a small, but not particularly meaningful, positive association between age and delinquency existed for self-reported delinquency. Also, for the age range studied (thirteen through seventeen), official statistics in India indicate increased involvement with age. But this is not a strong relationship. Thus, the age-delinquency curve commonly reported in American texts on delinquency showing a rather substantial increase in arrests from early to late teens with a steady decline beginning around age nineteen does not appear in India. Instead, in India comparatively high arrest rates are found for persons in early to mid-twenties. In that regard, it appears that a ten-year delay in official reaction to misconduct takes place in India compared to the United States. American (perhaps western) youths begin their misconduct earlier (or at least come to official attention earlier) than do young people in economically developing societies such as India. Why this might be the case is part of the issue we seek to address below.

THE EXPLANATORY PROBLEM

Criminological theory has traditionally been directed to either explaining "Why they do it?" (the etiology question) or variations in rates of crime (the epidemiology question). Often, however, the explanatory focus of particular theories has not been clear or the explanatory question has been confused (see Gibbons, 1994). Even though these are indeed different problems, the behaviors to which the speculations are directed are by no means unrelated. Assuming that rates are measures of frequencies of behavior (but see Hartjen, 1978), differences in these frequencies ultimately reflect differences in the relative existence, strength, etc., of the precipitating conditions (etiology) that produce the behavior reflected in them. On the one hand, we seek to explain the "behavior," on the other, we seek to explain variations in the "conditions" that produce the behavior. This distinction has not always been made clear in criminological inquiry.

When addressing the question of etiology, what we seek to explain is the relative probability that individuals will be involved in delinquent behavior at all, or delinquency of some specific kind. Any theory of etiology seeking to address either or both of these questions would ultimately have to argue that individuals who comply with the explanatory conditions of the theory (e.g., are exposed to "conditions" X, Y, Z or have "characteristics" X, Y, Z) will likely engage in any delinquent act (or do so with greater or lesser frequency) than they would if they did not so comply. In this regard, measured at the individual level, we should find a positive relationship between the putative causal condition and relative probabilities of delinquent behavior. Conversely, according to control theories (such as "social bond" or "reintegrative shaming" theory) a negative relationship between the control dimension and probabilities of delinquency would be found. The discussion in Chapter Six indicates that in terms of these ideas, the delinquent behavior of youths in such highly different societies as the United States and India does indeed probably stem from common etiological origins. This observation, of course, does not speak to the universal etiology of delinquent behavior, but it suggests that this conduct has common etiological dimensions.

When confronting the question of epidemiology, however, we are faced with quite a different explanatory problem. What we seek to explain is the relative rate of involvement in delinquent acts by persons within a population aggregate (e.g., as defined by gender, age, nation of residence). Two issues are of concern. One is the prevalence of delinquency within a population aggregate. Measured as the percentage of persons admitting acts on a self-report survey or, for example, arrested as offenders, prevalence is a measure of delinquent persons and can serve only as a proxy for delinquent acts. Second, the incidence (absolute or average number) of delinquent acts exhibited by the members of a population aggregate is a mathematical function of prevalence and the number of delinquent acts, totally or of a certain type, accumulated by the aggregate over some period of time, such as a year. Although counts of how often individuals are arrested may be used to estimate incidence, about the only direct measure we have of this dimension is the frequency with which respondents say they committed various offenses.

To the extent that delinquency rates (prevalence and incidence) reflect the occurrence of actual delinquent acts, regardless of how these are estimated, a theory of epidemiology would lead us to predict that (all else being equal) if individuals within some population aggregate (e.g., country) exhibit mild or low degrees of some causal force (e.g., degree of association with delinquent others) and/or high levels of some control condition (e.g., low levels of bonding), and/or if substantial numbers of the individuals within the population aggregate exhibit such characteristics, the aggregate as a whole should produce low rates of delinquency, either in terms of the proportion engaged in this conduct and/or the numbers of delinquent acts they commit. Conversely, where the members of an aggregate (or large numbers of them) are (or are heavily) induced and reinforced to commit delinquent acts, and/or are not greatly impeded from so doing, rates of delinquency should be high.

However, regardless of the levels of delinquency inducing/reinforcing conditions and/or levels of delinquency impeding conditions within any population aggregate, some individuals will be subjected or exposed to inducing or reinforcing conditions more so than others. We would expect that these individuals would have a higher probability of delinquency, or frequent delinquency, involvement than would other members of the aggregate. What accounts for the relatively higher rate of delinquency among some persons within a population aggregate or why some population aggregates have higher rates than other aggregates are two separate questions, both of which require distinct theories of epidemiology. But, whatever explains the delinquency involvement of individuals within any population aggregate in itself cannot answer either of these questions. Thus, any attempt to explain the "within" or "across" aggregate distribution of delinquency requires a theory (or addition to the etiological theory) that explains the relative distribution of delinquency inducing/impeding conditions within and across population aggregates, whether they be high, low, or medium delinquency-rate aggregates as such.

Any theory purporting to be a general or universal theory of etiology would have to apply equally to the delinquency involvement of individuals in any population aggregate. Otherwise the theory only explains why some individuals do it in some kinds of population aggregates and not others. Assuming that such notions as differential association, various motivational arguments such as strain theory, and control theories such as bond theory do enhance our understanding of "why they do it," an adequate understanding of why more of them do "it" or do more of "it" (or "it" of some kind or another) in one population aggregate compared to another would require that we explain why the members of one aggregate have higher levels of differential association, experience more intense or frequent strain, and/or are subject to lower levels of social control than those of another.

A theory of epidemiology, in other words, is not a theory of delinquency in the same sense that an etiological theory can be understood to be. Rather, a theory of epidemiology explains the relative variations in the etiological conditions that produce (or allow for) differences in rates of delinquent forms of behavior across population aggregates.

In this regard, the combination of variables discussed in Chapter Six explain the occurrence of delinquent behavior on the part of juveniles in both the United States and India. But they do not tell us why these rates vary to the extent that and in the ways that they do. The path models depicting the operation of these causal conditions imply that, while equally explanatory in the etiological sense, differences in types and levels of strain, involvement with delinquent peers, and bonding to family and school may explain why rates of delinquency among youths in India and the United States are not the same. In what follows, we seek to explore some aspects of these differences.

FAMILY, PEERS, AND COMMUNITY

If high levels of strain, frequent involvement with delinquent peers, and weak social controls are responsible for (help to explain) high rates of delinquent behavior, and if these variables explain the delinquent behavior of youths in

India and the United States to a similar extent and in a similar manner, then the variations in rates of delinquency (overall or for specific offense-type prevalence and/or incidence frequencies) between youths in these two countries are a function of differences in the socioeconomic conditions of the two societies that produce differences in levels of strain, involvement with delinquent as opposed to conventional others, and social controls.

Comparison of the American and Indian survey samples on the various measures used to assess strain, control, and delinquent peer associations indicates that real (if not dramatic) differences in the forces that promote or deter delinquent behavior may exist between India and the United States (see Table 7.1).

Table 7.1
Comparison of Indian 1990 and United States 1978 Respondents on
Conventional Bonding and Delinquent Peer Involvement

| Measure | India | | U.S. | | |
	Mean	S.D.	Mean	S.D.	t
Exp. Del. Peers	14.27	11.50	22.11	7.95	11.97
Peer Involvement	5.96	4.24	7.90	3.84	7.13
Family Involvement	9.09	3.93	10.11	3.34	4.49
School Involvement	9.43	3.63	6.84	3.40	-11.90
Sample N	428		701		

Note: Missing cases excluded in computations. NS = Not significant, all others significant <.01.

Indian youths appear to be similar to American youths as far as involvement with family is concerned. This is a bit surprising given the readily apparent cohesiveness of Indian compared to American families and probably reflects the way this dimension was measured (i.e., "How much time do you spend with family members?") rather than a true assessment of "involvement." On the other hand, Indian youths are clearly much more involved than are Americans with conventional school activities and far less involved with delinquent peers. Given the relative importance of differential association in the explanation of delinquency etiology, these differences are particularly significant.

To some extent, at least, differences in rates of delinquency between American and Indian youths are a function of differences in the extent to which youths in the two countries associate with others engaged in delinquency. Indeed, this is especially significant insofar as many forms of delinquency likely to be noticed by or reacted to by authorities is concerned—especially conduct such as substance use and public "rowdiness." This, in turn, might be why official rates of delinquency are so disparate for the two countries and why official and self-report rates are at such apparent variance in India. Comparatively, Indian youths are simply not in situations where they associate with other youths who promote delinquent behavior nor, by virtue of their being associated with such youths (e.g., delinquent gangs), are they likely to become similarly identified as delinquent by others. To the extent that this is true, understanding the differences in delinquency rates across societies such as India and the United States requires that we address the socioeconomic contexts in which peer associations likely to result in delinquency do or do not materialize.

In an earlier study of delinquency in India, Hartjen and Priyadarsini (1984) argued that economically developed compared to economically developing societies were likely to produce different rates of actual delinquency as well as societal reactions to it by virtue of differences in socio-interactional characteristics related to their level of economic development. Specifically, they argued that the affluence and alienation associated with economic development promote and facilitate delinquency, and, at the same time, help support and make necessary the extensive use of official social control agencies to deal with such behavior. Conversely, the poverty and social interdependency associated with economically developing (pre-modern) societies reduces rates of delinquent behavior and generates informal, extralegal, modes of societal reaction to it. Thus, both the official and behavioral rates of delinquency are likely to be high in countries such as the United States and western European nations and low in countries like India and other Third World societies.

These arguments were, admittedly, rather gross over-generalizations based on the sparse comparative knowledge available at that time. But the research in comparative criminology that has accumulated over the past ten years has done nothing to fundamentally alter these observations. In fact, the accumulated evidence supports the general claims made by Hartjen and Priyadarsini. In that regard, Third World societies such as India are likely to have social interactional forms relating to etiological dimensions that differ from those found in economically developed countries such as the United States. Whether these forms are a product of economic development or merely coincidental to it is not the issue here, although the matter deserves considerably more attention by criminologists than it has so far received. For the present, given the arguments of strain, learning, and control theories, what concerns us here is the apparent differences in the family and peer-association characteristics of the United States and India and how these might be reflected in delinquency rates for the two societies.

FAMILY AND PEERS IN THE UNITED STATES

Perhaps the fundamental question to be answered here is not why rates of delinquency in India are so low but why those in the United States are so high. Given that numerous people have sought to answer that question, our inquiry here is limited to a more modest investigation of the comparative differences and similarities in the rates we find between the two societies. Perhaps, however, in exploring that issue we can cast light on the more frequently investigated problem of delinquency rates in the United States.

It is a sociological truism that a primary function of the family is to act as a mechanism of social control. This occurs both directly (through physical proximity, economic arrangements, and immediate discipline/reward) and through the family's central role in the socialization of children (see Bell, 1983). Criminologists have also long recognized the importance the family has for delinquency—see e.g., Levitan et al., 1988; Lincoln & Straus, 1985; Rosen, 1985; Sommers et al., 1994; Van Voorhis et al., 1988; Wells and Rankin, 1988; McCord, 1990. Criminological research accumulated on the relationship between family factors and delinquency clearly indicates that a host of variables associated with family structure, operation, inter-personal relationships, and the like are related to delinquent conduct.

This research, in turn, suggests that in communities where families inadequately perform their social control/socialization function or where this ability has in some way been usurped or impeded, rates of crime and delinquency are likely to be high (see e.g., Cernkovich & Giordano, 1987; Laub & Sampson, 1988; Liska & Reed, 1985; Matsueda & Heimer, 1987; Messner & Rosenfeld, 1994; Zhang & Messner, 1995). This applies both to societies as a whole as well as to population aggregates within particular societies. The United States in the latter half of the twentieth century appears to be a society where both situations apply.

There are two reasons why delinquency rates would be higher in one society compared to some other in terms of the social-control and socialization activities of families. One, all else being equal, high delinquency rates are likely to occur when the restraining force of strong family controls along with the conventional bonding these controls presuppose are weak or absent. Weak family controls, of course, do not necessarily predispose youths to commit delinquent acts, but they could make deviance, if not more likely, more readily pursuable given the lack of sufficient constraints (physical or internalized) to impede delinquency when occasions for its commission occur (Rankin & Wells, 1991). Assuming that all youngsters are to some degree exposed to delinquent motivations and/or opportunities, the probability that more or fewer will act upon these motivations or opportunities would vary depending upon the nature and extent to which they are constrained. The family seems to be primary in this regard. Indeed, it is quite possible that the age generation differences in the peak arrest rates between Indian and American youths has to do with the differences in the ages at which family controls are lessened for youths in the two countries.

Two, and perhaps more importantly where delinquency is concerned, the lack of the group identity and cohesion that a strong family bond presupposes, not only facilitates, but make it more likely, that youths will seek social/emotional contacts elsewhere. Whether this produces some kind of "strain" motivating youths to seek out deviant others with whom to identify and thereby become similarly involved in deviance is not the issue here (Agnew, 1991). But, in societies where meaningful and legitimate alternatives (such as jobs, active participation in significant social activities, etc.) are not provided to young people (or large segments of them) and/or are not held out as desirable routes of self-identity and esteem, spending one's time "hanging out" and coming to identify with one's peers become a readily adaptable alternative. Only a thin line divides the gang member who defines the gang as his or her family from the teenager whose mall-crawling associates are similarly so perceived. Juveniles who return from school to homes where parents are absent, not concerned with their activities, unwilling to involve their children in their pursuits or to even supervise their children's activities, may tend to seek out and find others like themselves—adrift and alone (Hirschi, 1969; Mansnerus, 1993; Wooden, 1995). This is also not necessarily delinquency promoting in itself. But, such social arrangements could heighten one's orientation to peers and promote detachment from the most direct and meaningful mechanism of conventional social control and socialization the family provides.

Several decades ago, Albert Cohen (1955) argued that the sense of rejection that American working-class boys experienced because of their failure to live up to the middle-class measuring rod of the school compelled them to reject their rejectors, seek consolence with others similarly afflicted, and then rebel against middle-class society by acts of delinquency. For the bulk of youths in contemporary America (and western Europe), rejection and rebellion can hardly serve to account for their delinquency. Yet perhaps a more fitting description for most contemporary American youths is the concept "set adrift" (rendered socially meaningless, uninvolved, relegated to pointless time-filling activities [see e.g., Alwin, 1988; Covington, 1982; Inciardi et al., 1993; Gaines, 1992]). School, of course, consumes much of their time. And some youths do become heavily committed to school and the conventionality it provides. They are likely to "stay out of trouble" and become the economic successes of their generation. But for many youths, school is meaningless, simply a place to be, "mess around" in, or to escape from. For many others (especially middle class) the challenge of schooling is absent, hardly something to consume their time. Filling it becomes a daily occupation. Boredom has become a malaise felt throughout the adolescent world (Gaines, 1992; Mansnerus, 1993).

This is particularly important when coupled with socio-economic arrangements that cater to and actively facilitate the association of young people away from or not actively under the supervision of adults who (supposedly) care (i.e., parents). All of the ingredients for mischief exist (boredom, opportunity, lack of restraint). It takes but a little desire, a dare, a wish for some excitement or relief from boredom, to turn mischief into delinquency. In societies where even "good school-attending kids" spend hours "hanging out" in video arcades, roaming the corridors of shopping malls, attending unsupervised parties, going out with the "guys," on a date, or just "goofing off," the possibilities for delinquency become enormous. One's peers become the measuring rod of one's actions, morality, and judgment (Levitan et al., 1988). As Thornberry et al. (1994) suggest, circumstances are ripe wherein "delinquent" peer involvement becomes a kind of self-fulfilling reward system promoting delinquent behavior, further peer involvement, acceptance of deviance and continued delinquency. Parents and various "theys" are to be feared, no doubt. But being caught or having something "bad" happen to you is rare; the probability of that is difficult to judge and often converted into a positive badge of identity anyway (Lemert, 1951; Werthman, 1970; Jensen, 1980).

For most, this situation results in the relatively mild forms of delinquency revealed in self-report surveys. But for many youths, unsupervised peer associations and a general cultural orientation that *"It don't matter any way!"* make the probability exceedingly high that some youths will be exposed to and succumb to serious involvement with drugs and more ambitious forms of criminality. One does not learn to steal a car from peers if an interested parent is observing his or her activity. One does not become acquainted with the joys of marijuana or "crack" if one is being observed by adults ready and willing to intervene. One does not steal unneeded clothing out of desire or on a dare if some conventional parent seriously keeps tabs on the contents of one's bedroom. And one does not shoot or get shot by a schoolmate if a parent had taught that the use of violence is not the solution to interpersonal disputes and prevented the kind of peer associations conducive to the acquisition and use of firearms.

OTHER COUNTRIES

Limited research on delinquency in countries as diverse as Japan and the former Soviet Union also indicate that broad socioeconomic conditions relating to social controls, motivations, and delinquent peer associations are responsible for substantial increases in delinquency rates in these countries in the past few decades.

Japan, for example, has exceptionally low crime rates compared to other industrialized countries. Delinquency rates in that country remain extremely low. However, Charles Fenwick (1983) notes that these rates dramatically increased between 1951 and 1979 (also see Suzuki, 1981; National Police Agency, 1989). This increase, Fenwick argues, was a consequence of socioeconomic changes in Japan at that time, lessening the integrative forces of work, school, family, and community for substantial numbers of Japanese youths. This, in turn, decreased the social controls these institutions had and opened up opportunities as well as providing motivations for delinquency. While true of all the integrative institutions in Japanese society, for many youths the breakdown of integrative constraints previously provided by the family was especially acute. According to Fenwick (1983: 124):

Historically, the Japanese family has been a highly revered institution that has played a major role in defining prescriptions and proscriptions for action. The threat of exclusion from the family and/or community has been one of the cornerstones for conformity within this society. . . . In conjunction with work and community ties, strong family attachments have traditionally provided adolescents with high levels of group consciousness, thereby reducing the probability of crime and delinquency.

But, as Fenwick notes, in post-World-War-II Japan the traditional concepts of community and attachment to family underwent rapid alteration. For many youths, these changes appear to have resulted in crime and delinquency, producing the noticeable increase in official rates.

A seemingly different set of circumstances, although with similar socioeconomic consequences, appears to have led to a sizable growth in criminality on the part of youths in the former Soviet Union. Finckenauer and Kelly (1992), for example, report that in the early 1990s a tremendous and highly noticeable increase in youth crime and delinquency occurred in the former Soviet Union (also see Kuznietzova, 1989; Voigt & Thornton, 1990). This increase, they argue, was largely a result of the emergence of youth subcultures and juvenile gangs with the decline of the Komosmols and the socioeconomic chaos that accompanied the transformation from a planned to a market economy. Formally serving as a kind of national rallying force for Soviet youth, by the 1980s the Komosmols had begun to lose their integrative force, both because of internal corruption and outside forces. With that decline, youth "subcultures" emerged as a way of providing Soviet youths a sense of community and place to express their individuality. But, at the same time, they offered youths peer associations conducive of and reinforcements for delinquency.

Along with this, economic dissatisfaction and insecurity heightened pressures to deviate as well as allowed justifications for theft and other forms of illegal activity. But perhaps equally significant was the breakdown of the extended family throughout the Soviet Union. According to Finckenauer and Kelly (1992: 255):

> The increasing urbanization—accompanied by a breaking down of the traditional family structure with two-parent, extended families—has lead to large numbers of urban children having to fend for themselves a great deal of the time. They are often left unsupervised because their mothers work. In addition, the high divorce rate leaves many children growing up in single-parent, usually fatherless homes. This combination, just as it has in American cities, creates the fertile soil out of which juvenile delinquency grows.

FAMILY AND PEERS IN INDIA

In contemporary American criminological research, theories of social control have received comparatively little support as explanations of the primary or immediate cause of delinquency. And, on the face of it, it is unlikely that they ever will. But, arguments made by Hirschi (1969) and numerous others (for summaries of this research, see Thornton & Voigt, 1992: 230–250) that poor or inadequate parenting is a major (if indirect) factor in delinquency etiology cannot be denied (VanVoorhis et al., 1988; Wells & Rankin, 1988). As such, socioeconomic situations conducive of such inadequacy would surely produce high rates of youth crime and delinquency. Contemporary America appears to be just such a society, and many European countries seem not to be far behind. It appears that India, on the other hand, has not as yet been so affected.

Social control theories would also imply that the emergence of a youth subculture and high rates of delinquency in post-World-War-II United States and European countries reflect the disintegration of the family and its consequent inability to instill conventional values and exercise adequate control over young people. Some suggest that this was an unintended consequence of post-war economic affluence (Friday, 1980; Friday & Hage, 1976). But why this may have happened remains highly speculative and is not immediately germane to our argument. Whatever the case, the central idea contained in Braithwaite's (1989) notions of crime and reintegrative shaming is pertinent. As Braithwaite argues, a sense of shame is critical to the effect actual or threatened negative sanctions may have on retarding deviance. Shame, in turn, requires both a sense of identity and commitment. This is something families have traditionally imparted to their members. In societies where families no longer fulfill this function and the ability of other institutions (e.g., schools) to do so is lacking or weak, the threat of shame loses its force as a psychological mechanism of control. Indeed, that force itself could become perverted. Being "deviant" becomes one's identity (Polk & Schafer, 1972; Wells, 1989; Paternoster & Lovanni, 1989).

In societies where the family and one's place in it have central importance to one's life, where shaming one's self shames one's family, and where such shame has consequences far beyond the actual punishment one may receive for the specific deviance, integrative social control can very much serve to repress deviance, regardless of what stimuli or opportunities one may experience to deviate. India at the end of the twentieth century remains such a society (Misra & Agnihoti, 1985). A substantial body of anthropological research exists on Indian society and culture. Much of this information would appear quite dated for understanding delinquency in contemporary India. But more recent studies do not depict a society fundamentally different from that described in any of the post-independence era investigations so that the accumulated body of this research can be drawn upon for our purposes (see e.g., Ashby, 1974; Karve, 1986; Lannoy, 1971; Mandelbaum, 1970; Singer & Cohn, 1968). Moreover, contemporary Indian social scientists have contributed a large number of observations and commentary about Indian society, particularly as regards women and family relationships. Collectively these publications provide a rich source of descriptive (and, occasionally, hard) data on the sociocultural entity called India. It is beyond the scope of this study to offer an extensive discussion of India's social system and culture. But two interrelated aspects of Indian society and culture as described in this literature are particularly significant in understanding the differences and similarities in delinquency rates between India and the United States: (1) the prominence of the Indian family in people's lives, and (2) the opportunity structures affecting the associations of Indian youths.

Family Control in Indian Society
The measure of family bonding used in the 1990 survey employed "time spent with family" as a measure of this bond. Respondents in both the Indian and American samples indicated similar associational time. This would imply that the importance of the family is equal in both societies. This is not so. It is not the amount of time spent with family members (immediate and distant relatives) but the meaning of "family" to Indians that is most significant and central to understanding its force as a mechanism of social control in that society.

Study after study has shown that historically the family (regardless of form, e.g., joint, extended, stem, and nuclear) has been the central locus of social/economic life in India. In spite of urbanization, industrialization, and westernization throughout the society, for the great bulk of Indians the family still so remains. As Roopnarine et al. (1992: 300) observes ". . . family life changes very slowly in India and is bound by intricate webs of traditions, customs, and patriarchal tendencies that do not seem to respond well to industrialization and legislation. . . ." Thus, while India is indeed "modernizing," its modernization appears to be unique. The traditional system of family and community has not been destroyed. Instead it has become an important channel of change in its own right (Gore, 1968; Ishwaran, 1970). Thus, probably more than any other force, the family and the place it occupies in Indian society also remains the central locus of social control throughout the society. Why the family has such a powerful force in Indian society has primarily to do with marriage and economic well-being. The two, of course, are interrelated.

Given the caste/subcaste (jati) organization of Indian society and the economic dependency of children, particularly daughters, the primary function of extensive family relationships (regardless of the specific form of family in which one at the moment lives) is to find appropriate mates for daughters (to "marry them off" as Indians say). In a study of family structure in South India, Caldwell et al. (1984) observe that the primary purpose of the stem-joint family found in the community they investigated centers on the marriage of daughters. According to Caldwell et al. (1984: 225), besides providing a training institution for new daughter-in-laws who almost always move into the household of their husbands' parents, at least temporarily, the major significance of the family

. . . is to act as an engine for marrying off the daughters of the family. By definition, there is a single household budget, the product of all members' labor, which indisputably can be used by the patriarch to provide dowries and other marriage expenses. None of the patriarch's sons can question this use of the amount, let alone opt out from financial responsibility, while he is a member of the household.

Indeed, even in situations where sons are no longer living in the household, contributing to the economic expenses of marrying off a sister or a niece and helping find her an appropriate husband are moral obligations not easily ignored.

This is necessary not only to secure the daughter's economic future but also to relieve the family of the burden of her upkeep. But more importantly, marriage ties between families within jatis strengthen bonds among all members of the jati. Virtually everyone is related in some way to virtually every other person in the jati or at least recognized as a member of the "clan." This, in turn, enhances the economic strength of the jati as far as sharing resources, securing jobs, government positions, seats in the university, housing, and the like are concerned. In discussing the continuity and changes in the caste system in India, Mencher (1970: 199), for example, notes:

Today, the caste groupings do serve new functions in what is perhaps a more competitive sphere than before. In urban areas in the south, informal caste groupings help their fellows at least in providing social forums, and on occasion, in more crucial matters. If a member of the caste has risen in importance either in government or in private business, he will make use of these informal relationships within his caste group in selecting recipients for favors (assuming his close relatives are not in the bidding) or in deciding whom to hire.

Much like the "old school tie" of western societies, being a respected member of the right jati can do much for one's economic position. Having a sister or daughter married to an influential member of the jati can help bring tremendous rewards. Maintaining family respectability, therefore, is not only essential to finding the right husbands for daughters but to establish the well-being of all in the family. Ramu (1977: 101) suggests the social control implications this may have:

. . . the individual becomes totally obligated to his family for his family supports his educational, occupational and marital endeavors. In view of such critical support extended by the family, a person becomes relatively dependent on his family and his behavior conforms to general expectations.

The central issue here is not simply one of parenting. Rather, it concerns the way in which societies integrate individuals into the larger social system and foster their commitment to conventionality. Indeed, poor, inadequate, or clearly "bad" parenting can be found in India as much as it can in the United States or in any other society for that matter. And children victimized by neglectful, abusive, or simply incompetent parents are as likely to exhibit the psychological and behavioral characteristics found among such children universally—including involvement in delinquency (National Seminar on Child Abuse in India, 1988; "Child Abuse: Tragically Widespread," 1987; Mehta, 1984; Jabbi, 1986; Institute of Psychological & Educational Research, 1985; Lokeshwar et al., 1979). In this regard, "poor parenting" can be considered both a motivating as well as control-related etiological variable in the explanation of delinquent behavior in India as it is in the United States. But it has little to do with rates of delinquency directly. In this regard, rather than the quality of parenting per se, it is the degree to which youths in any society develop a stake in conventionality and the extent to which they associate and identify with non-delinquent as opposed to delinquent peers that, in part at least, is reflected in their rates of delinquency. The critical difference between India (and possibly other Third World countries) and western nations like the United States is the role families play in fostering that stake in conventionality and peer associations.

Quite clearly, children victimized by poor parenting in countries like the United States have few options other than formal agencies of welfare or control to pick up the slack, heal the wounds, intervene on their behalf, and the like. No matter the degree of commitment a society makes or the extent of the dedication and skill of those involved in child-welfare and other substitute family agencies, such substitutions can be but "poor cousins" to real cousins, uncles, brothers, etc., who may not only have a greater emotional relationship with the youth but also possibly a greater economic stake in them or the consequences their victimization may have for the family as a whole. Both authors have witnessed, been informed about, and even directly experienced the kind of Indian family pulling together in situations of crises and need that would, at best, be extremely unusual in American society, if only because such pulling together is seen to be unneeded since other ways of handling the problem exist (e.g., medical insurance, unemployment compensation, etc.).

In one instance, for example, the nephew of one of the authors became critically ill in India and suffered the added consequences of a misdiagnosis and botched surgery (by another family member, no less!). The man's immediate family was financially capable of bearing the cost of medical treatment (although at great sacrifice). But medical supplies, equipment, and facilities in India were simply inadequate to save the man's life. It was only because other relatives in India and abroad at their own expense rallied to his cause by giving blood, getting needed medicine or equipment on airplanes (sometimes in the hands of strangers), using whatever influence they had to bring together medical specialists, and the like, that his life was saved. In western societies, members of one's immediate family may spend literally thousands of dollars to save the life of a loved one. But it is doubtful that distant relatives in far corners of the world would do much, or that such intervention would even be necessary in the first place. Thus, the kind of social interdependency such necessity predisposes would be less likely to form.

While merely illustrative, the above case demonstrates the wide context of family ties as opposed to parenting skills to which such notions as Braithwaite's reintegrative shaming and Hirschi's social bond theories allude. And it is in this context that the family in India can be understood as an effective mechanism of social control as far as reducing rates of delinquency is concerned.

The individualistic orientation characteristic of western societies not only makes the individual's deviance relatively inconsequential to the members of his or her family but also makes their evaluation of the individual relatively meaningless—at least as a mechanism of control. One may not, of course, want to "hurt" one's mother or whatever. And one may feel ashamed or embarrassed at the deviance of one's son or daughter. But the behavior of one or the feelings of the other are hardly likely to have any significant consequence for the life or life chances of either in most cases.

By contrast, in societies such as India where the family plays such a central role in one's economic and social life, what the members of the family think of you and your behavior counts. And that family consists of more than parents and immediate siblings. Also, your deviance reflects on the other members of the family. In the United States having a murderer in the family may be a skeleton to hide in the closet if only to save embarrassment. In India that member could seriously impede the ability of others to secure jobs, spouses, or any of the other goals in life for generations to come.

Peer Involvement Among Indian Youth
Perhaps more important than the emotional and direct control over the behavior of family members is the importance family (and in India, jati) membership has in channeling associations. As our, and almost all other, research shows, delinquent peer involvement is the most important immediate correlate of delinquency. No matter how it is measured, this variable persistently explains more of the variance in delinquency than any other and often exceeds the combined explanatory power of all other dimensions investigated. Comparatively, as an etiological variable, social control is relatively unimportant. However, this does not mean it is inconsequential. Indeed, the integrated model developed by Elliott et al. (1985) and employed in this analysis suggests that, if anything, it is the effect social control has on one's peer (and other) associations that makes it a significant predictor of delinquency.

The 1990 survey attempted to assess the extent to which Indian and American respondents associated with delinquent and conventional others. Comparing various dimensions in this regard, it is clear that American youths are significantly more involved with peers, especially delinquent peers, and less often engage in conventional school activities compared to Indian youths (see Table 7.1). Thus, in spite of their relatively higher scores on frequency of involvement with family, it is apparent that American youths are much more peer oriented than are Indian respondents.

The crucial factor appears to center on the difference in the scores American and Indian respondents have on involvement in school activities. The fundamental importance of these scores is that while associating with members of their own age cohort, Indian youths are more likely than Americans to be doing so within the relatively channeled setting of the school and, possibly, family. Thus, participating with peers is less likely to involve participating with deviant ones or with peers in deviant activities.

Equally important, once school is over, Indian children are presented with very few places to go or few things to do except under the supervision of relatives or other interested adults. And this extends to evenings and weekends. Indian juveniles simply have no occasion to "hang out" with groups of other juveniles. And even for those who may want to, there are few places for them to do so.

India (even cities in India) simply offers juveniles few places to be outside of parental supervision when not in school. In spite of the growing westernization of India and the emergence of a distinct middle class with the growth of accompanying amenities such as restaurants, bars, and readily available consumer goods, India has not (as yet) developed an alienated youth subculture or provided youths with the means (e.g., their own car) and places (e.g., video arcades, shopping malls, teenage hangouts, etc.) where they have opportunities to congregate with other youths or find opportunities for trouble. This is particularly reflected in the differences in the kinds of delinquency American and Indian youths most frequently commit.

Specifically, American youths report substantially higher rates of public order and substance abuse offenses compared to Indians. Moreover, they are arrested at substantially higher rates than Indians for behavior related to these kinds of activities or other behaviors oriented to subcultural displays of status (such as shoplifting, stealing cars to demonstrate driving skills to other youths, dressing in ways that hint of rebellion against the adult world, and the like).

To some extent this reflects cultural differences between the two societies. Drinking behavior among Indian youths, for example, is comparatively infrequent because India's Muslim and Hindu cultural histories are not conducive to the consumption of alcohol or the use of drugs. These substances are, of course, used by Indians. But the atmosphere fostered by advertising and the ready availability of alcohol or its use common to western nations are not found in India. Going out to get drunk or illegally buying "booze" is simply something few Indian high-school youths would ever contemplate or to which peer pressure would subject them (Priyadarsini & Hartjen, 1982).

Similarly, teen-age dating (if not marriage, although it is illegal) is still extremely rare in India. Consequently, all the potential delinquency associated with such activity is forestalled.

Entertainment, a seemingly all-consuming interest of American youths, is a family, not an age-generational, activity in India. Groups of unsupervised teenagers are not found flooding out of theaters late at night with no other purpose or direction but to "get into mischief." Instead, the whole family (or segments of it) goes to the cinema together. Movies are not tailored to age-differentiated audiences. Indeed, to a western observer they all look to be very much alike in any case. But Indians adore them, and every seat in every theater for every showing is taken. At the same time that they depict a well-recognized fantasy world, Indian films also promote a cultural (if not national) solidarity and support of traditional values regarding family life and respect of elders that western films have long discarded.

The cultural and socioeconomic variations between Indian and American societies resulting in the variable delinquency rates they exhibit could be described at length. But perhaps the rather extreme case of Indian girls can be used to best illustrate the social-control/delinquent-peer involvement features of Indian compared to American society and their respective rates of delinquency.

THE CASE OF INDIAN GIRLS

That women and girls are decidedly less criminal or delinquent than their male counterparts everywhere seems to have been well established (Adler, 1984; Berger, 1989). What may differ, however, is the relative size of the gender gap across countries or social systems. In most economically developed societies, the gap is relatively narrow compared to that reported for most traditional or Third World nations (Bowher, 1981; Hartnagel, 1982). This is particularly apparent when the delinquency of boys and girls in India and the United States is compared.

Table 7.2
Offense Category Prevalence Rates for India 1987 and United States 1978
Respondents, by Gender

| | Percent Admitting | | | |
| | Boys | | Girls | |
Offense Category	U.S.	India	U.S.	India
Total Delinquency	85	84	76	65
Status Offenses	56	56	46	33
Property Crimes	30	35	13	12
Personal Crimes	17	20	10	6
Substance Abuse	49	19	40	7
Theft Offenses	22	15	11	6
Home Delinquency	18	27	15	13
Public Delinquency	43	19	31	7
Sample N	663	1013	584	1040

Note: Percentages rounded to nearest whole number.

Table 7.2 Continued
Phi Coefficients for Offense Categories by Sample Group

Offense Category	U.S. Boys/ Girls	India Boys/ Girls	Boys U.S./ India	Girls U.S./ India	India Boys/ U.S. Girls	U.S. Boys/ India Girls
Total Delinquency	.11	.22	NS	.12	.09	.22
Status Offenses	.10	.23	NS	.13	NS	.23
Property Crimes	.20	.28	−.05*	NS	.24	.22
Personal Crimes	.10	.20	Ns	.06	.13	.18
Substance Abuse	.09	.19	.32	.41	−.23	.48
Theft Offenses	.15	.16	.09	.10	NS	.24
Home Delinquency	NS	.18	−.10	NS	.14	.07
Public Delinquency	.12	.18	.26	.31	−.25	.43

NS = not statistically significant, * = significant <.05, all others significant <.01.

Table 7.2 presents prevalence rates by gender for Indian and American respondents based on the 1987 India survey comparison. The data presented in this table show that in both societies, girls are less delinquent than boys, regardless of how such activity is measured. However, the extremely low arrest and self-reported offense rates for girls in India are striking. Indeed, using the findings from the 1987 survey, when rates for the genders are compared cross-culturally, American girls and Indian boys have very similar prevalence rates, if not similar offense-specific patterns. Indian girls, however, are exceedingly distinct, both from Indian boys as well as American girls as far as their lack of delinquency is concerned. As we argued in an earlier report focusing on this finding (see Hartjen & Kethineni, 1993), this distinctiveness undoubtedly reflects the unique social position of girls in India vis-a-vis such variables as social control, opportunity structures, and associations.

Assuming these differences in rates are reflective of reality, what explains the exceedingly low rates for Indian girls? The information presented in Table 7.3 is suggestive. Drawing upon the 1990 comparative survey findings, this table presents mean scores and t-tests for the various sample groups on the delinquent and conventional bonding scales. Clearly Indian girls are distinctive as far as conventional bonding and practically nonexistent peer and particularly delinquent-peer involvements are concerned—both compared to Indian boys and American girls and boys. In short, Indian girls exhibit all the characteristics we would associate with noninvolvement in delinquent behavior according to leading theories of etiology. That these characteristics are common to Indian girls generally is reflected in the low rates of self-reported delinquency and, correspondingly, almost negligible arrest frequencies. This commonality, in turn, is a function of the particular socioeconomic position girls and women occupy in Indian society and apparently in many other Third World countries as well.

Table 7.3
Comparison of Indian 1990 and United States 1978 Respondents on Conventional and Delinquent Peer Involvement Scales, by Gender

| | U.S. | | | | India | | | |
| | Boys | | Girls | | Boys | | Girls | |
Measure	Mean	SD	Mean	SD	Mean	SD	Mean	SD
Exp. Del. Peers	22.79	8.09	21.35	7.73	16.93	13.40	11.69	8.58
Peer Involvement	7.85	3.94	7.97	3.72	7.50	4.27	4.42	3.67
Family Involvement	10.08	3.28	10.14	3.42	8.51	3.70	9.71	4.09
School Involvement	6.12	3.38	7.65	3.23	8.63	3.75	10.29	3.29
Sample N	371		330		221		227	

T-Tests of Difference in Mean Scale Scores by Comparison Group

Measure	U.S. Boys/ Girls	India Boys/ Girls	Boys U.S./ India	Girls U.S./ India	U.S Boys/ India Girls	India Boys/ U.S. Girls
Exp. Del. Peers	2.40	4.58	5.56	12.99	14.99	−4.18
Peer Involvement	−0.42*	7.19	0.91*	10.23	9.88	−1.22*
Family Involvement	−0.23*	−3.17	5.22	1.29*	1.14*	−5.24
School Involvement	−6.13	−4.85	−8.14	−9.07	−14.43	3.15

Note: Missing cases excluded in computations, *= Not significant, all others significant <.01.

Females, especially unmarried girls, are at the bottom of India's social structure (Caplan, 1985; Hale, 1989; Jain, 1975; Krishnaraj & Chanana, 1989; Murkhopadhyay, 1984; Somjee, 1989). The birth of a male child is an occasion for great joy in Indian households. One girl is also desired for religious and cultural reasons, but the birth of girls generally is met with sorrow and resignation. To be the parents of many girls (and no boys) would be an economic disaster and looked upon as a curse.

Because of neglect, wanton abuse, reported instances of infanticide, etc., infant mortality rates among females are considerably higher than among males. Comparatively few Indian girls go to college and even those attending high school (as in the self-report surveys) are relatively privileged. But as Hale

(1989: 379) notes: "The educational qualifications achieved by a girl are commonly treated as commodities for the marriage market rather than as intrinsically valuable. Her achievements become something which she confers upon her husband rather than herself." Not surprisingly, literacy rates for females are lower than those of males. Out-of-household employment of women is in low-status, menial, low-wage jobs when compared to males (Desai & Krishnaraj, 1987; Devi & Ravindran, 1983; Lebra et al., 1984: 82–94; Radha & Ravindran, 1983). Many Indian women are compelled to work, usually in the family farm, business, or cottage industry. Elsewhere, out-of-house employment is often sought by poor Indian wives and daughters to augment the family income and by members of the middle/upper class to "give them something to do." But, it is expected that wages will be turned over to the male household head and that the working woman will still fulfill all her womanly duties (observing rituals, cooking, cleaning, childrearing, catering to males, etc.).

To an extent few westerners can fully realize, childhood socialization for the vast majority of Indian females is almost exclusively directed to preparing them for marriage and their eventual departure from the household. Whatever else one may be or do, the central purpose of existence for most of India's women is to be a good wife, mother, daughter-in-law, and homemaker. Few "love marriages" actually occur in spite of a growing recognition of this possibility. And males and females do increasingly interact with one another in schools and universities. But Indian children still expect marriages to be arranged for them by members of their family, increasingly with their consent as to the choice of mate however. And being "married off" is the ultimate (and desired) destiny of most Indian girls, usually to become the lowest-level servant in the home of their mother-in-law. Lannoy (1971: 128) characterizes the situation regarding marriage and its impact on interpersonal relationships as follows:

> The vast majority of adolescents know with certainty that their parents will arrange marriage for them. This has an enormously important influence on their behavior and upon their initiative in relationships. Girls, for instance, are seldom faced with the need to make difficult decisions on their own, either in their own families or in the families into which they marry, because important problems will be deliberated on by everyone. Where boys and girls have opportunities of mixing, at modern co-educational institutions, their relationships tend to remain very much in the category of nervous, titillating, and tentative skirmishes. Deeper attachments are still rare because they are socially disapproved of, and involve a greater element of hazard than they do in the West.

The exceedingly repressed position of females in India (to western eyes at least) presupposes their low delinquency (and adult crime) rates in at least two ways: (1) by subjecting them to almost continuous family social control and (2) thereby limiting their opportunities to deviate or to associate with others who transmit and reinforce delinquent orientations and skills (Hagan et al., 1987; Sethi & Allen, 1984).

Indeed, the few case studies of female criminality available in the Indian criminological literature almost universally suggest that much of the crime and delinquency Indian girls commit occurs within the context of the family (e.g., killing a spouse or other family member), is occasioned by others in the family (e.g., being the accomplice of a male sibling or a spouse), or is directed to fulfilling family obligations (e.g., stealing food to feed their children).

Particularly after puberty, Indian girls are rarely alone or allowed to venture out on their own. Almost invariably they are chaperoned by relatives or a responsible adult. In extreme cases, they are virtually sequestered in their husband's home awaiting the birth of their first child. Rarely are teen-age girls found "hanging out" with other girls, especially unrelated ones and, except in the context of school, associating with a mixed-sex group of peers. With one's marriage prospects largely circumscribed by jati (and increasingly class), the problem of "being popular with boys" is largely outside their realm of concerns. The kinds of delinquency girls encounter as a consequence of the dating-rating complex endemic to the lives of American teen-agers simply does not exist. "Dating," to the extent it occurs at all, is largely reserved for westernized affluent children, whose marital prospects have not already been determined by their mid-twenties. It is not something fourteen-year-old girls are expected to do.

In this regard, the patriarchal social order of Indian society, especially as it affects women, is indeed repressive—assertions that this "repression" actually allows women to fulfill their "female essence" notwithstanding (e.g., Lannoy, 1971: 130; Thomson, 1990). Insofar as involvement in delinquency is concerned, especially the more serious forms of public misconduct likely to come to the attention of authorities, the oppression of women and girls in India acts as a deterrent (Singer & Levine, 1988).

On the other hand, being oppressed itself, as well as the socio-economic strain it could produce, may serve to motivate Indian girls to deviate. But to whatever extent this may be true, fatalistic cultural beliefs, perceptions of few if any options, and lifelong socialization probably reduce these motivations for most. Where they do exist, acting on them is exceedingly difficult since peer support would normally be absent and few opportunities may present themselves to engage in undetected delinquency in any case. As such, the cultural orientations of India as well as the social structural location of women in Indian society make delinquent behavior on their part, especially the kind of peer-inspired misconduct so prevalent in the United States, something Indian girls are unlikely to attempt or be in positions to learn or successfully carry out when tried (Hartnagel, 1982). More likely, they become the unrecognized victims of crimes committed by adults against them.

CONCLUSION

A substantial body of criminological theory and research exists concerning the amounts and distributions of crime in the United States and European countries. While some information is available on the international dimensions of crime, very little is known about youth crime and delinquency and practically no comparative inquiries exist that allow us to test the generalizability of our knowledge regarding the epidemiological dimensions of delinquency as such, much less the adequacy of our theories to account for delinquency rates throughout the world. The preceding discussion has sought to address that problem.

In doing so, we have contrasted delinquency rates in India with those of (largely) the United States and several other countries. As a case example, India is appropriate for this kind of analysis, in part, because knowing something about the extent and distribution of delinquency in the second largest country of the world is criminologically intriguing in its own right. India also provides a striking contrast socially, economically, and culturally to other countries— about whose delinquency rates and correlates considerable knowledge already exists. The simple fact that India is socially, economically, and culturally distinctive would lead us to immediately expect that its crime and delinquency rates would be distinctive also. That does appear to be the case given the information we now have on hand.

Assuming that etiological theories regarding the occurrence of delinquent behavior are valid and hold universally, an explanation of the distinctive quality of delinquency rates in India (or anywhere) requires us to explain variations in the existence and operation of the causal and/or enabling conditions responsible for delinquent acts. Employing the integrated theory model developed by Elliott et al. (1985) as our conceptual scheme, we argue here that when compared to the United States and other western nations, India's seemingly low rates of delinquency (or at least serious delinquency) are a function of the distinctive integrative features of Indian society. Using the language of social control, we suggest that the family-jati socioeconomic organization of Indian society provides an integrative web of social controls that not only restricts and channels the interactions and relations of youths in India but also (and perhaps more importantly) fosters a social bonding mechanism of interdependence and relatedness that has either disappeared in modern western countries or has been rendered unnecessary or inoperable. Very simply, in contrast to the "set adrift" adolescents of western economically developed societies, Indian youths are strongly dependent upon and integrated into a network of family, jati, and community relationships unlike any their western counterparts experience. As a consequence, Indian youths are much less likely to associate with, be influenced by, or have opportunities to acquire deviant skills and orientations from peers than are the youth of western nations. While peers largely form the nexus of American adolescents' focus, relatives and elders are much more significant to Indian youth. Thus, to the extent that social learning and control theory have explanatory relevance, this may explain why the conditions conducive of delinquency (lack of control and heavy involvement with peers) are less common in India and why, consequently, rates of delinquency are comparatively low.

Obviously such integrative control is imperfect in India also, since individual youths also commit the spectrum of delinquent acts youths commit in other societies. In that respect the "system" fails in the case of Indians as the different "system" fails in the case of American and European youths. Nevertheless, the lack of a youth problem in a large, impoverished, rapidly changing country that has a substantial urban population and is faced with a host of serious social problems should give criminologists occasion to pause. If the arguments of Hirschi and Sutherland are indeed relevant to our understanding of why some kids do it, why comparatively few do very much of it in a country like India suggests that we have much to learn about how social bonds and delinquent peer associations are or are not formed in human societies. This knowledge is prerequisite to any adequate explanation of criminal epidemiology.

CHAPTER EIGHT

Conclusion: Some Comments on the Comparative Study of Delinquency

The need for comparative and international inquiry on crime and justice has long been recognized in criminology (Cavan, 1968; Clinard & Abbott, 1973; Chang, 1976; Friday, 1973; Gurr, 1976; Igbinovia, 1989; Shelley, 1981b; Toby, 1979; Mannheim, 1965). However, a truly international field of criminological inquiry has yet to exist. A number of things probably explain why this remains the case. Nevertheless, it is inevitable that the scope of criminological research and theory in the century ahead will be considerably broader and more inclusive than it has been to date. In this chapter we seek to offer some thoughts regarding this future enterprise generally and particularly as it pertains to the study of delinquency and societal reaction to young offenders.

Considerable research has already been done in comparative (cross-national, international) criminology, and if one were to add commentary from the other social sciences to it, the literature would be extensive. Practically every issue regarding comparative inquiry has been addressed, ranging from its desirability and feasibility to the specific methodological problems and advantages such research entails (Ali, 1986; Beirne, 1983; Bennett & Lynch, 1990; Bennett & Wiegand, 1994; Friday, 1973; Gertz & Gertz, 1992; Jacovetta, 1981; Krohn, 1987; Marshall & Marshall, 1983; Newman & Ferracuti, 1980; Selke, 1992; Shelley, 1981c; Skogan, 1984; Van Dijk et al., 1990; Wilkins, 1980). It is not our purpose to enter into the debate on the prospects of ever achieving a truly international criminology. Obviously, we believe it is both feasible and desirable, although also rife with difficulties (as we have commented upon throughout this book). But before closing our discussion, some commentary seems appropriate on a few of the issues concerning the comparative study of delinquency that we found most vexing in the present inquiry. Specifically, these concern the focus of inquiry, units of study, and the problem of data.

One of the fundamental difficulties facing anyone conducting international comparative research is the apparent vast differences in laws defining criminal and delinquent behaviors and the systems of justice various countries have developed to deal with offenders. This problem is by no means unique to international comparative criminology. The diverse laws and legal systems in the United States, for example (Bartollas & Miller, 1994; Champion, 1992), make any generalizations about delinquency in that country highly problematic if one were to insist upon identical definitions of and ways of counting "delinquency," although such generalizations are routinely made by American criminologists. Yet many people consider this to be a particularly serious impediment to cross-national inquiry, although some research suggests it may not be as problematic as we might think (Bennett & Lynch, 1990; Bennett & Wiegand, 1994).

Diverse definitions of delinquency can produce methodological hurdles. However, we do not share the sentiment that this fact negates the possibility of comparative research (Beirne, 1983). Rather, researchers must be clear as to the focus of their inquiry. As with criminology generally, two areas of inquiry are of interest in comparative research: behavior and societal reaction to it.

The fundamental concern of criminology has traditionally been the criminal/delinquent *behavior* of individuals. In that realm, two issues have been addressed: the etiology of criminal/delinquent acts and the epidemiology of these acts. Criminologists have, and rightly so, debated the appropriate definition of these behaviors to guide our research (Hartjen, 1972; Schwendinger & Schwendinger, 1970). No universally accepted definition can be found in the discipline. By default, most criminologists seem to have simply relied upon whatever definition authorities employ to compile the statistics that criminologists then analyze (as we have done here) or they have bypassed the issue by focusing on behaviors that few would deny fall within the proper realm of criminological interest.

How appropriate either strategy might be for criminological, much less comparative criminological, research is not a matter we can address here. Our point, very simply, is that if our interest is in understanding the occurrence of and/or relative frequency of "behavior," its legal/social definition as criminal or delinquent is of secondary importance. Obviously, the legal or illegal status of some activity in some society could affect its occurrence and/or frequency of occurrence, although there is considerable debate in criminology as to whether or to what extent this is so (see e.g., Braithwaite, 1989). The legal/illegal status of some activity could also affect whether or not it is included in some official counts of criminal/delinquent behavior and thereby render these accounts problematic when one tries to compare them from different countries—as we have cautioned throughout this report. Alternative ways of measuring criminal/delinquent behaviors (such as self-report surveys) should be used in comparative research.

Nevertheless, since our central concern is with the behavior of youths in two or more social environments, criminologists (comparative or otherwise) are free to choose to study whatever behaviors they find of interest—whether or not these behaviors are actually defined as illegal (or similarly so defined) in the legal codes of the social environments (countries) studied. Other criminologists have the right to question the inclusion or exclusion of various acts, of course. Undoubtedly the claim made by Schwendinger and Schwendinger (1970) that things like sexism, racism, and imperialism should fall within the proper realm of criminological interest would appeal to many. Others may favor Wilkins' (1980) argument that "social harms" be the focus of comparative study. More likely, Gibbons' (1994:45–51) suggestion that the law be used as our defining standard would be comfortable to most criminologists. In the study of "delinquent" behavior around the world, however, neither approach is *ipso facto* wrong (e.g., Rafter, 1992). For example, in the self-report inquiry conducted here, we included the act of "truancy" even though skipping school without a legitimate excuse is not an offense (status or otherwise) in India. But whether truancy is or is not "illegal" in the countries selected for comparative inquiry is of little consequence. If truancy is of interest to the researcher (for whatever reasons), its legal/illegal status could affect the kind of data sources one relies upon to investigate this behavior. But that fact alone does not render truancy a form of activity to be necessarily included or excluded from the research. The same is true of taking another person's life, whether it be called murder, homicide, manslaughter, or whatever, and whether or not it is defined as any of these things in an identical fashion across societies. Since few criminologists will ever directly observe the behaviors we hope to study, the rather unsatisfactory definitions of our discipline's realm provided by legal codes around the world will have to be used as guidelines for selecting the behavioral realm of our inquiry. They need not, however, dictate the exact dimensions of it.

But, what of legal codes and systems of justice? Although they have only been of marginal concern in this book, we would not mean to imply that they are marginal phenomena for comparative criminological research. Indeed, just the opposite! Whereas one concern of criminology is the behavior of "offenders," the equally intriguing and important realm of interest is the behavior of authorities in defining and responding to persons as "offenders."

While differences in legal codes and systems of justice could pose a problem for the comparative research of behavior, these differences are at the very heart of comparative research on criminal justice. Why do these differences exist? What impact does one approach have compared to another? What policy implications are found in the community-corrections approach taken in one country for dealing with offenders in some other? These, and a host of similar questions are of immediate relevance to comparative "criminal justice" research (see e.g., Bayley, 1985; Hackler, 1991; Los & Anderson, 1981; Selke, 1992; Terrill, 1984). Indeed, criminologists focusing on countries such as the United States have spent considerable effort in "comparing" various ways of dealing with crime (e.g., intensive parole versus regular parole, reactive policing versus community policing, retained versus public defense attorneys, etc.). Cross-national comparative research on the forms and operations of criminal justice systems in diverse societies simply offers a wider realm for similar research. Undoubtedly the problems of carrying out any such research multiply when cultural/legal/political borders are crossed, but the principles of such research are the same.

More directly, how different countries deal with "offenders" is of interest for its own sake. Here the concern is with the legal/social status (societal reaction to) of behavior, not the behavior itself (see e.g., Field, 1994; Lushing, 1982). Clearly, just as reaction may affect the occurrence of behavior, the occurrence of behavior may affect how it is viewed, defined, and reacted to in any society. An apparent increase in drug use behavior for example could spark new laws and/or more repressive police practices. Factors other than the type or frequencies of various acts occurring in some locality (e.g., media attention, political campaigns) could, of course, also affect societal reactions (Hartjen, 1977). And these should be a matter of direct criminological (as opposed to only sociological or political science) inquiry. Whatever the case, the focus of inquiry is on how societies (or those groups within them able to shape public policy) define and react to behaviors, why they do so, and what impact their reactions have on such activity and the lives of societal members (Chambliss & Seidman, 1982; Hartjen, 1978; Morden, 1980; Quinney, 1970).

In short, the interests of comparative criminology are the same as those of criminology generally. While diversity of laws and systems of justice may complicate the task of studying "criminal" or "delinquent" behaviors around the world, they need not negate it. And they open up a host of possibilities to study the subject of social control and the notion of justice. Whether the two (behavior/reaction) are universally (or in any way) related, of course, remains a matter for future comparative research to investigate also.

UNITS OF STUDY OR ARE NATIONS NECESSARY?

National borders are, of course, artificial constructs that circumscribe aggregates of people who may, but do not necessarily, share common cultures or social systems. With the possible exception of so called "radical," "Marxist," "conflict," etc. perspectives, no theory of criminal behavior or justice exists in criminology that uses "political state" as an explanatory dimension (Greenberg, 1981; Inciardi, 1980). What is assumed (but far from established) is that various aspects of culture (e.g., religious beliefs) and/or social systems (e.g., stratification system) affect criminal/delinquent behavior (if not its genesis, at least its rate) and possibly also the nature and operation of the legal-judicial systems of countries. As such, comparing the artificial constructs of nations (e.g., Canada vs. India) would seem to make no sense. And from the point of view of explanatory theory it does not. Why then compare delinquency rates cross-nationally when cross-culture or cross-society holds more theoretically relevant meaning?

Probably the best commentary on this point was offered by Melvin Kohn (1987) in his presidential address to the American Sociological Association. As Kohn indicates, the unit "nation" is perhaps irrelevant as far as explaining behavior (or rates of behavior) is concerned. One could instead study youths in culturally distinct environments (i.e., by income levels)—within and across countries—and test the explanatory ability of some etiological theory regarding some relevant criminological variable (i.e., child-rearing practices). Indeed, as argued here, whatever "causes" delinquency in one environment should be found operative in any other. To the extent that features of the different "cultures" affect the causal dimension, we should then find variations in rates across the units of study, the variations in culture then being explanatory of the variations in rates.

But unless comparative criminality is willing to adapt an ethnographic methodology, relatively little research of this kind is likely to materialize. And without large-scale survey research to accompany the ethnography, any extensive statements about variations in rates would be near impossible. Like it or not, almost all data pertaining to rates are gathered by and disseminated by governments in the form of arrest, court, or corrections statistics. That means nation states for the most part. In some places, breakdowns of these data adequate to distinguish cultural or social category groups (e.g., ethnic categories, income levels) distinct from the general national aggregate may exist. However, whether they can be compared meaningfully to a similar group designated in the statistics of some other country remains questionable. In most cases the question is mute anyway, since such categorizations are often absent from official statistics. Thus, until considerably more financial support is available to criminologists to conduct research around the world in which samples of research populations can be selected on the bases of theoretically relevant criteria, comparative criminological research will largely be cross-national criminological research relying on highly dubious government generated statistics as a principal source of data, with all the benefits and limitations that this entails.

On the other hand, since laws and systems of justice are by their very nature nation-state (government) creations, for comparative criminal justice research, the nation is, by definition, the ideal unit of analysis and the data it generates to count "offenses" and "offenders" the object of our inquiry. In that regard, cross-national research is essentially comparative criminal justice research (Scott & Zatz, 1981). Thus, for example, comparing how the political entities Poland and New Zealand define and treat delinquency (as revealed in their laws and official statistics) is itself the topic of interest. Arguably, law and justice systems reflect political systems (Chambliss, 1984; Quinney, 1975; Turk, 1982) and as the latter vary so should the former. Cultural and social system factors not directly related to political systems surely also influence societal reactions. The issue here, however, is the role of political states (power structures) in directing the lives of the inhabitants of nations via the enactment and enforcement of criminal laws. In that regard, comparative criminology is not only a behavioral science but a political science as well.

THE PROBLEM OF DATA

Whatever else confounds comparative criminological research, the fundamental problem we face in developing a criminology that is truly international is the simple lack of information. If, according to Gordon Hawkins (1991) criminology (in the United States) can be described as "data-starved," comparative or international criminology can be described as data-famished and theory-anhydrous. And this is especially true with regard to the behavior of, and societal reaction to, the world's youth. Indeed, even in economically developed countries with extensive laws regarding juveniles and years of criminological research regarding them, little material is often available to the researcher from government sources. And, as for original research, only scattered and extremely limited inquiries have been carried out. David Farrington's (1992: 161) comments in lamenting the lack of hard data to trace, much less explain, changes in delinquency rates in England are pertinent to comparative inquiry generally.

> In order to advance knowledge in the future, repeated surveys of nationally representative samples of juveniles ... are needed. These should enquire about different types of self-reported offending and about possible causal factors such as demographic characteristics, family composition . . . parental supervision and discipline, economic deprivation, alcohol and drug use, opportunities for offending, truancy, and perceptions of the probability and consequences of being caught for offending.

Such data are most often lacking for individual, even economically developed, nations. For many of the nations of the world no such information exists at all. The "international" self-report survey involving thirteen western (economically developed) countries is, of course, revealing and a major step in gaining an international understanding of delinquency (Junger-Tas et al., 1994). However, a study of thirteen western, economically developed countries is hardly "international." What, of course, would be ideal would be a truly international self-report survey sampling youths in countries around the world along the lines of the one described by Farrington. Any such survey would be beneficial, although a longitudinal study would be ideal. That being unlikely, even surveys of selected countries conducted at ten-year intervals would be highly useful. Even a "one shot" survey of purposively selected (better yet, randomly drawn) countries (given that a census would likely be impossible) would provide the kind of data needed to make any reasonable claims about the nature, extent, and distribution of "delinquent" forms of behavior throughout the world.

Other than the technical matters of the instrument design, sampling format, and the like, conducting even a one-shot self-report survey, much less a decennial sequence of surveys, of this kind is highly unlikely at this point in history. The funding and political obstacles we would have to overcome to carry out such an inquiry are simply overwhelming. However, it need not be abandoned as a future major criminological undertaking.

Farrington also notes that the self-report data we would want to gather should be supplemented by information from official records. As highly desirable as this may be, one of the remarkable things the comparative researcher discovers early in the game is how few countries actually publish, or even provide in archival form, such information (aside from how useful it might be). If we lack self-report data, we also lack reasonably available official data as well. Some "international" data sets exist, such as World Health Organization, INTERPOL, United Nations, etc. (see Bennett & Lynch, 1990; Block, 1984; Kalish, 1988). But these tend to lack age breakdowns allowing us to investigate "youth crime" as opposed to "total crime" in the contributing countries, and, even then, the offense categories often exclude much of the petty sorts of misconduct youths commit that may be of criminological or theoretical interest. Within countries, such information is often highly wanting where it does exist, but more often than not information of even remote relevance to criminological inquiry simply does not exist—no one collects it! This, of course, is more true of Third World compared to so-called developed nations. But even for many developed countries, national, comprehensive, reasonably reliable, and, to some extent, criminologically pertinent data cannot be found on such basic points as the number of persons between ages X and Y who are arrested each year, the number housed in correctional facilities (however these may be defined), or the number of youths formally charged, convicted, sentenced, and the like in "juvenile" or any other court.

Obviously criminologists cannot compel governments to collect information of interest to them or information of any kind at all. Indeed, the fact that some societies do not acquire offense and/or criminal justice statistics could be viewed as an important topic for cross-national criminal justice inquiry. Perhaps the country does not have a problem of proportions warranting the collection of data. Perhaps the government has something to conceal. Such questions have never been investigated in contemporary criminology. But, aside from the methodological issue of whether data can or cannot be compared, comparative criminology is likely to be plagued by having a world of comparative possibilities available to us with little information reasonably obtainable to draw upon in exploring them.

That simply means that comparative research will be severely hamstrung by being forced to rely on whatever data we can locate, beg, borrow, or in some cases "steal," (as was done often in the present inquiry) and/or be collected on our own (as was also attempted here). In the latter case, it makes breaking through the bureaucratic (much less language, etc.) barriers of government officials suspicious of criminologists wishing to investigate matters of possible sensitive concern. For example, it took almost three years after the grant was awarded for the Indian government to approve Hartjen's request to conduct the self-report survey of 1987. Whether the political maneuvering leading to the passage of the 1986 delinquency law had something to do with the delay or whether it was simply the work of a single gatekeeper bureaucrat cannot be known.

In other cases, convincing granting agencies to finance a study of youths in some foreign country is near impossible. The standard funding agencies devoted to criminological research in the United States, for example, show little interest in studies of children in countries like Uganda, Chili, Jordan, or even China (except insofar as the behavior of people in these countries has some direct relevance to the interests of the United States). It is doubtful, in turn, if India's Social Science Research Council would fund Indian criminologists to study delinquency in the United States. And that is true of virtually every other country. In short, even for those who would want to collect it, funds to gather the needed data for a truly comparative criminological enterprise are likely to be lacking in the foreseeable future.

These rather negative comments would seem to suggest that not only is comparative criminological research of possible dubious scientific merit but near to impossible to pursue in any case. Neither of these conclusions is, of course, true. Yet, in many ways, they are nearly so. But, as suggested by S. Priyadarsini in her review of this work, rather than focusing on what we cannot accomplish, future comparative research in criminology would best concentrate on what can be done and what insights and understanding we might gain from that attempt.

THE UNIVERSALITY OF DELINQUENCY

Before closing our discussion, we would like to return to a topic touched on throughout this book. Even though differences exist in delinquency rates, striking cross-national similarities also exist. These similarities may be indicative of a certain universality in the behavior of young people. Very simply, rates of youth crime and delinquent behavior appear to vary greatly both within and across national boundaries. But to the extent that we have any information at all, young people everywhere seem to engage in similar kinds of behavior with strikingly similar demographic distributions. In short, while adolescents throughout the world are not equally "delinquent," they are remarkably similar as to the kinds of crimes they commit as well as the relative prevalence and incidence distributions of this conduct as far as such variables as age, gender, social class, residence, and the like are concerned. If differences in social-economic-cultural arraignments are responsible for differences in rates of delinquent behavior, what about its universality? At this point, we can only offer some speculations on the matter.

The Etiology of Delinquent Behavior

No international or even cross-national study has ever been done testing the applicability of major etiological theories of criminal/delinquent behavior. Nor does any extensive research of this kind exist assessing the correlates of offense behavior conceivably related to the causal or enabling conditions. What we have is a handful of unrelated studies of varying sophistication and quality that attempt to test one or another causal variable or dimension on (usually) a single sample in specific countries. Outside the United States, the bulk of this research has been carried out in western European countries so that youths in Asia, Africa, South America, and elsewhere have received scant attention from criminologists. To make any conclusive statements about the "universality" of delinquency based on the existing body of research would, of course, be absurd. We can, however, offer a few speculations.

It is reasonable to argue that we do not yet have a general, scientifically validated, explanation of delinquent behavior in criminology (see Gibbons, 1994). But it is unreasonable to assume that the etiology of delinquency on the part of youths in the diverse countries of the world is the product of fundamentally different causal/facilitating conditions. Indeed, virtually all of the etiological research conducted around the world suggests that there are several commonalities in the etiology of delinquency. The few studies testing control and/or social learning theory in countries outside the United States have produced findings similar to those found by American research. All have supported the arguments of one or the other theory to some extent. It would thus appear that children everywhere who associate with delinquent peers and/or experience weak social bonds are likely to engage in delinquency. To the extent that these dimensions are part of a greater etiological nexus, it is quite likely that broad theoretical models incorporating these ideas may help explain the origins of delinquent acts everywhere to an extent criminological research has hitherto failed to do.

A much larger (relatively speaking) body of research has investigated a host of psychological, family, economic, situational, and other "background" dimensions as correlates of delinquent behavior. This research also suggests that youths who come to engage in delinquent acts or at least delinquent behavior serious or repetitive enough to bring them to the attention of authorities suffer the contingencies of poverty, social marginality, home-life discord and disruption, parental neglect and abuse, and psychological and emotional problems. In short, serious (if not all) delinquents tend to more often exhibit a host of traits likely to be associated with weak social/personal bonds and conducive of delinquent-peer group associations. Whether these traits cause them to be uncontrolled or involved with delinquent peers is not known. But what this research suggests is that similar kinds of social-emotional experiences (primarily concerning home and school) conspire to either produce or facilitate the kind of bonding/associational conditions that explain delinquency involvement. Although "strain" theories pertaining to some of these factors have not been strongly supported by existing research, perhaps new notions of strain will provide a more empirically sound framework allowing us to incorporate these findings into a more inclusive and powerful explanatory theory of etiology. Cross-national research can certainly help to more clearly identify what these factors might be.

Disregarding the issue of definitions of delinquency and realizing the national boundaries are likely to circumscribe our sample units, the problem of studying the etiology of delinquent behavior remains a vexing one. Existing research is largely based on samples of known offenders, sometimes compared to youths not so identified. While reasonable, given the pragmatic limitations affecting our research, drawing cross-national conclusions from this kind of inquiry requires a considerable leap of faith. Some good ethnographic research may help cast light on how various family arraignments, peer association patterns, child rearing patterns, or other such contingencies may relate to the delinquency of youths in various social settings. But it would take an extraordinary criminologist to conduct more than one such inquiry over the course of a career. Simply acquiring the necessary language skills, rapport, access, and the like to do such research would preclude carrying out much of it.

About the only readily usable data-gathering instrument that holds any promise of direct cross-national comparability of estimates of offense rates and types is the self-report survey. The primitive use of this instrument that we (and other researchers) have attempted in countries outside the United States suggests that this kind of research holds promise for testing etiological theory cross-nationally, but much more sophisticated instruments need to be developed. And, except for augmenting and partially validating official statistics, self-report research is of rather limited value as far as assessing the national extent and distribution of serious forms of criminal behavior.

Epidemiology: Variations in Rates

Very little (in the concrete sense) is actually known about the prevalence, incidence, and relative distribution of delinquent forms of behavior throughout the world. Indeed, even in countries where extensive criminological research has been carried out, we often have very little information about rates of offense behavior among young people. The fundamental information essential for a truly international science of criminology is simply lacking. Yet the little we do know or know about is suggestive.

As particularly revealed by self-report research, most children in most societies engage in a considerable amount of "mischief," "status-type," behaviors and mild forms of property and personal criminality. More or less of this misconduct may be committed by children in different societies, but such conduct as cheating on tests, experimenting with forbidden substances, defying parents, mild forms of vandalism, petty stealing, and fighting appears to be universal. Moreover, while variable, extreme differences in prevalence and incidence rates for most of this activity are not found. In that regard, the kind of delinquency best classified as "misconduct" rather than crime appears to be something young people as such engage in. While interesting for its own sake, this conduct could probably be excluded from future research focused on criminal forms of activity.

As far as crime is concerned, considerably greater differences in offense rates seem to exist across societies. Since most of our information in this regard is derived from official statistics, and since very little is known as to the organizational and other factors affecting the counting of crime in various societies, it is difficult to say how much of this variability is due to behavioral as opposed to labeling differences.

But criminal activity on the part of young people throughout the world does seem to be highly similar insofar as broad categories of crime are concerned. Localized departures from these broad dimensions may reflect idiosyncratic features of social systems that warrant special investigation. But youths everywhere seem to most often engage in property offenses, largely consisting of direct-predatory forms of theft that usually involve low levels of skill or organization such as purse snatching, residential burglary, shoplifting, and the like. More organized, frequent, and sophisticated forms of these activities (e.g., auto theft, armed robberies, burglaries of businesses, highjacking, etc.) may occur among youths belonging to delinquent gangs or among older youths who have acquired experience in criminal activity. The existence of gangs or numbers of career criminals may vary cross-nationally due to a variety of factors yet to be investigated, but, for the bulk of the world's juvenile population, petty, as opposed to serious repetitive, criminality appears to be more characteristic.

In spite of the considerable media and law enforcement attention youth violence has received in countries like the United States in recent years, other than fighting and occasional extortion, violent crime appears to be a relatively small part of youthful crime just about everywhere. Countries undergoing extreme political strife may produce exceptionally high rates of violent behavior by young people as a part or consequence of that strife, but, ordinarily, young people are relatively nonviolent compared to their engagement in other forms of crime and to adults.

Finally, engagement in substance abuse behavior, especially the use of alcohol and narcotic drugs, also shows considerable variability around the world. But aside from youthful experimentation, substance abuse is apparently fairly infrequent among most of the world's youth. In that respect, the image of the teenage addict is more of an anomaly than characteristic of young people throughout the world.

In short, an accurate behavioral profile of the "juvenile delinquent" that would probably most closely correspond to reality internationally would be someone engaged in mild mischief, occasionally in low-level theft or property crimes, who has experimented with one or a few illegal substances and has not committed serious or violent acts of criminal behavior at all. Future cross-national research needs to test the accuracy of this description, to assess the degree to which youths in various societies may depart from it, and explain why they do so.

Similar to forms of offense behavior, considerable uniformity probably also exists in the demographic distribution of delinquency. It would appear that the major demographic correlates of delinquency (gender, age, and social class) have much in common throughout the world.

Boys everywhere are more delinquent than girls and more seriously delinquent in terms of the kinds of behavior and frequency of misconduct they commit. Over all, boys and girls may be more similar than adult men and women insofar as types and frequencies of behavior are concerned, but the gender gap is only mildly influenced by age. Thus, while wide cross-national differences probably exist in the size of the gender gap (as with Indian compared to American youths), more young males everywhere manifest more, and more serious forms of, delinquent behavior than do young females. Comparative research regarding the situations of boys and girls in different societies as these are related to their relative rates may help us understand the reasons for and implications of the universal gender gap.

Whether or not laws and special systems of juvenile justice similar to those in the United States exist specifically defining acts such as truancy, consuming alcoholic beverages, or having sexual intercourse below specific ages, involvement in criminal and "delinquent" forms of behavior seems to vary by age in a similar pattern throughout the world. There are probably extreme differences to be found in this regard given the limitations of self-report research and the peculiarities of official statistics, but, in a general sense, involvement in misconduct seems to increase progressively from childhood to later adolescence, reaching a peak in late teens and then declining substantially thereafter. For example, when Indians are compared to American youths, the specific ages at which these events may occur could vary widely (reflecting cultural concepts of youth and the social-economic contingencies people in various countries face at different ages). However, it is likely that something similar to the age-criminality curve often used to depict the delinquency patterns of American youths would be found universally. Assuming this is the case, why it should be so and why the configuration of the age-delinquency curve may vary remain unknown. The theoretical and policy implications of such a possibility call for broader international inquiry in criminology.

Self-report findings in western nations have typically raised questions about a causal link between social class and delinquency, something our self-report data found for India also. In part, this may reflect the fact that self-report research taps a realm of comparatively innocuous behavior that young people everywhere commit regardless of their particular station in life. It could also mean that no such link actually exists. Research conducted from countries around the world having a variety of social/economic characteristics is needed to more adequately assess this putative association or lack thereof.

However, official arrest, court, and corrections statistics tell another story wherever they are collected. Invariably offenders are drawn from the ranks of the poor. In that regard, while involvement in delinquency is universal, one's chances of becoming officially so recognized are universally dependent on one's social status.

Whether this apparent fact reflects subtle differences in the actual delinquent activity of poor and more privileged youths or a kind of general use of the agencies of justice to repress the under class remains a matter of debate. Indeed, stealing chalk from an unattended classroom versus stealing food from a vender's cart are both "theft," but they are acts of fundamentally different kinds having fundamentally different potential consequences. As numerous studies in western societies also show, social class not only has implications for the types of delinquency youths may commit but for how different juveniles are viewed and reacted to. In this regard, comparative criminological research can not only cast light on why an apparent discrepancy in offense rates exists between economically developed versus economically developing nations but also on why the poor in all societies seem to bear the brunt of criminal justice attention.

CONCLUSION

This exercise in rather gross overgeneralization, given the lack of reliable data to support any claims whatsoever about delinquency around the world, is perhaps more a call for cross-national comparative research than an assertion of fact. Whether or not the world's young people are, or are not, similarly delinquent remains to be explored. Whatever the case, the implications of either finding are profound.

English-Language Version of 1987 Questionnaire

INDIAN INSTITUTE OF PUBLIC ADMINISTRATION
AMERICAN INSTITUTE OF INDIAN STUDIES
ADOLESCENT BEHAVIOR STUDY
We are conducting a study that compares the behavior of young people in India with youngsters in other countries. We would appreciate your helping us with this study by filling out the questionnaire given to you by the researcher. You are not identified on the questionnaire in any way and your answers are strictly confidential. So please try to answer each question as honestly as you can. If you have any difficulty with the questions, raise your hand and the researcher will try to help you.

Thank you for your help. Now please turn the page to PART I. Choose only one answer for each question.

PART I
First we would like to know something about the people who have agreed to help us with our study. Given below are several questions. Please check the most appropriate answer for each by placing a check mark (X) in the appropriate blank space provided.

1. How old are you?
    _____ 1. 8–10 years old
    _____ 2. 11–13 years old
    _____ 3. 14 years old
    _____ 4. 15 years old
    _____ 5. 16 years old
    _____ 6. 17 years old

2. How many years of school have you completed?
    _____ 1. 0–3 years of school
    _____ 2. 4–6 years of school
    _____ 3. 7–9 years of school
    _____ 4. 10 years of school
    _____ 5. 11 years of school
    _____ 6. 12 years of school

3. Is your father or guardian employed?
   _____ 1. yes
   _____ 2. no
   _____ 3. don't know
4. If your father or guardian is employed, what is his/her occupation? Please describe in detail.

   _____

   _____

   _____

5. Approximately what do you think is his/her income per month?
   _____ 1. less than Rs. 500
   _____ 2. between Rs. 500 and 999
   _____ 3. between Rs. 1000 and 1499
   _____ 4. Rs. 1500 or more
6. What is your religion?
   _____ 1. none
   _____ 2. Hindu
   _____ 3. Muslim
   _____ 4. Christian
   _____ 5. Any other (describe in detail)
7. I am a:
   _____ 1. Boy
   _____ 2. Girl

Thank you for your answers. Now please turn the page to PART II and answer each of the questions in that section.

PART II

Every community has certain rules of conduct that its citizens are expected to follow. However, scientific research shows that irrespective of age everyone violates some standards. Below is a list of acts. We would like to know which, if any, of these activities you have engaged in within the last year. Please put a check mark (X) in the appropriate blank space for each act that indicates how many times you have committed the act within the last three years.

Since you cannot be identified by the questionnaire, answer each question accurately and fully.

1. Have you ever intentionally damaged or destroyed public or private property? (vandalism)
   _____ 1. no
   _____ 2. once or twice
   _____ 3. several times
   _____ 4. very often

2. Have you ever stolen (or tried to steal) a motor vehicle such as a car or motorcycle? (auto theft)
　　_____ 1. no
　　_____ 2. once or twice
　　_____ 3. several times
　　_____ 4. very often
3. Have you ever stolen (or tried to steal) something worth more than Rs. 500? (grand theft)
　　_____ 1. no
　　_____ 2. once or twice
　　_____ 3. several times
　　_____ 4. very often
4. Have you ever knowingly bought, sold, or held stolen goods (or tried to do any of these things)? (stolen property)
　　_____ 1. no
　　_____ 2. once or twice
　　_____ 3. several times
　　_____ 4. very often
5. Have you ever thrown objects (such as rocks, bottles) at cars or people? (thrown objects)
　　_____ 1. no
　　_____ 2. once or twice
　　_____ 3. several times
　　_____ 4. very often
6. Have you ever run away from home? (run away)
　　_____ 1. no
　　_____ 2. once or twice
　　_____ 3. several times
　　_____ 4. very often
7. Have you ever tried to get something by lying about your age? (lying)
　　_____ 1. no
　　_____ 2. once or twice
　　_____ 3. several times
　　_____ 4. very often
8. Have you ever carried a concealed weapon other than a small knife? (weapon)
　　_____ 1. very often
　　_____ 2. several times
　　_____ 3. once or twice
　　_____ 4. no

9. Have you ever stolen (or tried to steal) something worth less than Rs. 50? (petty theft)
  _____ 1. very often
  _____ 2. several times
  _____ 3. once or twice
  _____ 4. no

10. Have you ever attacked someone with the idea of seriously hurting or killing him/her? (assault)
  _____ 1. no
  _____ 2. once or twice
  _____ 3. several times
  _____ 4. very often

11. Have you ever been involved in a gang fight? (gang fight)
  _____ 1. very often
  _____ 2. several times
  _____ 3. once or twice
  _____ 4. no

12. Have you ever sold marijuana or hashish ("pot," "grass," "hash")? (sold soft drugs)
  _____ 1. no
  _____ 2. once or twice
  _____ 3. several times
  _____ 4. very often

13. Have you ever cheated on a school test? (cheated)
  _____ 1. no
  _____ 2. once or twice
  _____ 3. several times
  _____ 4. very often

14. Have you ever stolen money or other things from your parents or other members of your family? (steal from family)
  _____ 1. no
  _____ 2. once or twice
  _____ 3. several times
  _____ 4. very often

15. Have you ever hit or struck one of your parents? (hit parent)
  _____ 1. very often
  _____ 2. several times
  _____ 3. once or twice
  _____ 4. no

16. Have you ever been loud, rowdy, or unruly in a public place? (disorderly conduct)
    _____ 1. no
    _____ 2. once or twice
    _____ 3. several times
    _____ 4. very often
17. Have you ever sold hard drugs such as heroin or cocaine? (sold hard drugs)
    _____ 1. no
    _____ 2. once or twice
    _____ 3. several times
    _____ 4. very often
18. Have you ever driven a car without the owner's permission? (joy ride)
    _____ 1. very often
    _____ 2. several times
    _____ 3. once or twice
    _____ 4. no
19. Have you ever used force to get money from another person? (extortion)
    _____ 1. very often
    _____ 2. several times
    _____ 3. once or twice
    _____ 4. no
20. Have you ever avoided paying for such things as movies, bus or train rides, and food? (avoid payment)
    _____ 1. no
    _____ 2. once or twice
    _____ 3. several times
    _____ 4. very often
21. Have you ever been drunk in a public place? (public drunkenness)
    _____ 1. no
    _____ 2. once or twice
    _____ 3. several times
    _____ 4. very often
22. Have you ever stolen (or tried to steal) something worth between Rs. 50 and Rs. 500? (moderate theft)
    _____ 1. no
    _____ 2. once or twice
    _____ 3. several times
    _____ 4. very often

23. Have you ever stolen (or tried to steal) something at school, such as books, pencils, or maps? (steal from school)
_____ 1. no
_____ 2. once or twice
_____ 3. several times
_____ 4. very often

24. Have you ever broken into a building or vehicle (or tried to break in) to steal something or just to look around? (break and enter)
_____ 1. very often
_____ 2. several times
_____ 3. once or twice
_____ 4. no

25. Have you ever begged for money or things from strangers? (begging)
_____ 1. no
_____ 2. once or twice
_____ 3. several times
_____ 4. very often

26. Have you ever skipped school without a legitimate reason? (truancy)
_____ 1. no
_____ 2. once or twice
_____ 3. several times
_____ 4. very often

27. Have you ever used substances like marijuana or ganja? (used soft drugs)
_____ 1. no
_____ 2. once or twice
_____ 3. several times
_____ 4. very often

28. Have you ever drunk alcoholic beverages such as beer or whisky? (drank alcohol)
_____ 1. very often
_____ 2. several times
_____ 3. once or twice
_____ 4. no

29. Have you ever used substances like heroin or cocaine? (hard drug use)
_____ 1. no
_____ 2. once or twice
_____ 3. several times
_____ 4. very often

30. Have you ever gotten into trouble with the police for anything that you have done yourself? (police trouble)
_____ 1. no
_____ 2. once or twice
_____ 3. several times
_____ 4. very often

31. Have you ever appeared before a judge or magistrate for something that you did? (court appearance)
_____ 1. no
_____ 2. once or twice
_____ 3. several times
_____ 4. very often

32. Have you ever been punished by a school official or head master for things you did? (school trouble)
_____ 1. very often
_____ 2. several times
_____ 3. once or twice
_____ 4. no

Thank you for helping us with our study. Please make sure you have answered all the questions.

English-Language Version of 1990 Questionnaire

YOUTH SURVEY

We are conducting a study that compares the attitudes, beliefs, and behavior of young people in India with youngsters in the United States. We would appreciate your helping us with this study by filling out the questionnaire given to you by the researchers. In order for our study to be valid, you must be open and honest in your answers. Your answers will be kept confidential, and no one outside our research team will ever see your responses. If you have any difficulty with the questions, raise your hand and the researcher will try to help you. Choose only ONE answer for each question.

PART I

1. What is your age? (Write in your age)

   _____

2. What is your gender? (Check (X) one answer only)
   _____ Boy
   _____ Girl

3. What is your religion? (Check (X) one answer only)

   _____ None
   _____ Hindu
   _____ Muslim
   _____ Christian
   _____ Any other (describe in detail)

   _____

4. What is your grade level (standard in school)? (Write your grade level in school)

   _____

5. What is your grade point average in school?
    (IF ANSWER CANNOT BE TRANSLATED INTO THE PERCENT-
    AGE SCALE BELOW, SELECT YOUR LETTER GRADE).
Check (X) one answer only.

_____ 60 % and above or   _____ Mostly A's
_____ 50–59 %   or   _____ Mostly B's
_____ 40–49 %   or   _____ Mostly C's
_____ 39 % and below or   _____ Mostly D's or F's

6. What is your father/guardian's income per month?
Check (X) one answer only.

_____ Less than Rs. 500
_____ Between Rs. 500 and 999
_____ Between Rs. 1000 and 1499
_____ Between Rs. 1500 and 1999
_____ Rs. 2000 or more

PART II
Please give us your best estimate of the exact number of times you've engaged
in each behavior during the last school year. Your answers to these questions
cover things which have happened during the last SCHOOL year.

Answers to these questions are confidential and you will not be identified by
this questionnaire. Circle ONE number for each question.

How many times in the LAST YEAR have you:

7. purposely   0 1 2 3 4 5 6 7 8 9 10 or more
damaged or destroyed
property that did not
belong to you?

8. stolen (or tried 0 1 2 3 4 5 6 7 8 9 10 or more
to steal) a motor
vehicle, such as a
car, motorcycle or bicycle?

9. stolen or tried   0 1 2 3 4 5 6 7 8 9   10 or more
to steal something
worth more
than Rs. 500?

10. knowingly   0 1 2 3 4 5 6 7 8 9   10 or more
bought, sold or held
stolen goods (or tried
to do any of these things)?

11. thrown objects   0 1 2 3 4 5 6 7 8 9   10 or more
(such as rocks, bottles)
at cars or people?

12. run away from   0 1 2 3 4 5 6 7 8 9   10 or more
home?

13. lied about your   0 1 2 3 4 5 6 7 8 9   10 or more
age?

14. carried a hidden   0 1 2 3 4 5 6 7 8 9   10 or more
weapon other than a
plain pocket knife?

15. stolen (or tried   0 1 2 3 4 5 6 7 8 9   10 or more
to steal) things worth
Rs. 50 or less?

16. attacked   0 1 2 3 4 5 6 7 8 9   10 or more
someone with the
idea of seriously
hurting or killing him/her?

17. been involved   0 1 2 3 4 5 6 7 8 9   10 or more
in gang fight?

18. sold marijuana   0 1 2 3 4 5 6 7 8 9   10 or more
or hashish ("pot,"
"grass," "ganja," "hash")?

19. cheated on   0 1 2 3 4 5 6 7 8 9   10 or more
school tests?

20. stolen money   0 1 2 3 4 5 6 7 8 9 10 or more
from your family
members?

21. hit (or threaten   0 1 2 3 4 5 6 7 8 9 10 or more
to hit) a teacher or
other adult at school?

22. hit (or threaten   0 1 2 3 4 5 6 7 8 9 10 or more
to hit) one of your
parents?

23. hit (or threaten   0 1 2 3 4 5 6 7 8 9 10 or more
to hit) other students?

24. been loud,   0 1 2 3 4 5 6 7 8 9 10 or more
rowdy, or unruly in a public
place (disorderly conduct)?

25. sold hard drugs   0 1 2 3 4 5 6 7 8 9 10 or more
such as heroin or
cocaine?

26. taken a vehicle   0 1 2 3 4 5 6 7 8 9 10 or more
(such as a car,
motorcycle or bicycle)
for a ride (drive)
without the owner's permission?

27. used force   0 1 2 3 4 5 6 7 8 9 10 or more
(strong-arm methods)
to get money or things
from other students?

28. used force   0 1 2 3 4 5 6 7 8 9 10 or more
(strong-arm methods)
to get money or
things from a teacher or
other adult at school?

29. used force   0 1 2 3 4 5 6 7 8 9   10 or more
(strong-arm methods)
to get money or things
from other people (not
students or teachers)?

30. avoided paying   0 1 2 3 4 5 6 7 8 9   10 or more
for such things as movies,
bus or train rides, and food?

31. been drunk in a   0 1 2 3 4 5 6 7 8 9   10 or more
public place?

32. stolen (or   0 1 2 3 4 5 6 7 8 9   10 or more
tried to steal)
things worth between
Rs. 50 and Rs. 500?

33. stolen (or tried   0 1 2 3 4 5 6 7 8 9   10 or more
to steal) something at school?

34. broken into a   0 1 2 3 4 5 6 7 8 9   10 or more
building or vehicle
(or tried to break in) to
steal something or just to look
around?

35. begged for   0 1 2 3 4 5 6 7 8 9   10 or more
money or things
from strangers?

36. skipped school   0 1 2 3 4 5 6 7 8 9   10 or more
without a
legitimate reason?

37. used soft drugs   0 1 2 3 4 5 6 7 8 9   10 or more
such as marijuana or
hashish ("pot," "grass,"
"ganja," "hash")?

38. drank alcohol   0   1   2   3   4   5   6   7   8   9   10 or more
beverages such as
beer, wine or whisky?

39. used hard drugs   0   1   2   3   4   5   6   7   8   9   10 or more
such as heroin or
cocaine?

PART III
NOW LET'S TALK ABOUT YOUR FRIENDS.

40. Is there a particular group of CLOSE FRIENDS that you run around
with? Check (X) one answer only.

_____ Yes   —————————>   IF YES, CONTINUE
_____ No   —————————>   IF YOU DO NOT HAVE A PARTICULAR
                                                 GROUP OF CLOSE FRIENDS, SKIP TO
                                                 QUESTION 47.

Keep in mind your particular group of CLOSE FRIENDS when answering
these questions.

41. Whom do you consider to be your CLOSE friends? Check (X) one
answer only.

_____ Sisters and brothers
_____ Cousins
_____ Classmates
_____ Neighbors

42. On the average, how many afternoons during the school week, from the
end of school to dinner, have you spent with your CLOSE friends?
(Circle ONE number only)   0   1   2   3   4   5   6

43. On the average, how many evenings during the school week, from
dinner to bed time, have you spent with your CLOSE friends? (Circle
ONE number only)   0   1   2   3   4   5   6

44. On the weekends, how much time have you generally spent with your CLOSE friends? (Circle ONE answer only)

A Great Deal	Quite a Bit	Some	Not Too Much	Very Little
5	4	3	10	13

45. How much have your CLOSE friends influenced what you've thought and done? (Circle ONE answer only)

A Great Deal	Quite a Bit	Some	Not Too Much	Very Little
5	4	3	2	1

46. How important has it been to you to have a group of CLOSE FRIENDS and be included in their activities?

Very Important	Pretty Important	Somewhat Important	Not Too Important	Not Important at All
5	4	3	2	1

PART IV
NOW LET'S TALK ABOUT SCHOOL

47. On the average, how many afternoons during the school week, from the end of school to dinner, have you spent studying? (Circle ONE number only) 0 1 2 3 4 5 6

48. On the average, how many evenings during the school week, from dinner time to bedtime, have you spent studying?

0 1 2 3 4 5 6

49. On the weekends, how much time have you generally spent studying?

A Great Deal	Quite a Bit	Some	Not Too Much	Very Little
5	4	3	2	1

50. How important has your school work been to you?

Very Important	Pretty Important	Somewhat Important	Not Too Important	Not Important at All
5	4	3	2	1

51. Have you been a member of any athletic teams at school?

_____ Yes ————————> IF YES, SKIP TO QUESTION 53
_____ No ————————> IF NO, ANSWER QUESTION 52, THEN
SKIP TO QUESTION 57

52.   How important is it to you to be on an athletic team at school?

Very Important	Pretty Important	Somewhat Important	Not Too Important	Not Important at All
5	4	3	2	1

SKIP TO QUESTION 57

53.   On the average, how many afternoons during the school week, from the end of school to dinner, have you spent on team activities?

0   1   2   3   4   5   6

54.   On the average, how many evenings during the school week, from the end of school to dinner, have you spent on team activities?

0   1   2   3   4   5   6

55.   On the weekends, how much time have you generally spent on team activities?

A Great Deal	Quite a Bit	Some	Not Too Much	Very Little
5	4	3	2	1

56.   How important have school athletics been to you?

Very Important	Pretty Important	Somewhat Important	Not Too Important	Not Important at All
5	4	3	2	1

PART V
NOW LET'S TALK ABOUT YOUR FAMILY

57.   On the average, how many afternoons during the school week, from the end of school to dinner, have you spent talking, working, or playing with your family members?

0   1   2   3   4   5   6

58.   On the average, how many evenings during the school week, from dinner time to bedtime, have you spent talking, working, or playing with your family?

0   1   2   3   4   5   6

59. On the weekends, how much time have you generally spent talking, working, playing with your family?

A Great Deal	Quite a Bit	Some	Not Too Much	Very Little
5	4	3	2	1

60. How important have the things you've done with your family been to you?

Very Important	Pretty Important	Somewhat Important	Not Too Important	Not Important at All
5	4	3	2	1

61. How much have your parents influenced what you've thought and done?

A Great Deal	Quite a Bit	Some	Not Too Much	Very Little
5	4	3	2	1

PART VI

NOW WE WOULD LIKE TO ASK YOU HOW IMPORTANT CERTAIN THINGS ARE TO YOU AND HOW YOU ARE DOING AT THESE THINGS. THIS SECTION HAS TWO PARTS. THE FIRST SECTION ASKS HOW IMPORTANT EACH GOAL IS TO YOU; THE SECOND SECTION ASKS HOW WELL ARE YOU DOING AT ACHIEVING THAT GOAL.

SECTION I	SECTION II
HOW IMPORTANT IS IT TO YOU?	HOW WELL ARE YOU DOING ACHIEVING THIS GOAL?

	Very Important	Somewhat Important	Not Important	Very well	O.K.	Not Well at all	Don't Know
62. to have a family that does lots of things together?	5	3	1	5	3	1	0

63.   to have other students
think of you as a good
student?

5	3	1	5	3	1	0

64.   to have parents you can
talk to about almost every-
thing?

5	3	1	5	3	1	0

65.   to do well in hard
subjects?

5	3	1	5	3	1	0

66.   to be asked to take
part in things your friends
do, such as going to parties
and games?

5	3	1	5	3	1	0

67.   to have parents who
comfort you when you're
unhappy about something?

5	3	1	5	3	1	0

68.   to do your own school
work without help from
anybody?

5	3	1	5	3	1	0

69.   to have your parents
think you do things well?

5	3	1	5	3	1	0

70.   to have teachers think
of you as a good student?

5	3	1	5	3	1	0

71.   to have friends ask to
spend time and do things
with you?

5	3	1	5	3	1	0

72.   to have a high
grade point average?

5	3	1	5	3	1	0

73.   to get along well with
your parents?

5	3	1	5	3	1	0

PART VII
THE NEXT SET OF QUESTIONS DEAL WITH YOUR FUTURE GOALS.

	Very Important	Somewhat Important	Not Important	Don't Know
How important is it to you:				
74. to have a good job/career after you've finished with school?	5	3	1	0
75. to go to college?	5	3	1	0

	Good	Fair	Poor	Don't Know
What do you think your chances are for:				
76. getting the kind of job you would like to have after finishing school?	3	2	1	0
77. completing a college degree?	3	2	1	0

PART VIII

THE NEXT SET OF QUESTIONS ASK ABOUT YOUR FEELINGS AND BELIEFS. PLEASE ANSWER HOW MUCH YOU AGREE OR DISAGREE WITH THESE STATEMENTS ABOUT YOU.

	Strongly Agree	Agree	Neither Agree nor Disagree	Strongly Disagree	Disagree	Don't Know
78. It's important to be honest with your parents, even if they become upset or you get punished.	5	4	3	2	1	0
79. To stay out of trouble, it is sometimes necessary to lie to teachers.	5	4	3	2	1	0
80. Making a good impression is more important than telling the truth to friends.	5	4	3	2	1	0
81. At school it is sometimes necessary to play dirty in order to win.	5	4	3	2	1	0
82. It's okay to lie if it keeps your friends out of trouble.	5	4	3	2	1	0
83. Making a good impression is more important than telling the truth to parents.	5	4	3	2	1	0
84. In order to gain the respect of your friends, it's sometimes necessary to beat up on other kids.	5	4	3	2	1	0

85. You can make it in school without having to cheat on exams/tests.	5	4	3	2	1	0
86. You have to be willing to break some rules if you want to be popular with your friends.	5	4	3	2	1	0
87. Sometimes it's necessary to lie to your parents in order to keep their trust.	5	4	3	2	1	0
88. It is important to do your own work at school even if it means some kids won't like you.	5	4	3	2	1	0
89. It may be necessary to break some of your parents' rules in order to keep some of your friends.	5	4	3	2	1	0
90. Making a good impression is more important than telling the truth to teachers.	5	4	3	2	1	0

PART IX

THE NEXT SET OF QUESTIONS WILL ASK YOU HOW YOUR PARENTS, FRIENDS, AND TEACHERS WOULD DESCRIBE YOU. HOW MUCH DO YOU THINK YOUR PARENTS WOULD AGREE WITH THAT DESCRIPTION OF YOU? PLEASE SELECT ONLY ONE ANSWER FOR EACH QUESTION.

THIS SECTION IS ABOUT YOUR PARENTS

	Strongly Agree	Agree	Neither Agree nor Disagree	Strongly Disagree	Disagree	Don't Know
How much would your PARENTS agree that you . . .						
91. are well liked	5	4	3	2	1	0
92. need help	5	4	3	2	1	0
93. are a bad kid	5	4	3	2	1	0
94. are a good citizen	5	4	3	2	1	0
95. get along well with other people	5	4	3	2	1	0
96. break rules	5	4	3	2	1	0
97. have a lot of personal problems	5	4	3	2	1	0
98. get into trouble	5	4	3	2	1	0
99. are likely to succeed	5	4	3	2	1	0
100. do things that are against the law	5	4	3	2	1	0

THE NEXT SECTION IS ABOUT YOUR FRIENDS (EVEN IF THEY ARE NOT CLOSE FRIENDS)

How much would your FRIENDS agree that you:

	Strongly Agree	Agree	Neither Agree nor Disagree	Strongly Disagree	Disagree	Don't Know
101. are well liked	5	4	3	2	1	0
102. need help	5	4	3	2	1	0
103. are a bad kid	5	4	3	2	1	0
104. are a good citizen	5	4	3	2	1	0
105. get along well with other people	5	4	3	2	1	0
106. break rules	5	4	3	2	1	0
107. have a lot of personal problems	5	4	3	2	1	0
108. get into trouble	5	4	3	2	1	0
109. are likely to succeed	5	4	3	2	1	0
110. do things that are against the law	5	4	3	2	1	0

THE NEXT SECTION IS ABOUT YOUR TEACHERS

		Strongly Agree	Agree	Neither Agree nor Disagree	Strongly Disagree	Disagree	Don't Know
How much would your TEACHERS agree that you:							
111.	are well liked	5	4	3	2	1	0
112.	need help	5	4	3	2	1	0
113.	are a bad kid	5	4	3	2	1	0
114.	are a good citizen	5	4	3	2	1	0
115.	get along well with other people	5	4	3	2	1	0
116.	break rules	5	4	3	2	1	0
117.	have a lot of personal problems	5	4	3	2	1	0
118.	get into trouble	5	4	3	2	1	0
119.	are likely to succeed	5	4	3	2	1	0
120.	do things that are against the law	5	4	3	2	1	0

PART X
THE NEXT SET OF QUESTIONS ASK YOU HOW YOUR PARENTS
WOULD REACT IF YOU DID EACH OF THE FOLLOWING THINGS.

	Strongly Dis-approve	Dis-approve	Neither Approve nor Dis-approve	Approve	Strongly Approve	Don't Know
How would your PARENTS react if you:						
121. kept promises you made to others	5	4	3	2	1	0
122. cheated on school tests	5	4	3	2	1	0
123. stole something worth less than Rs.5	5	4	3	2	1	0
124. sold hard drugs such as heroin and cocaine	5	4	3	2	1	0
125. returned money you found or any extra change a cashier gave you	5	4	3	2	1	0
126. used marijuana or hashish	5	4	3	2	1	0
127. stole something worth more than Rs.50	5	4	3	2	1	0
128. hit or threatened to hit someone without any reason	5	4	3	2	1	0

129. used alcohol	5	4	3	2	1	0
130. did a favor for someone without being asked	5	4	3	2	1	0
131. purposely damaged or destroyed property that did not belong to you	5	4	3	2	1	0
132. broke into a vehicle or building to steal something	5	4	3	2	1	0

PART XI

THE NEXT SET OF QUESTIONS ASK YOU HOW WOULD YOUR CLOSE FRIENDS REACT IF YOU DID EACH OF THE FOLLOWING THINGS. (IF YOU DO NOT HAVE CLOSE FRIENDS, SKIP TO QUESTION 145.)

	Strongly Dis-approve	Dis-approve	Neither Approve nor Dis-approve	Approve	Strongly Approve	Don't Know
How would your CLOSE FRIENDS react if you:						
133. kept promises you made to others	5	4	3	2	1	0
134. cheated on school tests	5	4	3	2	1	0
135. stole something worth less than Rs.5	5	4	3	2	1	0
136. sold hard drugs such as heroin and cocaine	5	4	3	2	1	0

137. returned money you found or any extra change a cashier gave you	5	4	3	2	1	0
138. used marijuana or hashish	5	4	3	2	1	0
139. stole something worth more than Rs.50	5	4	3	2	1	0
140. hit or threatened to hit someone without any reason	5	4	3	2	1	0
141. used alcohol	5	4	3	2	1	0
142. did a favor for someone without being asked	5	4	3	2	1	0
143. purposely damaged or destroyed property that did not belong to you	5	4	3	2	1	0
144. broke into a vehicle or building to steal something	5	4	3	2	1	0

PART XII

FOR THIS NEXT SET OF QUESTIONS, PLEASE TELL US HOW WRONG YOU THINK EACH OF THE FOLLOWING THINGS IS FOR YOU OR SOMEONE OF YOUR AGE.

How wrong is it for someone your age to:	Very Wrong	Wrong	A Little Bit Wrong	Not Wrong At All	Don't Know
145. cheat on school tests	4	3	2	1	0

146.	purposely damage or destroy property that does not belong to him or her	4	3	2	1	0
147.	use ganja or hashish	4	3	2	1	0
148.	steal something worth less than Rs.5	4	3	2	1	0
149.	hit or threaten to hit someone without any reason	4	3	2	1	0
150.	use alcohol	4	3	2	1	0
151.	break into a vehicle or building to steal something	4	3	2	1	0
152.	sell hard drugs such as heroin or cocaine	4	3	2	1	0
153.	steal something worth more than Rs.50	4	3	2	1	0
154.	give or sell alcohol to kids under 18	4	3	2	1	0

PART XIII
THINK OF YOUR CLOSE FRIENDS. (IF YOU DO NOT HAVE ANY CLOSE FRIENDS, SKIP THESE QUESTIONS.)

		All of Them	Most of Them	Some of Them	Very Few of Them	None of Them	Don't Know
During the last year how many of your CLOSE FRIENDS have:							
155.	cheated on school tests	5	4	3	2	1	0
156.	purposely damaged or destroyed property that did not belong to them	5	4	3	2	1	0

157.	used ganja or hashish	5	4	3	2	1	0
158.	stolen something worth less than Rs.5	5	4	3	2	1	0
159.	hit or threatened to hit someone without any reason	5	4	3	2	1	0
160.	used alcohol	5	4	3	2	1	0
161.	broken into a vehicle or building to steal something	5	4	3	2	1	0
162.	sold hard drugs such as heroin and cocaine	5	4	3	2	1	0
163.	stolen something worth more than Rs.50	5	4	3	2	1	0
164.	suggested you do something that was against the law	5	4	3	2	1	0
165.	used alcohol once in awhile	5	4	3	2	1	0
166.	sold or given alcohol to kids under 18	5	4	3	2	1	0

PART XIV
NOW WE WOULD LIKE TO ASK WHAT YOU THINK ABOUT YOUR CLOSE FRIENDS' BEHAVIOR. (IF YOU DO NOT HAVE CLOSE FRIENDS, DO NOT ANSWER THESE QUESTIONS.)

	Yes	Don't Know	No
167. If you found that your friends were leading you into trouble, would you still run around with them?	3	2	1

168.	If you found that your friends were leading you into trouble, would you try to stop these activities?	3	2	1

169.	If your friends got into trouble with the police, would you be willing to lie to protect them?	3	2	1

PART XV
THE NEXT SET OF QUESTIONS DEALS WITH YOUR CLOSE FRIENDS'
BEHAVIOR DURING THE LAST YEAR. (IF YOU DO NOT HAVE CLOSE
FRIENDS, DO NOT ANSWER THESE QUESTIONS.)

During the last year, how often have your close friends done any of the
following:

	Don't Know	Never	Once or Twice	Several Times	Often
170. Suggested that you should go drinking with them	0	1	2	3	4
171. Put pressure on you to drink	0	1	2	3	4
172. Put pressure on you to use drugs	0	1	2	3	4

THANK YOU FOR YOUR HELP!

Offense and Law-Violation Categories Used to Construct Arrest and Self-Report 1987 Scales

ARREST SCALES

Personal:
U.S.= murder and nondelinquent manslaughter, forcible rape, robbery, aggravated assault, other assault
India = murder, criminal homicide, rape, kidnapping and abduction, dacoity (gang robbery), robbery

Property:
U.S. = burglary, larceny-theft, motor vehicle theft, arson, forgery and counterfeiting, fraud, embezzlement,
India = burglary, thefts, criminal breach of trust, cheating (fraud), counterfeiting, excise act, customs act

Public Order:
U.S. = vandalism, weapons, prostitution and commercialized vice, sex offenses, gambling, offenses against family and children, disorderly conduct, vagrancy, curfew & loitering, runaways
India = riots, arms act, gambling act, explosives act, suppression of immoral traffic in women and children act, motor vehicles act, prevention of corruption act, railways act

Substance Abuse:
U.S. = drug abuse violations, driving under the influence, liquor laws, drunkenness
India = opium act, prohibition act

Other Offenses:
U.S. = all other offenses, suspicion
India = other IPC offenses (numbers computed), other SLL offenses

SELF-REPORT SCALES

Total Delinquency = summary of responses to 29 offenses
Status Offenses = Runaway, Lie About Self, Truancy
Property Crimes = Auto Theft, Break & Enter, Joy Ride,
Grand Theft, Moderate Theft, Petty Theft, Possess Stolen Property
Theft Offenses = Grand Theft, Moderate Theft, Petty Theft
Personal Offenses = Assault, Gang Fight, Hit Parent
Public Delinquency = Disorderly Conduct, Drunk in Public, Begging
Home Delinquency = Steal from Family, Hit Parent, Runaway
Substance Abuse = Drink Alcohol, Use Hard Drugs, Use Soft Drugs

Psychometric Properties of and Questionnaire Items Used to Construct Theory and Offense Scales 1990 Survey

INDEPENDENT VARIABLES

Strain

Family Aspirations/Achievement:
   Questions 62,64,67,69,73
   Coded 1,3,5 Scale Range = 5–25 (excluding "don't know" 0)
School Aspirations/Achievement:
   Questions 63,65,68,70,72
   Coded 1,3,5 Scale Range = 5–25 (excluding "don't know" 0)

Family and School Strain Scales (computed from above)

	Aspirations	Achievements	Score
Low Strain	5	5	1
	3	5	2
	3	3	3
	5	3	4
	3	1	5
High Strain	5	1	6

Scale ranges = 5–30 (excluding "don't know" 0)

Control
Family Normlessness:
   Questions 78,83,87,89
   Coded 1–5 Scale Range 4–20 (excluding "don't know" 0)
School Normlessness:
   Questions 79,81,85,88,89
   Coded 1–5 Scale Range 5–25 (excluding "don't know" 0)
Involvement with Family:
   Questions 57,58,59
   Coded, #s 57+58 = 0–6, 59 = 1–5 Scale Range 1–17

Involvement with School:
    Questions 47,48,49
    Coded, #s 47+48 = 0–6, 49 = 1–5 Scale Range 1–17

Learning
Peer Involvement:
    Questions 42,43,44
    Coded, #s 42+43 = 0–6, 44 = 1–5 Scale Range 1–17
 Attitudes Toward Deviance:
    Questions 145–154
    Coded 1–4 Scale Range 10–40 (excluding "don't know" 0)
 Exposure to Delinquent Peers:
    Questions 155–166
    Coded 1–5 Scale Range 12–60 (excluding "don't know" 0)
 Involvement with Delinquent Peers Index
    Computed IDPINDX = PI x (EDP—mean of EDP)
    Where PI = Peer Involvement Scale and EDP = Exposure to Delinquent
Peers Scale

OFFENSE SCALES
General Delinquency:
    Questions 8, 9, 10, 12, 14, 15, 16, 17, 18, 21, 22, 23, 24, 25, 26, 27, 28, 29,
32, 34, 35
    Coded 0–10 Scale Range 0–210
 Index Offenses:
    Questions 8, 9, 16, 17, 27, 28, 29, 34
    Coded 0–10 Scale Range 0–80
Minor Delinquency:
    Questions 12, 15, 21, 22, 24, 26, 35
    Coded 0–10 Scale Range 0–70
Substance Abuse:
    Questions 37, 38, 39
    Coded 0–10 Scale Range 0–30

Note: All corresponding NYS questionnaire items recoded as above.

1978 United States Sample

Scale Name	No. Items	Mean	SD	Alpha	Stand. Item Alpha
Strain Theory Scales					
Family Aspirations	5	22.16	3.34	.73	.74
Family Achievement	5	18.48	4.43	.77	.77
Academic Aspirations	5	19.63	4.15	.75	.75
Academic Achievement	5	16.28	4.64	.75	.76
Control Theory Scales					
Family Normlessness	4	15.31	2.59	.65	.70
School Normlessness	5	18.88	2.88	.64	.64
Family Activities	3	10.11	3.34	.67	.67
School Activities	3	6.84	3.40	.65	.68
Learning Theory Scales					
Peer Involvement	3	7.90	3.84	.74	.74
Attitudes Toward Deviance	10	32.94	5.09	.87	.88
Exposure Delinquent Peers	12	22.11	7.95	.88	.89
Offense Scales					
General Delinquency	21	15.02	70.84	.40	.82
Index Offenses	8	.90	5.90	.22	.54
Minor Offenses	7	4.50	21.39	.16	.52
Substance Abuse	3	4.82	7.33	.41	.49

1990 Indian Sample

	No. Items	Mean	SD	Alpha	Stand. Item Alpha
Strain Theory Scales					
Family Aspirations	5	21.84	3.69	.68	.69
Family Achievement	5	20.88	3.79	.68	.69
Academic Aspirations	5	22.05	3.57	.67	.70
Academic Achievement	5	21.09	3.66	.65	.66
Control Theory Scales					
Family Normlessness	4	12.75	3.52	.49	.47
School Normlessness	5	16.57	4.57	.54	.54
Family Activities	3	9.09	3.93	.72	.71
School Activities	3	9.43	3.64	.64	.63
Learning Theory Scales					
Peer Involvement	3	6.15	7.04	.40	.62
Attitudes Toward Deviance	10	34.88	10.07	.97	.97
Exposure Delinquent Peers	12	14.27	11.50	.96	.96
Offense Scales					
General Delinquency	21	4.29	11.68	.90	.91
Index Offenses	8	1.21	4.52	.82	.85
Minor Offenses	7	1.70	4.50	.68	.70
Substance Abuse	3	.39	1.96	.57	.70

References

Adler, Freda

1983   Nations Not Obsessed with Crime. Littleton, CO: Fred B. Rothman & Co.

1984   The Incidence of Female Criminality in the Contemporary World. New York: Free Press.

Agnew, Robert

1985   Social Control Theory and Delinquency: A Test of Theory. *Criminology* 23:47–61.

1990   Adolescent Resources and Delinquency. *Criminology* 28:535–566.

1991   The Interactive Effect of Peer Variables on Delinquency. *Criminology* 29:47–72.

Agnew, Robert, and Helene Raskin White

1992   An Empirical Test of General Strain Theory. *Criminology* 30:475–500.

Akers, Ronald L., James Massey, William Clarke, and Ronald M. Lauer

1983   Are Self-Report Studies of Adolescent Deviance Valid? Biochemical Measures, Randomized Response, and the Bogus Pipeline in Smoking Behavior. *Social Forces* 62:234–251.

Ali, Badr-El-Din

1986   Methodological Problems in International Criminal Justice Research. *International Journal of Comparative and Applied Criminal Justice* 10:163–176.

Allan, Emilie Andersen, and Darrell J. Steffensmeier

1989   Youth, Underemployment, and Property Crime. *American Sociological Review* 54:107–123.

Alwin, Duane E.

1988   From Obedience to Autonomy: Changes in Traits Desired in Children. *Public Opinion Quarterly* 54:33–52.

Archer, Dane, and Rosemary Gartner

1984   *Violence and Crime in Cross-National Perspective.* New Haven: Yale U. Press.

Ashby, Philip H.

1974   *Modern Trends in Hinduism.* New York: Columbia U. Press.

Bala, Nicholas

1992   The Young Offenders Act: The Legal Structure. In Raymond Corrado, Nicholas Bala, Rick Linden and Marc LeBlanc (eds.) *Juvenile Justice in Canada: A Theoretical and Analytical Assessment*, pp. 21–74. Toronto: Butterworths.

Barak-Glantz, Israel L., and Elmer H. Johnson (eds.)

1983   *Comparative Criminology.* Beverly Hills, CA: Sage.

Bartollas, Clemens, and Stuart J. Miller

1994   *Juvenile Justice in America.* Englewood Cliffs, NJ: Prentice Hall.

Bayley, David H.

1969   *The Police and Political Development in India.* Princeton: Princeton U. Press.

1985   *Patterns of Policing: A Comparative International Analysis.* New Brunswick, NJ: Rutgers U. Press.

Bazemore, S. Gordon

1991   Beyond Punishment, Surveillance, and Traditional Treatment: Themes for a New Mission in U.S. Juvenile Justice. In Jim Hackler (ed.) *Official Responses to Problem Juveniles: Some International Reflections*. Onati: The Onati International Institute for the Sociology of Law, pp. 129–158.

Beirne, Piers

1983   Generalization and Its Discontents: The Comparative Study of Crime. In Israel L. Barak-Glantz and Elmer H. Johnson (eds.) *Comparative Criminology*. pp. 19–38. Beverly Hills, CA: Sage.

Bell, Robert R.

1983   *Marriage and Family Interaction* (6th ed.). Homewood, IL: Dorsey Press.

Bennett, Richard R., and James P. Lynch

1990   Does a Difference Make a Difference? Comparing Cross-National Crime Indicators. *Criminology* 28:153–181.

Bennett, Richard R., and R. Bruce Wiegand

1994   Observations on Crime Reporting in a Developing Nation. *Criminology* 32:135–148.

Bensinger, Gad J.

1991   The Juvenile Court of Cook County: Past, Present, and Future. In Jim Hackler (ed.) *Official Responses to Problem Juveniles: Some International Reflections*. Onati: The Onati International Institute for the Sociology of Law, pp. 159–174.

Berger, Ronald J.

1989   Female Delinquency in the Emancipation Era: A Review of the Literature. *Sex Roles* 21:375–399.

Bernard, Thomas J.

1984   Control Criticisms of Strain Theories: An Assessment of Theoretical and Empirical Adequacy. *Journal of Research in Crime and Delinquency* 21:351–372.

1992   *The Cycle of Juvenile Justice*. New York: Oxford U. Press.

Black, Donald J., and Albert J. Reiss

1970   Police Control of Juveniles. *American Sociological Review* 35:63–77.

Block, Richard (ed.)

1984   *Victimization and Fear of Crime: World Perspectives*. Washington, DC: Department of Justice, Bureau of Justice Statistics.

Bordua, David (ed.)

1967   *The Police: Six Sociological Essays*. New York: John Wiley & Sons.

Bowher, Lee H.

1981   The Institutional Determinants of International Female Crime. *International Journal of Comparative and Applied Criminal Justice* 5:41–50.

Braithwaite, John

1981   The Myth of Social Class & Criminality Reconsidered. *American Sociological Review* 46:36–57.

1989   *Crime, Shame and Reintegration*. Cambridge: Cambridge U. Press.

Brownfield, David

1986   Social Class and Violent Behavior. *Criminology* 24:421–438.

Bursik, Robert J., Jr.

1988   Social Disorganization and Theories of Crime and Delinquency: Problems and Prospects. *Criminology* 26: 519–552.

Caldwell, John C., P.H. Reddy, and Pat Caldwell

1984   The Determinants of Family Structure in Rural South India. *Journal of Marriage and the Family.* February: 215–229.

Canadian Center for Justice Statistics

1990   Sentencing in Youth Courts, 1984–85 to 1988–89. *Juristat Service Bulletin* 10 (No. 1) Ottawa, Ontario (Canada): Statistics Canada.

1994   Youth Custody in Canada, 1992–93. *Juristat Service Bulletin* 14 (No. 11) Ottawa, Ontario (Canada): Statistics Canada.

Canter, Rachelle J.

1982   Sex Differences in Self-Reported Delinquency. *Criminology* 20:373–394.

Caplan, Patricia

1985   *Class and Gender in India.* London: Tavistock.

Cavan, Ruth S., and Jordan T. Cavan

1968   *Delinquency and Crime: Cross-Cultural Perspectives.* Philadelphia: Lippincott.

Census of India

1981   New Delhi: Government of India.

Central Bureau of Correctional Services

1970   *Juvenile Delinquency: A Challenge.* New Delhi: Department of Social Welfare, Government of India.

Cernkovich, Stephen A., and Peggy Giordano

1987   Family Relationships and Delinquency. *Criminology* 25:295–321.

Cernkovich, Stephen A., Peggy Giordano, and Meredith D. Pugh

1985   Chronic Offenders: The Missing Cases in Self-report Delinquency Research. *Journal of Criminal Law and Criminology* 76:705–732.

Chambliss, William, and Robert Seidman

1982   *Law, Order, and Power.* 2nd ed. Reading, MA.: Addison Wesley.

Chambliss, William J. (ed.)

1984   *Criminal Law in Action.* 2nd ed. New York: John Wiley & Sons.

Champion, Dean J.

1992   *The Juvenile Justice System: Delinquency Processing and the Law.* New York: Macmillan Publishing Co.

Chang, Dae H., and Donald L. Blazicek

1986   *An Introduction to Comparative and International Criminology.* Durham, NC: The Acorn Press.

Chang, Dae H. (ed.)

1976   *Criminology: A Cross-Cultural Perspective* (2 vols.). Durham, NC: Carolina Academic Press.

Channabasavanna, S.M., M.K. Isaac, and M.S. Bhaskar

1981   Juvenile Delinquency: A Socio-demographic Study. *Indian Journal of Criminology and Criminalistics* 1:47–49.

Chesney-Lind, Meda, and Randall G. Shelden

1992   *Girls, Delinquency, and Juvenile Justice.* Pacific Grove, CA: Brooks/Cole.

Cheung, Y.W., and A.M.C. Ng

1988 Social Factors in Adolescent Deviant Behavior in Hong Kong: An International Theoretical Approach. *International Journal of Criminology and Applied Criminal Justice* 12:27–45.

"Child Abuse: Tragically Widespread"

1987 *India Today*. January 31:116–119.

Cho, Byung In, and Richard J. Chang

1992 The Youth Crime Problems in the Republic of Korea. *International Journal of Comparative and Applied Criminal Justice* 16:301–316.

Clinard, Marshall B.

1978 *Cities with Little Crime: The Case of Switzerland.* Cambridge: Cambridge U. Press.

Clinard, Marshall B., and Daniel J. Abbott

1973 *Crime in Developing Countries.* New York: John Wiley.

Cohen, Albert

1955 *Delinquent Boys: The Culture of the Gang.* New York: The Free Press.

Conger, Rand D.

1976 Social Control and Social Learning Models of Delinquent Behavior: A Synthesis. *Criminology* 14:17–40.

Corrado, Raymond R., and Susan D. Turnbull

1992 A Comparative Examination of the Modified Justice Model in the United Kingdom and the United States. In Raymond R. Corrado, Nicholas Bala, Rick Linden & Marc LeBlanc (eds.) *Juvenile Justice in Canada: A Theoretical and Analytical Assessment*, pp. 75–136. Toronto: Butterworths.

Corrado, Raymond R., Nicholas Bala, Rick Linden, and Marc LeBlanc (eds.)

1992 *Juvenile Justice in Canada: A Theoretical and Analytical Assessment.* Toronto: Butterworths.

Covington, Jeanette

1982 Adolescent Deviation and Age. *Journal of Youth and Adolescence* 11:329–344.

Department of Justice

1992 *Imprisonment as "The Last Resort:" The New Zealand Experience.* Wellington, NZ.

Desai, Nura, and Maithreyi Krishnaraj

1987 *Women and Society in India.* Delhi: Ajanta.

Devi, Radha D., and M. Ravindran

1983 Women's Work in India. *International Social Science Journal* 35:683–701.

Doleschal, Eugene

1981 Crime and Delinquency Research in Selected European Countries. In Louis I. Shelley (ed.) *Readings in Comparative Criminology.* Carbondale and Edwardsville, IL: Southern Illinois U. Press, pp. 217–234.

Dull, Thomas R.

1983 Friends' Use and Adult Drug and Drinking Behavior: A Further Test of Differential Association Theory. *The Journal of Criminal Law and Criminology* 74: 1608–1619.

Dunford, Franklin W., and Delbert S. Elliott

1984   Identifying Career Offenders Using Self-reported Data. *Journal of Research in Crime and Criminology* 21:37–86.

Ebbe, Obi N.I.

1992   Juvenile Delinquency in Nigeria: The Problem of Application of Western Theories. *International Journal of Comparative and Applied Criminal Justice* 16:353–370.

Edwards, William J.

1992   Predicting Juvenile Delinquency: A Review of Correlates and a Confirmation by Recent Research Based on an Integrated Theoretical Model. *Justice Quarterly* 9:553–584.

Elliott, Delbert S., and Suzanne S. Ageton

1978   *The National Youth Survey. Project Report No. 4A, The Social Correlates of Delinquent Behavior in a National Youth Panel (revised)*. Boulder, CO: Behavioral Research Institute.

1980   Reconciling Race & Class Differences in Self-Reported and Official Estimates of Delinquency. *American Sociological Review* 45:95–110.

Elliott, Delbert S., Suzanne S. Ageton, David Huizinga, Brian A. Knowles, and Rachelle J. Canter

1983   *The Prevalence and Incidence of Delinquent Behavior: 1976–1980*. Boulder, CO: Behavior Research Institute.

Elliott, Delbert S., and David Huizinga

1983   Social Class & Delinquent Behavior in a National Youth Panel, 1976–1980. *Criminology* 21:149–177.

Elliott, Delbert S., David Huizinga, and Suzanne S. Ageton

1985   *Explaining Delinquency & Drug Use*. Beverly Hills, CA: Sage.

Elliott, D.S., D. Huizinga, and S. Menard

1989   *Multiple Problem Youths: Delinquency, Substance Abuse, and Mental Health Problems*. New York: Springer-Verlag.

Empey, LaMar T., and Mark C. Stafford

1991   *American Delinquency: Its Meaning and Construction*, 3d ed. Belmont, CA: Wadsworth.

Erickson, Maynard

1972   The Changing Relationship between Official and Self-reported Measures of Delinquency: An Exploratory-predictive Study. *Journal of Criminal Law, Criminology and Police Science* 63:388–395.

Erickson, Maynard, and LaMar T. Empey

1963   Court Records, Undetected Delinquency, and Decision Making. *Journal of Criminal Law, Criminology and Police Science* 54:456–469.

Evans, Robert C., Gary D. Copus, Thomas E. Sullenberger, and F. Peter Hodgkinson

1993   Self-Concept Comparison of English and American Delinquents. *International Journal of Offender Therapy and Comparative Criminology* 37:297–317.

Farrington, David P.

1986   Age & Crime. In Michael Tonry & Norval Morris (eds.) *Crime & Justice: An Annual Review of Research*, Vol. 7, Chicago: U. of Chicago Press, pp. 189–250.

1992   Trends in English Juvenile Delinquency and Their Explanation. *International Journal of Comparative and Applied Criminal Justice* 16:151–163.

Feld, Barry C.

1994   Juvenile Justice Swedish Style: A Rose by Another Name? *Justice Quarterly* 11:625–650.

Fenwick, Charles R.

1983   The Juvenile Delinquency Problem in Japan: Application of a Role Relationship Model. *International Journal of Comparative and Applied Criminal Justice* 7:119–128.

Finckenauer, James O., and Linda Kelly

1992   Juvenile Delinquency and Youth Subcultures in the Former Soviet Union. *International Journal of Comparative and Applied Criminal Justice* 16:207–230.

Friday, Paul C.

1973   Problems in Comparative Criminology: Comments on the Feasibility and Implications for Research. *International Journal of Criminology and Penology* 1:151–160.

1980   International Review of Youth Crime and Delinquency. In Graeme R. Newman (ed.) *Crime and Deviance: A Comparative Perspective,* pp. 100–129. Beverly Hills, CA: Sage.

1992   Delinquency in Sweden: Current Trends and Theoretical Implications. *International Journal of Comparative and Applied Criminal Justice* 16:231–246.

1995   The International Division and International Scholarship. *The Criminologist* 20:10–11.

Friday, Paul C., and Jerald Hage

1976   Youth Crime in Postindustrial Societies: An Integrated Perspective. *Criminology* 14:347–368.

Fu, Hualing

1992   Juvenile Delinquency in Post-Mao China. *International Journal of Comparative and Applied Criminal Justice* 16:265–272.

Gaines, Donna

1992   *Teenage Wasteland: Suburban Dead End Kids.* New York: Harper & Row.

Gertz, Marc G., and Laura Gertz

1992   Impediments to Cross-National Research: Problems of Reliability and Validity. *International Journal of Comparative and Applied Criminal Justice* 16:57–66.

Gibbons, Don C.

1994   *Talking About Crime and Criminals: Problems and Issues in Theory Development in Criminology.* Englewood Cliffs, NJ: Prentice Hall, eds. Gibbons, Don C., and Marvin D. Krohn

1991   *Delinquent Behavior,* 5th ed. Englewood Cliffs, NJ: Prentice Hall.

Ginsberg, Irving J., and James R. Greenley

1978   Competing Theories of Marijuana Use: A Longitudinal Study. *Journal of Health and Social Behavior* 19:22–34.

Gomme, Jan M., Mary E. Morton, and W. Gordon West

1987   Rates, Types & Patterns of Male & Female Delinquency in an Ontario County. *Canadian Journal of Criminology* 26:313–323.

Gore, M.S.

1968   *Urbanization and Family Change.* Bombay: Popular Prakashan.

Greenberg, David F.

1978   Delinquency and the Age Structure of Society. In Peter Wickman and Phillip Whitten (eds.) *Readings in Criminology*. Lexington, MA: D.C. Heath, pp. 66–86.

Greenberg, David (ed.)

1981   *Crime and Capitalism*. Palo Alto, CA: Mayfield.

Grove, Walter R., Michael Hughs, and Michael Gurken

1985   Are Uniform Crime Reports a Valid Indicator of the Crimes? An Affirmative Answer with Minor Qualifications. *Criminology* 3:451–501.

Groves, W. Byran, and Graeme Newman

1986   Criminal Justice and Development: Some Critical Observations. *International Journal of Comparative and Applied Criminal Justice* 1:1–16.

Gurr, Ted Robert

1976   *Rogues, Rebels & Reformers*. Beverly Hills, CA: Sage.

Hackler, James C.

1970   Testing a Causal Model of Delinquency. *Sociological Quarterly* 11:511–521.

Hackler, Jim

1991   Using Reintegrative Shaming Effectively: Why Fiji Has a Juvenile Justice System Superior to the U.S., Canada, and Australia. In Jim Hackler (ed.) *Official Responses to Problem Juveniles: Some International Reflections*. Onati: The Onati International Institute for the Sociology of Law, pp. 109–128.

Hackler, Jim (ed.)

1991   *Official Responses to Problem Juveniles: Some International Reflections*. Onati: The Onati International Institute for the Sociology of Law.

Hagan, John

1993   The Social Embeddedness of Crime and Unemployment. *Criminology* 31:465–492.

Hagan, John, and Fiona Kay

1990   Gender and Delinquency in White-collar Families: A Power-Control Perspective. *Crime and Delinquency* 36:391–407.

Hagan, John, John Simpson, and A.R. Gillis

1987   Class in the Household: A Power-Control Theory of Gender & Delinquency. *American Journal of Sociology* 92:788–816.

Hale, Sylvia M.

1989   The Status of Women in India: Review Article. *Pacific Affairs* 62:364–381.

Hardt, Robert H., and Sandra Peterson-Hardt

1977   On Determining the Quality of the Delinquency Self-Report Method. *Journal of Research in Crime and Delinquency* 14:247–261.

Hartjen, Clayton A.

1972   Legalism and Humanism: A Reply to the Schwendingers. *Issues in Criminology* 7:59–69.

1977   *Possible Trouble: An Analysis of Social Problems*. New York: Praeger.

1978   *Crime and Criminalization*, 2nd ed. New York: Praeger/HRW.

1983   Self-Reported Delinquency in India: A Study of High School and Approved School Boys in Tamil Nadu. *International Journal of Comparative and Applied Criminal Justice* 7:225–235.

1986 Crime and Development: Some Observations on Women and Children in India. *International Annals of Criminology* 24:39–57.

Hartjen, Clayton A., and Sesharajani Kethineni

1993 Culture, Gender and Delinquency: A Study of Youths in the United States and India. *Women & Criminal Justice* 5:37–70.

I.P. Juvenile Justice in India. In Donald J. Shoemaker (ed.) *Handbook on International Juvenile Justice*. Westport, CT: Greenwood.

Hartjen, Clayton A., and S. Priyadarsini

1984 *Delinquency in India: A Comparative Analysis*. New Brunswick, NJ: Rutgers U. Press.

Hartnagel, Timothy F.

1982 Modernization, Female Social Roles, and Female Crime: A Cross-National Investigation. *The Sociological Quarterly* 23:477–490.

Hassall, Ian B., and Gabrielle M. Maxwell

1991 The Family Group Conference. In Office of the Commissioner for Children (ed.) *An Appraisal of the First Year of the Children, Young Persons and Their Families Act 1989*. Wellington, NZ, pp. 1–13.

Hatch, Alison, and Curt T. Griffiths

1992 Youth Crime in Canada: Observations for Cross-Cultural Analysis. *International Journal of Comparative and Applied Criminal Justice* 16:165–183.

Hawkins, Gordon

1991 Sutherland Award Address Given at Meetings of American Society of Criminology.

Hindelang, Michael J., Travis Hirschi, and Joseph G. Weis

1979 Correlates of Delinquency: The Illusion of Discrepancy Between Self-Report and Official Measures. *American Sociological Review* 44:995–1014.

1981 *Measuring Delinquency*. Beverly Hills, CA: Sage.

Hirschi, Travis

1969 *Causes of Delinquency*. Berkeley, CA: U. of California Press.

1987 Review. *Criminology* 25:193–201.

Igbinovia, Patrick Edabor

1989 Criminology in Africa. *International Journal of Offender Therapy and Comparative Criminology* 33: v-x.

Inciardi, James A. (ed.)

1980 *Radical Criminology: The Coming Crises*. Beverly Hills, CA: Sage.

Inciardi, James A., Ruth Horowitz, and Anne E. Pottieger

1993 *Street Kids, Street Drugs, Street Crime: An Examination of Drug Use and Serious Delinquency in Miami*. Belmont, CA: Wadsworth.

Institute of Psychological and Educational Research

1985 *Humanizing Child Labor*. Calcutta.

Ishwaran, K. (ed.)

1970 *Change and Continuity in India's Villages*. New York: Columbia U. Press.

Jabbi, M.K.

1986 Child Marriages in Rajasthan. *Social Change* 16:3–9.

Jackson, Elton F., Charles R. Tittle, and Mary Jean Burke

1986   Offense-Specific Models of the Differential Association Perspective. *American Journal of Sociology* 78:562–575.

Jacovetta, R.G.

1981   Research Problems and Issues in Comparative Corrections. *International Journal of Comparative and Applied Criminal Justice* 5:205–211.

Jain, Devaki (ed.)

1975   *Indian Women*. New Delhi: Ministry of Information and Broadcasting.

Jejurikar, N.D., and N.S. Shonvi

1985   Socio-economic Factors in Adolescent Delinquency. *International Social Work* 28:21–29.

Jensen, Gary F.

1980   Labeling and Delinquency: Toward a Reconciliation of Divergant Findings. *Criminology* 18:121–129.

Junger-Tas, Josine

1992   Juvenile Delinquency in the Netherlands: Trends and Perspectives. *International Journal of Comparative and Applied Criminal Justice* 16:207–229.

1994   Self-Reported Delinquency in Thirteen Western Countries: Some Preliminary Conclusions. In Josine Junger-Tas, Gert-Jan Terlouw, and Malcolm M. Klein (eds.). *Delinquent Behavior Among Young People in the Western World: First Results of the International Self-Report Delinquency Study.* New York: Kugler, pp. 370–380.

Junger-Tas, Josine, and Richard L. Block (eds.)

1988   *Juvenile Delinquency in the Netherlands*. Berkeley, CA: Kugler.

Junger-Tas, Josine; Gert-Jan Terlouw, and Malcolm M. Klein (eds.)

1994   *Delinquent Behavior Among Young People in the Western World: First Results of the International Self-Report Delinquency Study.* New York: Kugler.

The Juvenile Justice Act 1986

1988   Madras, India: Government of Tamil Nadu.

Kaiser, Gunther

1992   Juvenile Delinquency in the Federal Republic of Germany. *International Journal of Comparative and Applied Criminal Justice* 16:185–204.

Kaliappan, K.V., and K. Senthilathiban

1984   Anxiety Among Delinquents. *Indian Journal of Criminology* 12:58–60.

Kalish, Carol B.

1988   *International Crime Rates*. Washington, DC: Bureau of Justice Statistics, Special Report.

Kandel, Denise

1973   Adolescent Marijuana Use: Role of Parents and Peers. *Science* (September): 1067–1070.

Kannappan, R., and K.V. Kaliappan

1987   The Use of Jessness Inventory with South Indian Delinquents. *Indian Journal of Criminology* 15: 20–24.

Karve, Irawati

1986   *Kinship Organization in India*. London: Asia Publishing House.

Klein, Malcolm W.

1994   Epilogue. In Josine Junger-Tas, Gert-Jan Terlouw & Malcolm W. Klein (eds.) *Delinquent Behavior Among Young People in the Western World: First Results of the International Self-Report Delinquency Study.* New York: Kugler, pp. 381–386.

Klein, Malcolm W. (ed.)

1989   *Cross-National Research in Self-Reported Crime and Delinquency.* Boston: Kluwer Academic Publishers.

Kohn, Melvin L.

1987   Cross-National Research as an Analytic Strategy. *American Sociological Review* 52:713–731.

Kosambi, D.D.

1969   *Ancient India: A History of Its Culture and Civilization.* New York: Meridian Books.

Kratcoski, Peter, and Lucille Kratcoski

1991   The Impact of Social Change on Juvenile Justice Policy in the United States. In Jim Hackler (ed.) *Official Responses to Problem Juveniles: Some International Reflections.* Onati: The Onati International Institute for the Sociology of Law, pp. 189–204.

Krisberg, Barry

1988   *The Juvenile Court: Reclaiming the Vision.* San Francisco, CA.: National Council on Crime and Delinquency.

Krishna, K.P., and Satyendra Kumar

1981   Adjustment Problems Among Truants. *Indian Journal of Criminology* 9:36–43.

Krishnamurti, S., and K. Alagamalai

1975   *A Hand Book of Criminal Law,* 12th ed. Madras: S. Subbiah Chetty & Co.

Krishnaraj, Maithreyi, and Karuna Chanana (eds.)

1989   *Gender and the Household Domain: Social and Cultural Dimensions.* New Delhi: Sage.

Krohn, Marvin, Gordon P. Waldo, and Theodore G. Chiricos

1975   Self-Reported Delinquency: A Comparison of Structured Interviews and Self-Administered Checklists. *The Journal of Criminal Law and Criminology* 65:545–553.

Krohn, Marvin D., Lonn Lanza-Kanduce, and Ronald L. Akers

1984   Community Context and Theories of Deviant Behavior: An Examination of Social Learning and Social Bonding Theories. *The Sociological Quarterly* 25:354–372.

Krohn, Melvin L.

1987   Cross National Research as an Analytic Strategy. *American Sociological Review.* 52:713–731.

Kulshresktha, V.B., and R. Bhushan

1981   Delinquency in the Perspective of Personality Traits and Social Environment. *Perspectives in Psychological Research* 4:35–37.

Kundu, R., and G. Bhaumik

1982   Introversion, Extraversion and Neuroticism: The Outstanding Personality Correlates of Juvenile Delinquent Boys. *Indian Journal of Criminology* 10:37–41.

Kuznietzova, N. F.

1989   Criminal Liability of Juveniles in the USSR. Paper Presented at Meetings of the American Society of Criminology.

LaFree, Gary, and Christopher Birkbeck

1991   The Neglected Situation: A Cross-National Study of the Situational Characteristics of Crime. *Criminology* 29:73–98.

LaGrange, Randy L., and Helene Raskin White

1985   Age Differences in Delinquency: A Test of Theory. *Criminology* 23:19–45.

Lahri, S.K.

1983   Differential Personality Patterns of Normal and Delinquent Children. *Indian Journal of Criminology and Criminalistics* 3:23–24.

Lakshmanna, M.

1982   Roots of Delinquency. *Social Welfare* 29:4–7.

Lannoy, Richard

1971   *The Speaking Tree: A Study of Indian Culture and Society.* New York: Oxford U. Press.

Laub, John, and Robert J. Sampson

1988   Unraveling Families and Delinquency: A Reanalysis of the Gluecks' Data. *Criminology* 26:355–380.

Lebra, Joyce, Jay Paulson, and Jana Everett (eds.)

1984   *Women and Work in India: Continuity and Change.* New Delhi: Promilla and Company.

Lemert, Edwin M.

1951   *Social Pathology.* New York: McGraw-Hill.

Leschied, Alan

1991   Canadian Juvenile Justice Reform: Is Fair and Equal Always Effective? In Jim Hackler (ed.) *Official Responses to Problem Juveniles: Some International Reflections.* Onati: The Onati International Institute for the Sociology of Law, pp. 83–90.

Leschied, Alan W., and Peter G. Jaffe

1991   *The Young Offenders Act—A Revolution in Canadian Juvenile Justice.* Toronto: U. of Toronto Press.

Levitan, Sar A., Richard S. Belous, and Frank Gallo

1988   *What's Happening to the American Family?* Baltimore: Johns Hopkins U. Press.

Lincoln, Alan Jay, and Murray Straus

1985   *Crime and the Family.* Springfield, IL: Charles C. Thomas.

Liska, Allen E., and Mark D. Reed

1985   Ties to Conventional Institutions and Delinquency: Estimating Reciprocal Effects. *American Sociological Review* 50:547–560.

Loeber, Rolf

1987   The Prevalence, Correlates & Continuity of Serious Conduct Problems in Elementary School Children. *Criminology* 18:615–642.

Loeber, Rolf, and Howard N. Snyder

1990   Rate of Offending in Juvenile Careers: Findings of Constancy and Change in Lambda. *Criminology* 28: 97–109.

Los, Maria, and Palmer Anderson

1981   The 'Second Life': A Cross-Cultural View of Peer Subcultures in Correctional Institutions in Poland and the United States. In Louise I. Shelley (ed.) *Readings in Comparative Criminology*. Carbondale and Edwardsville: Southern Illinois U. Press, pp. 189–200.

Lushing, Susan

1982   Comparative Criminal Justice—Search and Seizure, Interrogation, and Identification of Suspects in India: A Research Note. *Journal of Criminal Justice* 10:239–245.

Lyery, Robert Richard, and James K. Skipper, Jr.

1981   Differential Rates of Rural-Urban Delinquency: A Social Control Approach. *Criminology* 19:385–399.

Maitra, A.K.

1981   The DAP Differentials of the Delinquents. *Psychological Research Journal* 5:59–66.

Manard, Scott, and Delbert S. Elliott

1994   Delinquent Bonding, Moral Beliefs, and Illegal Behavior: A Three-Wave Panel Model. *Justice Quarterly* 11:173–188.

Mandelbaum, David G.

1970   *Society in India: Continuity and Change*. Berkeley: U. of California Press.

Mannheim, Hermann

1965   *Comparative Criminology* (2 vols.). London: Routledge & Kegan Paul.

Mansnerus, Laura

1993   Kids in the 90's: A Bolder Breed. *New York Times* (April 4): Section A: 14–15.

Marcos, Anastasios C., Stephen J. Bahr, and Richard E. Johnson

1986   Test of a Bonding/Association Theory of Adolescent Drug Use. *Social Forces* 65:135–161.

Markwart, Alan

1992   Custodial Sanctions under the Young Offender Act. In Raymond Corrado, Nicholas Bala, Rick Linden and Marc LeBlanc (eds.) *Juvenile Justice in Canada: A Theoretical and Analytical Assessment*. Toronto: Butterworths, pp. 229–282.

Marshall, Ineke Haen, and Chris E. Marshall

1983   Toward a Refinement of Purpose in Comparative Criminological Research: Research Site Selection in Focus. *International Journal of Comparative and Applied Criminal Justice* 7:80–97.

Massey, James L., and Marvin D. Krohn

1986   A Longitudinal Examination of an Integrated Social Process Model of Deviant Behavior. *Social Forces* 65: 106–134.

Matsueda, Ross L.

1988   The Current State of Differential Association Theory. *Crime and Delinquency* 34:277–306.

Matsueda, Ross L., and Karen Heimer

1987   Race, Family Structure and Delinquency. *American Sociological Review* 52:826–840.

Maxwell, Gabrielle M., and Allison Morris

1993   *Family, Victims and Culture: Youth Justice in New Zealand*. Wellington, NZ: Institute of Criminology, Victoria, University of Wellington.

Maxwell, Gabrielle M., and Jeremy P. Robertson

1991 Statistics on the First Year. In Office of the Commissioner for Children (ed.) *An Appraisal of the First Year of the Children, Young Persons and Their Families Act 1989.* Wellington, NZ, pp. 14–23.

McCord, Joan

1990 Crime in Moral and Social Contexts. *Criminology* 28: 1–26.

Mehta, M.N.

1984 Child Abuse and Neglect. Paper Presented in the Plenary Session of the 21st National Conference of the Indian Academy of Pediatrics, Bombay.

Mencher, Joan P.

1970 A Tamil Village: Changing Socioeconomic Structure in Madras State. In K. Ishwaran (ed.) *Change and Continuity in India's Villages.* New York: Columbia U. Press, pp. 197–218.

Messner, Steven F.

1982 Societal Development, Social Equality, and Homicide: A Cross-National Test of a Durkheimian Model. *Social Forces* 61:225–239.

Messner, Steven F., and Richard Rosenfeld

1994 *Crime and the American Dream.* Belmont, CA: Wadsworth Publishing Company.

Misra, V.D.

1981 Direction of Aggression and Reaction to Frustration in Juvenile Delinquents. *Indian Journal of Criminology* 9:110–113.

Misra, L.A., and V.S. Agnihotri

1985 The Community Practices of Informal Social Controls. *Indian Journal of Criminology* 13:96–102.

Mitra, N.L.

1988 *Juvenile Delinquency and Indian Justice System.* New Delhi: Deep & Deep Publications.

Moffitt, Terrie E., and Phil A. Silva

1988 Self-Reported Delinquency: Results from an Instrument for New Zealand. *Australian and New Zealand Journal of Criminology* 21:227–240.

Moffitt, Terrie E., Phil A. Silva, Donald R. Lynam, and Bill Henery

1995 Self-Reported Delinquency at Age 18: New Zealand's Dunedin Multidisciplinary Health and Development Study. In Josine Junger-Tas, Gert-Jan Terlouw, and Malcolm M. Klein (eds.). *Delinquent Behavior Among Young People in the Western World: First Results of the International Self-Report Delinquency Study.* New York: Kugler, pp. 354–366.

Morden, Peter

1980 Towards a Weberian Criminology for Developing Countries. *Canadian Criminology Forum* 2:35–46.

Morris, Allison, and Gabrielle M. Maxwell

1993 Juvenile Justice in New Zealand: A New Paradigm. *Australian and New Zealand Journal of Criminology* 20:72–90.

Murkhopadhyay, Maitrayee

1984 *Silver Hackles: Women & Development in India.* Oxford: Oxfam.

Nagla, B.K.

1981 The Juvenile Delinquent in Society. *Indian Journal of Criminology* 9:44–50.

Nagpaul, Hans

1984   Patterns of Homicide in North India: Some Sociological Hypotheses. *International Journal of Offender Therapy and Comparative Criminology* 2:147–157.

Natalino, Kathleen W.

1981   Methodological Problems in Self-Report Studies: Black Adolescent Delinquency. In Gary F. Jensen (ed.) *Sociology of Delinquency*. Beverly Hills, CA: Sage, pp. 63–78.

National Police Agency

1989   *Summary of the White Paper on Crime*. Tokyo: Research and Training Institute, Ministry of Justice, Government of Japan.

National Seminar on Child Abuse in India

1988   *Background Papers*. New Delhi: National Institute of Public Cooperation & Child Development.

Natt, B., and P.C. Malik

1973   *Law and Material on the Code of Criminal Procedure*. Lucknow: Eastern Book Co.

Newman, Graeme R., and Franco Ferracuti

1980   Introduction: The Limits and Possibilities of Comparative Criminology. In Graeme R. Newman (ed.) *Crime and Deviance: A Comparative Perspective*. Beverly Hills, CA: Sage, pp. 7–16.

Newman, Graeme R. (ed.)

1976   *Comparative Deviance: Perceptions and Law in Six Cultures*. New York: Elsevier.

1980   *Crime and Deviance: A Comparative Perspective*. Beverly Hills, CA: Sage.

Osgood, D. Wayne, Patrick M. O'Malley, Jerald G. Bachman, and Lloyd D. Johnston

1989   Time Trends and Age Trends in Arrests and Self-Reported Illegal Behavior. *Criminology* 27:389–418.

Panakal, J.J., and S.D. Gokhale (eds.)

1989   *Crime and Corrections in India*. Bombay: Tata Institute of Social Science.

Paternoster, Raymond, and Ruth Triplett

1988   Disaggregating Self-Reported Delinquency and Its Implications for Theory. *Criminology* 26:591–625.

Paternoster, Raymond, and LeeAnn Lovanni

1989   The Labeling Perspective and Delinquency: An Elaboration of the Theory and Assessment of the Evidence. *Justice Quarterly* 6:359–394.

Patterson, E. Britt

1991   Poverty, Income Inequality, and Community Crime Rates. *Criminology* 29:755–776.

Patterson, Gerald R., and Thomas J. Dishion

1985   Contributions of Families and Peers to Delinquency. *Criminology* 23:63–79.

Pepinsky, Harold E., and Paul Jesilow

1984   *Myths That Cause Crime*. Cabin John, MD: Seven Locks Press.

Polk, Kenneth, and Walter E. Schafer

1972   *Schools and Delinquency*. Englewood Cliffs, NJ: Prentice Hall.

Poole, Eric D., and Robert M. Regoli

1979 Parental Support, Delinquent Friends, and Delinquency: A Test of Interaction Effects. *Journal of Criminal Law & Criminology* 70:188–193.

Priyadarsini, S., and Clayton A. Hartjen

1982 Legal Control and Alcohol in the United States and India. *The International Journal of the Addictions* 17:1099–1106.

Quinney, Ricard

1970 *The Social Reality of Crime.* Boston: Little, Brown.

1975 *Criminology: Analysis and Critique of Crime in America.* Boston: Little, Brown.

Radha, D., and M. Ravindran

1983 Women's Work in India. *International Social Science Journal* 35:633–701.

Rafter, Nicole Hahn

1992 Criminal Anthropology in the United States. *Criminology* 30:525–546.

Ram, P.K.

1986 Cognitive Style in Father Absent Delinquents. *Indian Journal of Criminology* 14:152–154.

Ramu, G.N.

1977 *Family and Caste in Urban India: A Case Study.* New Delhi: Vikas Publishing House Pvt LTD.

Ranchhoddas, R., and D.K. Thakore

1953 *Law and Crime*, 18th ed. Bombay: The Bombay Law Reporter Office.

Rankin, Joseph H.

1977 Investigating the Interrelations Among Social Control Variables and Conformity. *The Journal of Criminal Law and Criminology* 67:470–480.

Rankin, Joseph H., and Edward L. Wells

1991 The Preventive Effects of the Family on Delinquency. In Ronald J. Berger (ed.) *The Sociology of Juvenile Delinquency.* Chicago: Nelson-Hall, pp. 171–187.

Ravinder Nath, K.V., and B. David

1982 A Comparative Study of the Intelligence of Delinquents. *Indian Journal of Criminology* 10:31–36.

Reid, Douglas L.

1989 A Path Analytic Examination of Differential Association Theory. *Journal of Drug Education* 19: 139–156.

Reinarman, Craig, and Jeffrey Fagan

1988 Social Organization and Differential Association: A Research Note from a Longitudinal Study of Violent Juvenile Offenders. *Crime and Delinquency* 34:307–327.

Reiss, Albert J.

1971 *The Police and the Public.* New Haven, CT: Yale U. Press.

Roberts, Albert R. (ed.)

1989 *Juvenile Justice: Policies, Programs, and Services.* Chicago: The Dorsey Press.

Roopnarine, Jaipoul L., Enaget Talukder, Deepa Jain, Prieti Joshi, and Parul Srivastav

1992 Personal Well-being, Kinship Tie, and Mother-Infant and Father-Infant Interactions in Single-Wage and Dual-Wage Families in New Delhi, India. *Journal of Marriage and the Family* 54:293–301.

Rosen, Lawrence

1985   Family and Delinquency: Structure or Function. *Criminology* 23:553–574.

Sampson, Robert J.

1985   Sex Differences in Self-Reported Delinquency and Official Records: A Multiple-Group Structural Modeling Approach. *Journal of Quantitative Criminology* 1:345–367.

Sandhu, Harjit

1987   Low Rates of Delinquency and Crime in India: A Case for Strong Social Controls. *Indian Journal of Criminology* 15:2–16.

Schwartz, Ira M.

1989   *(In)Justice for Juveniles: Rethinking the Best Interests of the Child.* Lexington, MA: Lexington Books.

Schwendinger, Herman, and Julia Schwendinger

1970   Defenders of Order or Guardians of Human Rights? *Issues in Criminology* 5:123–157.

Scott, Carolyn, and Marjorie S. Zatz

1981   Comparative Deviance and Criminology. *International Journal of Comparative Sociology* 22:238–255.

Sekar, K., S. Chamundi Eswari, I.A. Shariff, D. Muralidhar, and V. Indramma

1983   Antisocial Behavior Among School Children: Further Validation of a Detecting Instrument. *Indian Journal of Criminology* 11:99–106.

Selke, William L.

1992   Program Concepts from International Corrections. *International Journal of Comparative and Applied Criminal Justice* 16:87–100.

Sen, A.

1982   Juvenile Delinquents and Mental Health Problems. *Social Change* 12:13–19.

Sethi, Renuka R., and Mary J. Allen

1984   Sex-Role Stereotypes in Northern India and the United States. *Sex Roles* 11:615–626.

Shane, Paul G.

1980   *Police and People: A Comparison of Five Countries.* St. Louis: C.V. Mosby Co.

Sharda, Neel K.

1988   *The Legal, Economic and Social Status of the Indian Child.* New Delhi: National Book Organization.

Shariff, I.A., and Sekar, K.

1982   Social Predictions in Juvenile Delinquency. *Indian Journal of Criminology* 10:42–46.

Shelley, Louise I.

1981a   *Crime & Modernization: The Impact of Industrialization and Urbanization on Crime.* Carbondale and Edwardsville: Southern Illinois U. Press.

1981b   *Readings in Comparative Criminology.* Carbondale and Edwardsville: Southern Illinois U. Press.

1981c   Introduction. In Louise I. Shelley (ed.) *Readings in Comparative Criminology.* Carbondale and Edwardsville: Southern Illinois U. Press, pp. xix–xxxiv.

Sheu, Chuen-Jim

1988   Juvenile Delinquency in the Republic of China: A Chinese Empirical Study of Social Control Theory. *International Journal of Criminology and Applied Criminal Justice* 12:59–71.

Shim, Young-Hu

1987   Hidden Delinquency in Korea. *Crime and Delinquency* 33:425–432.

Shoemaker, Donald J.

1990   *Theories of Delinquency: An Examination of Explanations of Delinquent Behavior*, 2nd ed. New York: Oxford U. Press.

1992   Delinquency in the Philippines: A Description. *Philippine Sociological Review* 40:83–103.

1994   Male-Female Delinquency in the Philippines: A Comparative Analysis. *Youth and Society* 25:299–329.

I.P.   *Handbook on International Juvenile Justice*. Westport, CT: Greenwood.

Shukla, K.S.

1979   *Adolescent Thieves: A Study in Socio-Cultural Dynamics*. New Delhi: Leeladevi Publications.

1982   Juvenile Delinquency in India: Research Trends and Priorities. *Indian Journal of Criminology and Criminalistics* 2:103–113.

Singer, Milton, and Bernard S. Cohn (eds.)

1968   *Structure and Change in Indian Society*. New York: Wenner-Gren Foundation.

Singer, Simon L., and Murray Levine

1988   Power-Control Theory, Gender and Delinquency: A Partial Replication with Additional Evidence on the Effects of Peers. *Criminology* 26:627–648.

Singh, Prakash, and Padma Agrawal

1986   Family Environment and Delinquency. *Indian Journal of Criminology* 14:143–150.

Sinha, L.N.K., and K.P. Krishna

1982   Some Personality Correlates of Cheating Behavior. *Indian Journal of Criminology* 10:30–33.

Skinner, William F.

1986   Delinquency, Crime, and Development: A Case Study of Iceland. *Journal of Research in Crime & Delinquency* 23:268–294.

Skogan, Wesley G.

1984   Reporting Crime to the Police: The Status of World Research. *Journal of Research in Crime & Delinquency* 21:113–137.

Smith, Douglas

1986   The Neighborhood Context of Police Behavior. In A. Reiss and M. Tonry (eds.) *Communities and Crime*. Vol. 8. Chicago: U. of Chicago Press, pp. 313–342.

Smith, Douglas A., and Laura A. Davidson

1986   Interfacing Indicators and Constructs in Criminological Research: A Note on the Comparability of Self-Reported Violence Data for Race & Age Groups. *Criminology* 24:473–488.

Somjee, Geeta

1989   *Narrowing the Gender Gap*. New York: St. Martin's Press.

Sommers, Ira, Jeffrey Fagan, and Deborah Baskin

1994   The Influence of Acculturation and Familism on Puerto Rican Delinquency. *Justice Quarterly* 11:207–228.

Souryal, Sam S.

1992   Juvenile Delinquency in the Cross-Cultural Context: The Egyptian Experience. *International Journal of Comparative and Applied Criminal Justice* 16:329–352.

Stapleton, Aday, and Ito Stapleton

1982   An Empirical Typology of American Metropolitan Juvenile Courts. *American Journal of Sociology* 88: 549–564.

Steffensmeier, Darrell J., and Renee Hoffman Steffensmeier

1980   Trends in Female Delinquency: An Examination of Arrest, Juvenile Court, Self-Report, and Field Data. *Criminology* 18:62–83.

Sutherland, Edwin H., and Donald R. Cressey

1978   *Criminology* 10th ed. Philadelphia: Lippincott.

Suzuki, Y.

1981   Japan. In V.L. Steward (ed.) *Justice & Troubled Children Around the World*, Vol. 3. New York: New York U. Press.

Terrill, Richard J.

1984   *World Criminal Justice Systems: A Survey*. Cincinnati, OH: Anderson.

Thilagaraj, R.J.

1987   Goal Perception of Delinquents and Non-Delinquents: A Comparative Study. *Indian Journal of Criminology* 2:145–148.

Thomson, John Adam

1990   India Toward the Year 2000. *Asian Affairs* 21:162–173.

Thornberry, Terence P., Alan J. Lizotte, Marvin D. Krohn, Margaret Farnworth, and Sung Joon Jang

1994   Delinquent Peers, Beliefs, and Delinquent Behavior: A Longitudinal Test of Interactional Theory. *Criminology* 32:47–84.

Thornton, William E., Jr., and Lydia Voigt

1992   *Delinquency and Justice,* 3rd ed. New York: McGraw-Hill.

Tittle, Charles R., Wayne J. Villemez, and Douglas A. Smith

1978   The Myth of Social Class and Criminality: An Empirical Assessment of the Empirical Evidence. *American Sociological Review* 43:643–656.

Tittle, Charles R., and Robert F. Meier

1990   Specifying the SES/Delinquency Relationship. *Criminology* 28:271–300.

Toby, Jackson

1979   Delinquency in Cross-Cultural Perspective. In LaMar T. Empey (ed.) *Juvenile Justice: The Progressive Legacy and Current Reforms*. Charlottesville, VA: U. of Virginia Press, pp. 105–149.

Turk, Austin T.

1969   *Criminology and Legal Order*. Chicago: Rand-McNally.

1982   *Political Criminality: The Defiance and Defense of Authority*. Beverly Hills, CA: Sage.

Van Dijk, Jan J.M., Pat Mayhew, and Martin Killias

1990   *Experiences of Crime Across the World*. Deventer, The Netherlands: Kluwer.

Van Voorhis, Patricia, Francis T. Cullen, Richard A. Mathers, and Connie Chenoweth Garner

1988   The Impact of Family Structure and Quality on Delinquency: A Comparative Assessment of Structural and Functional Factors. *Criminology* 2: 235–262.

Vatuk, Sylvia

1972   *Kinship and Urbanization*. Berkeley: U. of California Press.

Vaughn, Michael S., and Frank F.Y. Huang

1992   Delinquency in the Land of the Rising Sun: An Analysis of Juvenile Property Crimes in Japan During the Showa Era. *International Journal of Comparative and Applied Criminal Justice* 16:273–300.

Verma, Arvind

1993a The Phenomenon of Crime in India. Paper presented at meetings of American Society of Criminology, Phoenix, Arizona.

1993b The Problem of Measurement of Crime. *Indian Journal of Criminology* 21:51–58.

Voigt, Lydia, and William E. Thornton, Jr.

1990   Social Change, Anomie, and Crime-USSR and USA: A Network Systems Comparison. Paper Presented at the International Conference on Important Problems of Deviant Behavior: Theory and Method. Moscow, USSR.

Vold, George B., and Thomas J. Bernard

1986   *Theoretical Criminology*, 3rd. ed. New York: Oxford U. Press.

Walter, Michael, and Fischer Wolfgang

1989   Juvenile Delinquency Structures and Forms of Dealing with It in Budapest and Hamburg. *International Journal of Offender Therapy and Comparative Criminology* 33:1–20.

Warner, Barbara D., and Glena L. Pierce

1993   Reexamining Social Disorganization Theory Using Calls to the Police as a Measure of Crime. *Criminology* 31:493–517.

Warr, Mark, and Mark Stafford

1991   The Influence of Delinquent Peers: What They Think or What They Do? *Criminology* 29:851–866.

Weisheit, Ralph A.

1984   Women and Crime: Issues and Perspectives. *Sex Roles* 11:567–581.

Wells, L. Edward

1989   Self-Enhancement Through Delinquency: A Conditional Theory of Self-Derogation. *Journal of Research in Crime and Delinquency* 26:226–252.

Wells, L. Edward, and Joseph H. Rankin

1988   Direct Parental Controls and Delinquency. *Criminology* 26:263–285.

Werthman, Carl

1970   The Function of Social Definitions in the Development of Delinquent Careers. In Peter G. Garabedian and Don C. Gibbons (eds.) *Becoming Delinquent*. Chicago: Aldine.

Wiebe, Paul D.

1975   *Social Life in an Indian Slum*. New Delhi: Vikas.

Wilkins, Leslie T.

1980   World Crime: To Measure or Not to Measure? In Graeme R. Newman (ed.) *Crime and Deviance: A Comparative Perspective*. Beverly Hills, CA: Sage, pp. 17–41.

Williams, Frank P. III, and Marilyn D. McShane

1988   *Criminological Theory*. Englewood Cliffs, NJ: Prentice Hall.

Williams, Jay R., and Martin Gold

1972   From Delinquent Behavior to Official Delinquency. *Social Problems* 20:209–229.

Winfree, L. Thomas, Jr., Curt T. Griffths, and Christine S. Sellers

1989   Local Learning Theory, Drug Use, and American Indian Youths: A Cross-Cultural Test. *Justice Quarterly* 6:395–418.

Winfree, L. Thomas, Jr., G. Larry Mays, and Teresa Vigil-Backstrom

1994   Youth Gangs and Incarcerated Delinquents: Exploring the Ties Between Gang Membership, Delinquency, and Social Learning Theory. *Justice Quarterly* 11:229–256.

Wooden, Wayne S.

1995   *Renegade Kids, Suburban Outlaws: From Youth Culture to Delinquency*. Belmont, CA: Wadsworth.

Zhang, Lening, and Steven F. Messner

1995   Family Deviance and Delinquency in China. *Criminology* 33:359–388.

Index

Age and arrest patterns
    comparison of Indian and U.S., 68–
        69
    differences between Indian survey
        and UCR, 28
    in England, 72
    in Federal Republic of Germany, 72
    in India, 63–67
    in Korea, 74
    variations in, 165
Age/criminal offense relationship, in self-
    reporting, 85–89
Ahmedabad, number of juvenile arrests
    in, 61, 62
Alcoholism, 145, 164
Andra Pradesh, number of juvenile arrests
    in, 61, 62
Apprentice Act (1850), 35
Arrest rates
    age and gender variations in India,
        63–65
    annual rates for IPC crimes, 26
    in Canada, 71–72
    in China, 73
    comparing, 27–29
    comparison of Indian and U.S.
        arrest rates by age, 68–69
    comparison of Indian and U.S.
        arrest rates by gender, 69–71
    in Egypt, 74
    in England, 72
    in Federal Republic of Germany, 72
    generalizations from, 25–27
    India and the U.S. compared, 67–71
    in Japan, 73
    in Korea, 73–74
    in the Netherlands, 72
    in Nigeria, 74

number of juvenile arrests compared
    with total numbers, 57–60
regional variations, 60–63
self-report surveys versus official
    findings, 129
in the Soviet Union (former), 73
summary of world patterns, 74–75
in Sweden, 72–73
trends in, 66–67
use of, to augment self-report
    surveys, 21–23
Arrest scales, 197

Bombay, number of juvenile arrests in,
    61, 62
Bonding, delinquent versus conventional
    peer, 118–23

Calcutta, number of juvenile arrests in,
    61, 62
Canada
    arrest rates in, 71–72
    delinquency law in, 40–42
    delinquency processing in, 51–52
    self-reported delinquency study in,
        103
Caste system, 14
Children, Young Persons and Their
    Families Act (1989) (New
    Zealand), 42–44
Children's Act (1960), 36
China
    arrest rates in, 73
    self-reported delinquency study in,
        103
Chi Square statistics, use of, 85, 93
Cluster analysis, 119–20
Code of Criminal Procedure (1861), 35

Code of Criminal Procedure (1973), 37
Community, relationship of delinquency
     to peers, family and, 132–34
Comparative inquiry/research
     growing recognition of, 5, 153
     on an international basis, 5–6
Comparative inquiry/research, problems
     with
     in arrest statistics, 27–29
     defining offense behavior, 163–66
     diverse definitions of delinquency,
        154
     diverse laws/legal systems, 154–56
     diverse views of delinquent
        behavior, 154–55
     lack of data, 158–61
     units of study versus nation states,
        156–58
Control theory, 108, 109, 110, 125–26
Costs of confining juveniles
     in India, 48
     in the United States, 49
Crime/criminal offense, types committed.
     See Offenses, types committed
Crime in India
     arrest statistics in, compared with
        UCR, 27–29
     compared with similar documents,
        22–23, 27
     number of juvenile arrests compared
        with total numbers, 57–59
Crime in the United States, 22, 27

Data collection
     analysis of, 29–30
     problems with the lack of, 158–61
Dating, teenage, 145, 150
Delinquency, explanations for
     conclusions, 151–52
     distribution patterns, 129–30
     etiology versus epidemiology, 130–
        32
     in India, 132–34, 139–46
     in Japan, 137
     social position of Indian girls,
        impact of, 146–51
     in Soviet Union (former), 138–39
     in the U.S., 135–37
Delinquency and relationship to family/
     peers
     in India, 132–34, 139–46

in Japan, 137–38
in the U.S., 135–37
Delinquency in India, survey of research
     on, 7–10
Delinquency law(s)
     in Canada, 40–42
     comparative inquiry and problems
        with diverse, 154–56
     in India, 35–38
     in New Zealand, 42–44
     summary of, comparing the
        countries, 55–56
     in the United States, 39–40
Delinquency processing
     in Canada, 51–52
     in India, 44–48
     in New Zealand, 52–55
     summary of, comparing the
        countries, 55–56
     in the United States, 48–51
Delinquency rates
     distribution patterns, 129–30
     in Japan, 137
     overall, 127–29
Delinquent behavior
     See also Etiology of delinquent
        behavior
     comparative inquiry and problems
        with diverse views, 154–55
     traditional views of, 3–4
Delinquent juvenile
     comparative inquiry and problems
        with diverse definitions, 154
     defined, 37
Demographic characteristics
     comparison of Indian and U.S.
        samples, 17, 29–30
     universality in, 163–64
Differential association theory, 4, 118–23
Dispositions
     in Canada, 51–52
     in India, 44–46
     in New Zealand, 52–55
     statistics, use of, 23–24
     in the United States, 48–51
Distribution patterns, 129–30

Egypt, arrest rates in, 74
Employment rates
     for females, 149
     for juveniles, 14